n1139016

Th

European Law and the Individual

European Law
and the Individual

Edited by

F.G. Jacobs

Professor of European Law
University of London King's College

1976

NORTH-HOLLAND PUBLISHING COMPANY

AMSTERDAM – NEW YORK – OXFORD

Library of Congress Catalog Card Number: 76-8480
North-Holland ISBN: 0-7204-0473-8

Published by:
NORTH-HOLLAND PUBLISHING COMPANY
AMSTERDAM – NEW YORK – OXFORD

Distributors for the U.S.A. and Canada:

ELSEVIER/NORTH-HOLLAND, INC.
52 VANDERBILT AVENUE
NEW YORK, N.Y. 10017

Library of Congress Cataloging in Publication Data
EUROPEAN LAW AND THE INDIVIDUAL.
Papers presented at a workshop held in 1975 and sponsored by the University of London Institute of Advanced Legal Studies.
1. Law – European Economic Community countries – Congresses. I. Jacobs, Francis Geoffrey, 1939 – II. London. University. Institute of Advanced Legal Studies.
Law   341.24'2   76-8480
ISBN 0-7204-0473-8

PRINTED IN THE NETHERLANDS

Table of Contents

v

Foreword

For some years the University of London Institute of Advanced Legal Studies has arranged, with the support of the Ford Foundation, an annual "workshop" which enables lawyers from United Kingdom universities to meet and discuss in depth a subject of current interest. The general subject is determined by the interests of the Ford visiting professor from the U.S.A.; in 1975 the visitor was Professor Eric Stein, and the subject European Community Law.

Having been asked to select a particular topic and to invite the speakers, I took the opportunity to focus discussion on the area of Community law which can loosely be called "social". This seemed to be a relatively neglected area of the law; it had been made topical by recent developments, particularly by far-reaching decisions of the Court of Justice of the European Communities; and it seemed an appropriate area for the development of teaching and research, which it was the purpose of the workshop to stimulate.

It is hoped that the same purpose will be promoted by the publication of this book, which comprises revised versions of ten of the papers presented at the workshop. The papers fall broadly into two groups, dealing respectively with the substantive law and with the remedies available to the individual, although the latter question goes beyond the area of social law. Thus, while the topics dealt with are disparate, they have a unifying theme, which is the concern of European law with the individual.

King's College, London
December 1975

F.G. Jacobs

Contributors to this volume

Professor Walter van Gerven
Catholic University of Louvain
Tiensestraat 41
3000 Louvain
Belgium

T.C. Hartley
Department of Law
London School of Economics and Political Science
Houghton Street
Aldwych
London WC2A 2AE
England

Dr. R. Plender
Faculty of Laws
University of London King's College
Strand
London WC2R 2LS
England

Professor K. Lipstein
Clare College
University of Cambridge
Cambridge CB2 1RH
England

P. Leleux
Legal Adviser
Commission of the European Communities
200 Rue de la Loi
1040 Brussels
Belgium

R. Wägenbaur
Legal Adviser
Commission of the European Communities
200 Rue de la Loi
1040 Brussels
Belgium

Professor Eric Stein
University of Michigan Law School
Legal Research Building
Ann Arbor
Michigan 48104
U.S.A.

Professor G. Joseph Vining
University of Michigan Law School
Legal Research Building
Ann Arbor
Michigan 48104
U.S.A.

M. Hilf
Legal Adviser
Commission of the European Communities
200 Rue de la Loi
1040 Brussels
Belgium

Lawrence Collins
Herbert Smith & Co.
62 London Wall
London EC2R 7JP
England

Professor O. Kahn-Freund
Roundabouts
Shottermill
Haslemere
Surrey GU27 3PP
England

The Legal Protection of Private Parties in the Law of the European Economic Community

WALTER VAN GERVEN

Introduction

It is the purpose of this contribution to describe how the legal protection of private persons, as provided for in the EEC Treaty,[1] has been gradually enlarged thanks to the broad interpretation of the relevant Treaty provisions by the Court of Justice. This interpretation has mainly been carried out in two respects. First, through the doctrine of direct effect of Treaty provisions and Community acts, whereby the legal protection of private parties before national courts has been considerably broadened, and, secondly, through the doctrine of tort liability of the Community in respect of wrongful normative acts of its institutions, whereby the legal protection of private parties before the Court of Justice has been equally enlarged.

Before sketching an outline of these two doctrines, as they presently stand, it should be recalled that under the Treaty of Rome the standing of private parties before the Court of Justice is conceived in a rather narrow way as will appear from the following summary of provisions concerning the main actions which can be introduced before the Court of Justice.[2] *First,* there is the appeal for annulment of binding Community acts (Article 173 EEC) and the appeal against inaction of Community institutions failing to act (Article 175). Such appeals can only be instituted by an individual or a company when the act which the Council or the Commission has accomplished or failed to accomplish was, or should have been,

F.G. Jacobs, ed. European Law and the Individual © 1976, North-Holland Publishing Company

addressed to him or, in the case of a regulation or a decision addressed to
another person (including a Member State), when the regulation or
decision was of direct and individual concern to the private person lodging
the appeal. Accordingly, such a person does not have the right to lodge an
appeal for annulment of an act which has a general import./However, if
such an act is used as a legal basis for an implementing Community act
which is addressed to him, he may, before the Court of Justice, raise the
illegality of the general act, by virtue of Article 184, asking the Court not to
apply it and, consequently, to annul the implementing act based on it.
Secondly, there is the action for damages brought against the Community in
case of non-contractual (i.e. tort) liability for acts or omissions on the part
of the Community institutions or servants (Article 215, para. 2). It is clear
that this action, which is to be brought before the Court of Justice, can be
instituted by a private party. As discussed below the Court has given
considerable impetus to this possibility by recognizing that such action can
also be initiated with respect to normative acts, i.e. acts having a general
import. *Thirdly,* there is the action for infringement of the Treaty by a
Member State (Article 169ff.). Such an action can only be instituted before
the Court of Justice by the Commission or by another Member State.
Accordingly, with the exception of the action for damages in tort, which is
one of the two topics considered hereinafter, a private person has a very
limited standing before the Court of Justice, namely only to the extent that
the Community act (or failure to act) is addressed to him individually or
affects him in an analogous manner.

The summary given so far concerns the possibility of actions before the
Court of Justice of the European Communities. Suit can also be brought,
however, by a private party before a national court, not because a Community act can be attacked directly before such a court – it cannot, the Court
of Justice having sole jurisdiction in that respect – but because the invalidity of a Community act can be ascertained in a particular case by a domestic court when such act is the basis of an implementing act of the national
authorities the validity whereof is challenged before the court, or is otherwise invoked by a litigating party in a suit against another private party
(e.g. in a suit for damages in connection with the EEC rules on competition).
Private parties may thus challenge before a domestic court the validity of a
national act by invoking the invalidity of the underlying Community act.
Moreover, they may also challenge the validity of a national act (or failure
to act) because of *conflict* with Community rules. Such issue may arise

before a domestic court, e.g. in a suit for annulment of the national act or against inaction on the part of the national authorities ('recours en carence'), *or* in a suit for payment of an amount of money which the plaintiff claims on the basis of a Community regulation (e.g. in the field of agricultural policy) but which is refused to him by the national authorities who are in charge of paying out, *or*, vice versa, in a suit for reimbursement of duties which have been imposed by the national authorities contrary to Community law, *or* in a suit for tort damages against the national authorities who, it is asserted, have committed a fault in applying Community legislation. Obviously, whether any one of these suits can be brought before a domestic court depends on the legal system of each of the Member States, which means that the degree of legal protection against acts or omissions of national authorities which are not in conformity with the Community rules varies from one Member State to another.

It is in connection with the examination before a national court of the conformity with Community rules of acts or failures to act on the part of national authorities that the doctrine of direct effect of Community provisions has become of importance. Indeed, the conflict with a Community rule will only be held to have practical consequences, e.g. result in the nullity, invalidity or irregularity of the national act or omission, if the Community rule is considered to be self-executing, i.e. to have a direct effect in the national legal order in the sense that nationals of the Member States may derive therefrom individual rights which are enforceable by the national courts. It should be clear, therefore, that the legal protection of private parties before the national courts against national acts which are in conflict with Community rules has increased considerably thanks to the broad interpretation of the concept of direct effect by the Court of Justice, as will be seen later. Why by the Court of Justice? Because it is, in the last instance, up to that Court to decide whether a Community rule has direct effect, when it is asked by a national court to give a preliminary ruling by virtue of Article 177.

The legal protection of private parties against Community acts, or failures to act, is accordingly rather limited: *except* for the action for damages instituted against the Community institutions on the basis of Article 215 (an action which has been declared admissible by the Court of Justice also in respect of normative acts), Community acts, or failures to act, can be challenged by private parties only within the rather narrow limits of Articles 173, 175 and 184. On the contrary the legal protection of private parties against national acts, or failures to act, seen in relation with

Community law is rather extensive before the national courts – though differing from one Member State to another according to the availability in each national system of appropriate procedures –, since the national courts can be asked to hold national acts, or failures to act, illicit either because they are based on invalid Community acts or because they are in conflict with existing Community rules; the more so as many Community rules are now held to have direct effect due to the broad interpretation of that concept by the Court of Justice.

The decisions of the Court of Justice, first in respect of the direct effect of Community rules and then in respect of the Community's liability for normative acts, will be shortly described hereinafter, as the action of the Court of Justice in both respects is a good example of how the Court has considerably enlarged the legal protection of individuals.

The Direct Effect of Community Provisions

The problem of the direct effect of Treaty provisions is a well known problem in international law: "According to a well-established principle of international law...", thus the Permanent Court of International Justice,

> an international agreement cannot, as such, create direct rights and obligations for private individuals. But it cannot be disputed that the very object of an international agreement, according to the intention of the contracting parties, may be the adoption by the parties of some definite rules creating individual rights and obligations and enforceable by the national courts.[3]

In other words, in international law the absence of direct effect of Treaty provisions is the general rule, from which the contracting parties may, however, deviate. The latter may result e.g. from the fact that the Treaty provision concerned, instead of being addressed to the contracting States, is clearly addressed to private parties by imposing an obligation on them or granting them a subjective right.[4]

In its first decision on the subject, rendered on 5 February 1963 in the *Van Gend & Loos* case, the Court of Justice clearly started from this rule by saying: "To ascertain whether the provisions of an international treaty extend so far in their effects it is necessary to consider the spirit, the general scheme and the wording of those provisions." It then went on to say that "the objective of the EEC Treaty, which is to establish a Common Market, the functioning of which is of direct concern to interested parties in the Community, implies that this Treaty is more than an agreement which creates mutual obligations between the contracting States". After citing a few indications from which it should appear that the Treaty addressed itself both to the Member States and their citizens the Court concluded

> that the Community constitutes a new legal order of international law for the benefit of which the States have limited their sovereign rights, albeit within limited fields, and the subjects of which comprise not only Member States but also their nationals. Independently of the legislation of Member States, Community law therefore not only imposes obligations on individuals but is also intended to confer upon them rights which become part of their legal heritage. These rights arise not only where they are expressly granted by the Treaty, but also by reason of obligations which the Treaty imposes in a clearly defined way upon individuals as well as upon the Member States and upon the institutions of the Community.[5]

Thus, the Court has from the outset taken a favourable view towards the direct effect of the EEC Treaty provisions. Its starting point amounts almost to a presumption, at least a 'prejugé favorable', in favour of such direct effect, which is based on the idea that the Community, to use the words of the Court, presents a new legal order in international law, going beyond the governments to the nations and the citizens of the Member States.

The decisions of the Court in respect of the direct effect of the EEC Treaty provisions should be seen against this background. They appear as successive applications of a general principle which in being applied is gradually expanded and better defined. In the *Van Gend & Loos* case the rule was first applied to a Treaty provision, Article 12, which

> contains a clear and unconditional prohibition which is not a positive but a negative obligation.... The very nature of this prohibition makes it ideally adapted to produce direct effects in the legal relationship between Member States and their subjects. The implementation of Article 12 does not require any legislative intervention on the part of the States.[6]

In later decisions the same reasoning was applied to other 'standstill' provisions.[7] In the second *Lütticke* case decided on 16 June 1966, the Court took a further step: it indicated that it was ready to consider also as self-executing a Treaty provision imposing a positive duty on the Member States, in that case the duty to adjust any tax on imported products to the lower rate applicable to domestic products. However, in order for such a provision imposing an obligation to act to have direct effect, the obligation must not be "subject in its implementation or effects, to the taking of any measure either by the institutions of the Community or by the Member States".[8] In other words, as stated by the Court in later decisions, it must appear that no 'discretion'[9] is left to the Community institutions or to the Member States leaving room for alternative decisions. A Treaty provision which gives such a discretion has no direct effect since it implies "the interposition between the rule of Community law and its implementation of legal acts implying a discretion".[10] Furthermore, for a provision to have direct effect, it should not be made subject to the expiration of a period of time. This further condition is obviously of great importance in view of the many obligations provided in the Treaty which had to be fulfilled at the end of the transitional period. The Court has made it clear that by the end of the transitional period, such provisions will have direct effect, provided, as said before, that no freedom of action or discretionary power is given to the Community institutions or Member States as to their implementation or their putting into effect.[11]

The latter proviso, necessity of further implementation indicating a freedom of action on the part of the Community institutions or the national authorities, is an important limitation on the direct effect of Treaty provisions. It has been pointed out by the Court, though, that the proviso does not imply that no direct effect is present whenever the enactment of implementing legislation is provided for: direct effect is excluded only when the obligation is *made dependent on,* not when it is merely meant to be made easier by, such implementation.[12] Whether further implementation is such a condition precedent will depend on the place and importance of the provision under review within the framework of the system. Thus, e.g. it has been decided by the Court that the rule on equal treatment of all Community nationals with nationals of the Member State concerned – which is one of the fundamental legal provisions of the Community – as applied to the rights of establishment and free services in Article 52 (read in conjunction with Article 54 and 57) and in Articles 59, para. 1, and 60, para. 3 (read in conjunction with Articles 63 and 66), is *not* made *dependent* on further implementation.[13] Although the implementation of these Articles, as provided in the Treaty, is important for making the exercise of the right of freedom of establishment more effective and the rendering of services easier, it has "become superfluous with regard to...the rule on nationality, since this is henceforth sanctioned by the Treaty itself with direct effect".[14] Accordingly, the requirement of further implementation is in itself no bar to direct effect but only if it is made a condition precedent to the direct effect of the provision. Similarly, it is no bar to direct effect that the concrete meaning of the provision under review depends on an assessment of the economic facts.[15] In other words the fact that loose words or concepts are used in the provision does not imply the existence of a freedom of decision which would prevent the provision from having direct effect, because determining the significance of such words or concepts is, according to the traditional view, 'only' a question of interpretation which can be decided by the courts. The same holds true for the presence in the provision of exceptions or restrictions whose scope can be determined by the courts and which are therefore not of a nature to prevent the direct effect of the provision.[16]

The present opinion of the Court of Justice in respect of the direct effect of *Treaty provisions* can thus be summarized as follows: provisions in an international treaty which like the EEC Treaty creates a new legal order addressing itself beyond the governments to the nations and the citizens of the Member States, have a direct effect not only when they explicitly so state but also when they create definite obligations (i.e. to attain a precise result) for individuals, Member States or Community institutions. The latter is true, regardless of whether the obligation is an obligation to abstain from doing something or an obligation to do something; *provided* that the obligation is complete and unconditional, which means that its fulfilment is *not* conditioned by the expiration of a time period and not made dependent on (as opposed to: only facilitated by) an intervention on the part of the Community institutions or the national authorities which implies a freedom of action to make one of at least two alternative decisions. An intervention merely consisting in the interpretation of loose concepts or in the determination of the scope of exceptions to the obligation concerned, is not an intervention implying a freedom of action, and therefore, is no bar to direct effect.

This summary suggests that, in respect of Treaty provisions, the initial statement of the Court that the direct effect of Treaty provisions depends on the spirit, the general scheme and the wording of the Treaty, has little practical significance: as to the *spirit* of the Treaty, the Court has declared once and for all that the Treaty addresses itself to the individuals beyond the heads of the Member States; as to the *general scheme*, meaning the framework of the Treaty within which the specific provision has to be

situated, it is primarily used to investigate the importance of the provision
in order to determine whether further implementation is a condition precedent to the fulfilment of the obligation: if the provision is important, its
fulfilment is not made dependent upon such implementation; and as to the
wording, unless the contrary were explicitly stated in the provision under
review, the wording has so far proved to be no actual bar to direct effect.

Not only provisions of the Treaty but also provisions set forth in regulations, directives or decisions issued by the Community institutions may
have a direct effect. This is most obvious, of course, for a *regulation* which,
according to Article 189, para. 2 "shall be binding in its entirety and
directly applicable in all Member States".[17] Thus, it was not too difficult
for the Court to decide that regulations "have direct effect on account of
their nature and of the function in the system of community sources of law
and as such can give rise to private rights which national courts are
bound to safeguard".[18] Whether a provision of a regulation has direct effect in a specific case and therefore gives rise to claims which can be enforced against a Member State by the individual, depends on the fulfilment of the conditions provided for in the provision "without a possibility
to subject their execution at the national level to provisions regarding
application other than those which may be laid down in the regulation itself".[19] It seems from this that the Court refers to the same criteria as
those used in respect of Treaty provisions, namely whether the fulfilment
of the obligation is made dependent upon its implementation by
national authorities disposing of a freedom of action enabling them
to add special provisions regarding the application of the rules concerned.
But the need for Member States to grant appropriate credits for the implementation of the obligation does not prevent direct application of the
obligation, especially since Article 5, para. (1) obliges Member States to
take all appropriate measures to ensure fulfilment of their obligations.[20]

The Court has taken a similar position in respect of *directives* and
decisions. To do so, it had first to set aside the distinction made in Article 189
between regulations on the one hand and directives and decisions on the
other hand. Regulations have a general application and shall be binding
in their entirety and directly applicable in all Member States. Directives
can only be addressed to Member States and are only binding as to the
result to be achieved, leaving to the national authorities the choice of form
and methods. Decisions have no general application but can be addressed
to Member States or individuals and are binding in their entirety upon the
addressees. The Court did not consider these differences to be sufficiently

important as regards the theory of direct effect. In respect of both directives and decisions, it stated that, although "regulations are directly applicable and may therefore certainly produce direct effects by virtue of their nature as law..., [I]t does not follow from this that other categories of legal measures mentioned in Article 189 could never produce similar effect", and that "it would be incompatible with the binding effect attributed to (decisions) (directives) by Article 189 to exclude in principle the possibility that persons affected might invoke the obligation imposed thereby".[21] This question of principle being settled, the next question becomes in which particular cases direct effect should be attributed to a provision of a directive or a decision. The answer given by the Court is that "one must examine whether the provision in question, by its legal nature, lay-out and wording, is capable of creating direct effects on the legal relations between the addressee of the measure and third parties".[22] Addressing itself to the provisions in question, the Court decided in one case that the obligation contained in a Council decision addressed to all Member States was "unconditional and sufficiently clear and precise to be capable of creating direct effect in the legal relations between the Member States and individuals",[23] and in another case that the obligation set forth in a directive was without reserve and unconditional and by its nature not requiring any further intervention on the part of the Community institutions or Member States; moreover the obligation was imposed in connection with an exception to one of the fundamental rules of the Treaty for the protection of individuals, so that the legal certainty of these private persons requires that they can invoke the obligation, even though it is contained in a normative act, a directive, which has no direct effect in its entirety.[24]

In conclusion, the Court has in principle no objection to declaring provisions in regulations, decisions and directives to have direct effect; it is willing by and large to apply the same criteria as in the case of treaty provisions to determine the direct effect in a particular case; but, especially in respect of directives which by their general nature are not binding in their entirety, it will examine whether the obligation in question is sufficiently related to the private person concerned so as to enable him to claim that it creates direct rights for him.

The Non-Contractual Liability of the Community for Normative Acts

Article 215, para. 2 EEC provides: "In the case of non-contractual liability, the Community shall, in accordance with the general principles common to the laws of the Member States, make good any damage caused by its institutions or by its servants in the performance of their duties." Apart from cases brought on the basis of this Article by Community employees against the Community in its capacity of employer,[25] Article 215 provides the legal basis for suits instituted on behalf of third persons who claim to have been damaged because of wrongful acts on the part of Community institutions or Community servants. Such wrongful acts, or torts, may consist, according to the Court of Justice, in the abusive application of powers, the non-performance of (non-contractual) obligations, the insufficient organisation of the service, inadequate supervision, the providing of erroneous information, the unlawful termination of staff contracts or the insufficient protection of rights of staff members,[26] the violation of internal rules.[27]

Actions for damages instituted against the Community on the basis of Article 215, para. 2, come within the sole jurisdiction of the Court of Justice (Article 178). It may occur, however, that in connection with the same factual situation a suit for damages is brought simultaneously against a Member State before a national court of that State. This will be the case when it is asserted that the Member State has mis-implemented or mis-applied the allegedly wrongful Community act so that damages can be asked from both, the Community (on the basis of Article 215) and the Member State concerned (on the basis of national provisions relating to the law on torts). According to the present case-law of the Court of Justice, the possibility of such a parallel suit before a national court does not paralyse the action before the Court of Justice.[28]

It is clear that Article 215, para. 2, supplies a convenient court action to private persons who claim to be harmed by acts (or failures to act) on the part of Community institutions or their employees. The protection so granted has been construed by the Court of Justice in the widest sense possible. This results from two important developments. The *first* development concerns the question whether the Court has jurisdiction to decide an action for damages based on Article 215 in respect of a Community act which (a) can *also* be the object of an appeal for annulment (Article 173) or an appeal against inaction (Article 175), or (b) given the limited standing of the individual, or because the two months limitation period has expired, can *not* be the object of an appeal for annulment or inaction. The Court of Justice in the third *Lütticke* case set forth for the first time the principle that an action for damages based on Article 215 is to be viewed as an independent form of redress. It has a specific function within the system of remedies and its application – on account of its special objective – is subject to particular conditions. The fact that a claim for damages under certain circumstances leads to a result similar to that arising on a claim pursuant to Article 175 does not cause its inadmissibility. Such a rule would be in conflict both with the independence of the claim and with the efficacy of the whole system of remedies as provided by the Treaty. Consequently, this exception of inadmissibility must be rejected.[29]

This does not mean that an action for damages on the basis of Article 215 will always be admissible in spite of the fact that the same Community act can or cannot be challenged before the Court of Justice by another procedure: if it should appear that the action for damages is nothing more than a disguised appeal for annulment or against inaction, the action will be declared inadmissible.[30]

The *second* development whereby the scope of legal protection provided by Article 215, para. 2, has been further enlarged, is the acceptance by the Court of Justice of the principle that private persons may seek and obtain damages from the Community because of wrongful normative acts of the Community. A normative act, in the words of the Court of Justice, is an act "which implies the existence of certain alternatives as regards economic policy".[31] They are Community acts, such as Regulations of the Council or of the Commission (with the exclusion of the provisions of the Treaties including the Act of Accession[32]), laying down general rules which have been enacted by a Community institution pursuant to its regulating power. The practical consequence of this development can hardly be overemphasized: because of it private persons who, according to Article 173, are only authorized to bring an action for annulment against an act which concerns them directly and individually, may now ask the Court of Justice, if not to review the validity of generally binding acts, then at least to review the regularity of such acts with a view to determining whether such persons have been unjustly harmed by the act under review and therefore whether they should be granted damages.

This second development appears to be the logical consequence of the first: pursuant to the first development a private person can use the action for damages based on Article 215, para. 2, in situations where he has not, or has no longer, the right to bring an appeal for annulment or against inaction; whenever the Community act concerned is a normative act – i.e. a generally binding act which by its nature does not normally concern the private person in a direct and individual manner (at least not in the narrow sense in which these notions have been construed by the Court of Justice[33]) – no appeal for annulment can be brought: thanks to the second development, however, an action for damages can be instituted by the individual against the normative act on the basis of Article 215, para. 2, if it appears, in the wording of that Article, that the normative act concerned constitutes vis-à-vis the plaintiff a tort "in accordance with the general principles common to the laws of the Member States".

To date seven decisions have been rendered by the Court of Justice regarding the liability of the Community for normative acts.[34] In each of these cases, the Court set forth the principle that "in the case of a normative action, the Community can be held liable for damages to private persons only when a higher rule of law, provided for their protection, is violated to a sufficiently qualified extent". By this token the Court acknowledged that such principle was "in accordance with the general principles common to the laws of the Member States". From an examination of the legal systems of the six original Member States and even more so of the legal systems of the present nine Member States, it appears that this holds true only if one is of the opinion that under the term 'general principles' in Article 215, general tendencies resulting from different specific rules serving an analogous function in the various Member States, rather than well established rules are to be understood, and furthermore, if one neglects the general principles in respect of Acts of Parliament for which normally no State liability exists in the Member States, even though, in the legal order of the Community, Regulations of the Council are, as to their nature and scope (but not their origin), very much comparable, in the legal order of the Member States, to laws enacted by Parliament.[35]

The scope of the general rule stated by the Court in respect of liability for normative acts is not yet clear. As can be seen from its wording it contains three elements: the Community will only be liable if

(i)   there has been a violation of a higher rule of law;
(ii) the violation is of an extent sufficiently qualified;
(iii) the higher rule of law provided for the protection of the private persons who claim to be harmed.

If these three elements are present, a tort has been committed by the Community institution concerned. However, for the Community to be liable in damages further proof must be given that damage has been caused and that there is a causal link between the wrongful act (or failure to act) and the damage incurred.[36]

As for the first of the three elements, a violation of a higher rule of law,[37] the Court has made it clear that the higher rule may consist in a Regulation of a higher rank, such as a Council Regulation which is at the basis of the Regulation of the Commission under review, or in a general principle which may or may not be stated in the Treaty or in another written provision.[38] Examples of a general principle laid down in the Treaty are the general prohibition of discrimination on the basis of nationality (Article 7) and the prohibition of discrimination between producers or consumers within the Community which is one of the basic principles in the field of the common agricultural policy (Article 40(3), para. 2).[39] An example of an unwritten general principle is the principle of legal certainty and the related principle of the legitimate reliance of individuals on previous statements or promises made by Community institutions.[40] It seems to result from the judments of the Court rendered to date that, in the case of a violation of a Regulation of a higher rank, the Court will base its finding of a violation on strictly legal arguments: as in the case of an appeal for annulment, the Court will analyse the terms of the higher and of the lower regulation to determine whether the latter is consistent with the former; whereas, in the case of a violation of a (written or unwritten) general principle, the Court seems willing to go farther and to re-appraise the economic considerations which guided the Community institution concerned, in order to decide whether, in the light of such considerations, the action of the institution was reasonable.[41]

Owing to the fact that in only one of the seven cases in which the question of liability for normative acts was raised and discussed, has the Court held a violation of a higher rule of law to be proven, the other two elements of the liability rule (sufficiently qualified violation of a rule provided for the protection of the plaintiffs) have not yet received much attention from the Court. This is even so, inexplicably, in the one instance in which the Court was of the opinion that the three elements were present and sufficiently proven, i.e. in the Comptoir National Technique Agricole (CNTA) case.[42] Accordingly, the following statements are based on conjecture. A sufficiently qualified violation occurs, it would seem, whenever the (higher) rule of law which is violated, is, on the one hand, sufficiently precise and well-established and, on the other hand, sufficiently important to make the violation a serious one. The rule which is violated has been provided for the protection of the plaintiff, if it is given not only for the protection of the general interest but also, be it only additionally, for the protection of the interests of individual citizens or undertakings.[43] As long as the Court has not shed more light on the latter two elements, a general comment may suffice here. It is that the Court, in later decisions, may use these two elements to limit its theory if it should appear, as is not at all unlikely, that the theory of liability for normative acts, as now accepted by the Court as a matter of principle, were to give rise to a large number of court actions against the Community on the basis of Article 215, para. 2.

A similar limitative effect may, of course, result from the interpretation of the two other conditions for Community liability to arise, to wit the existence of damage, and the existence of a causal link between the violation and the damage incurred. Since there is no reason to believe that the Court will in these respects apply different rules from those governing non-contractual liability for *non*-normative acts, these two further conditions need not be discussed here.[44]

[1] The subject of this paper is limited to the EEC Treaty.

[2] For a complete outline, see Kapteyn and Verloren van Themaat, *Introduction to the Law of the European Communities*, 1973, pp. 157ff.

[3] Permanent Court of International Justice, Jurisdiction of the Courts of Danzig, Advisory Opinion 1928, Series B, No. 15, pp. 17-18, cited by Kapteyn and Verloren van Themaat, *op. cit.*, p. 182.

[4] Kapteyn and Verloren van Themaat, *op. cit.*, p. 183.

[5] Case 26/62 *Van Gend & Loos* [1963] ECR 1 at 12.

[6] At p. 13.

[7] Case 6/64 *Costa v. ENEL* [1964] ECR 585 (in respect of Article 37 (2) and 53) and Case 13/68 *Salgoil v. Italian Ministry of Foreign Trade* [1968] ECR 453 (in respect of Articles 31 and 32 with the exception of the last sentence).

[8] Case 57/65 *Lütticke* [1966] ECR 205 (in respect of Article 95, para. 1 and 3). See also Case 33/70 *Sace, Rec.*, 1970, p. 1213 (in respect of Articles 9 and 13(2)) and Case 18/71 *Eunomia, Rec.*, 1971, p. 811 (in respect of Articles 9 and 16).

[9] Case 28/67 *Molkerei Zentrale* [1968] ECR 143 (in respect of Article 97); Case 13/68 *Salgoil* [1968] ECR 453 (in respect of Article 32, para. 2, last sentence and 33(1) and (2)).

[10] Case 28/67 *Molkerei Zentrale* [1968] ECR 143 at 156.

[11] Case 33/70 *Sace, Rec.*, 1970, p. 1213; Case 2/74 *Reyners* [1974] ECR 631 (in respect of Article 52); Case 33/74 *Van Binsbergen* [1974] ECR 1299 (in respect of Article 59, para. 1, and 60, para. 3); Case 36/74 *Walrave and Koch* [1974] ECR 1405 (in respect of Article 59, para. 1).

[12] Case 2/74 *Reyners, loc. cit.*

[13] *Ibid.*, and Case 33/74 *Van Binsbergen, loc. cit.*

[14] Case 2/74 *Reyners, loc. cit.*

[15] Case 27/67 *Fink-Frucht* [1968] ECR 223 (in respect of Article 95(2)).

[16] Case 41/94 *Van Duyn* [1974] ECR 1337 (in respect of Article 48).

[17] However the expression, as cited, in Article 189, para. 2, is not synonymous with 'having direct effect' in the sense of the court decisions under review: cf. the opinion of the Commission in Case 9/70 *Grad, Rec.*, 1970, p. 825, cited in English translation by Brinkhorst and Schermers, *Judicial Remedies in the European Communities Supplement*, 1972, on p. 49. See also the following sentence in the text from which it appears that also in the view of the Court, the two expressions do not cover each other entirely. See further Winter, "Direct Applicability and Direct Effect: Two Distinct and Different Concepts in Community Law", *Common Market Law Review*, 1972, pp. 425ff.

[18]   Case 43/71 *Politi, Rec.,* 1971, p. 1039; Case 84/71 *Marimex, Rec.,* 1972, p. 33; Case 93/71 *Leonesio, Rec.,* 1972, p. 287 cited in English translation by Brinkhorst and Schermers, *op. cit.,* pp. 54ff; Case 20/72 *Cobelex, Rec.,* 1972, p. 1055.

[19]   Case 93/71 *Leonesio, loc. cit.*

[20]   *Ibid.*

[21]   Case 9/70 *Grad, loc. cit.* (decision); Case 20/70 *Lesage* and Case 23/70 *Haselhorst, Rec.,* 1970, p. 861ff., and 881ff. respectively (decision); Case 41/74 *Van Duyn, loc. cit.* (directive).

[22]   *Ibid.* See also Case 33/70 *Sace, loc. cit.*

[23]   Case 9/70 *Grad, loc. cit.*

[24]   Case 41/74 *Van Duyn, loc. cit.*

[25]   Community servants are employed by the Community not by virtue of a private law contract but by virtue of public law provisions. The liability of the Community in the course of such a relationship is thus considered to be non-contractual.

[26]   Cf. preceding footnote.

[27]   See for an extensive discussion of these various categories of wrongful acts: Schermers, "The Law As It Stands on the Appeal for Damages", *Legal Issues of European Integration,* 1975, pp. 113ff., at pp. 114ff.

[28]   Case 43/72 *Merkur* [1973] ECR 1069. See, however, the earlier decision of the Court in Case 96/71 *Haegeman, Rec.,* 1972, p. 1015.

[29]   Case 4/69 *Lütticke, Rec.,* 1971, p. 325, cited in English translation by Brinkhorst and Schermers, *Supplement,* 1972, pp. 36ff. The Court adopted the same reasoning in respect of an appeal for annulment (Article 173) (Case 5/71 *Schöppenstedt, Rec.,* 1971, p. 979, cited in English translation by Brinkhorst and Schermers, *op. cit.,* pp. 38ff).

[30]   Thus Adv. Gen. Roemer in his Opinion in Case 5/71 *Schöppenstedt* cited before. See also Goffin and Mahieu, "L'arrêt Lütticke du 28 avril 1971...", *Cahiers de droit européen,* 1972, at pp. 75ff.

[31]   Case 5/71 *Schoppenstedt,* cited above.

[32]   Case 169/73 *Compagnie Continentale France* [1975] ECR 117.

[33]   See Kapteyn and Verloren van Themaat, *op. cit.,* pp. 167ff.

[34]   These decisions are: Case 5/71 *Schöppenstedt* cited above; Cases 9 and 11/71 *Cie d'Approvisionnement, Rec.,* 1972, p. 391; Case 59/72 *Wünsche* [1973] ECR 791; Case 43/72 *Merkur* [1973] ECR 1055; Cases 63-69/72 *Werhahn* [1973] ECR 1229; Case 153/73 *Holtz & Willemsen* [1974] ECR 675; Case 74/74 *CNTA* [1975] ECR 533.

[35]   For a summary of the status of the law in the nine Member States, see Gilsdorf, "Die Haftung der Gemeinschaft aus normativem Handeln", *Europarecht,* 1975, p. 73ff., on pp. 92-95.

[36]   Cf. Case 4/69 *Lütticke,* cited above: "According to Article 215, para. 2 and the general principles referred to in the provision, a number of conditions must be

fulfilled for the liability of the Community, to wit the existence of damages, the causal link between the asserted damage and the disputed behaviour of the institutions and the illegality of this behaviour."

[37] In the case *Cie d'Approvisionnement*, cited above, it was argued by the plaintiff that the Community is also liable for abnormal damage of a special nature due to conduct of the Community institutions which is not illegal. In other words, the plaintiff in that case was also arguing in terms of liability without fault. The Court said that 'in a situation as the one under review', the Community could not be held to be liable for legal conduct, thus leaving the door open for further developments.

[38] Case 153/73 *Holtz & Willemsen*, cited above.

[39] See the decisions of the Court in the cases *Schöppenstedt, Cie d'Approvisionnement, Merkur, Werhahn* and *Holtz & Willemsen*, all cited above.

[40] Case 74/74 *CNTA*, cited above, to be compared with: Case 169/73 *Compagnie Continentale France*, cited above.

[41] This conclusion is based on an examination of the relevant cases, as described in my article on "De Nietcontractuele Aansprakelijkheid van de Gemeenschap Wegens Normatieve Handelingen", to be published shortly in *Sociaal-Economische Wetgeving*.

[42] Case 74/74 *CNTA*, cited above.

[43] It would seem that the Court in using the concept of a rule of law provided for the protection of individuals makes use of the doctrine of German tort law known as the 'Schutznormtheorie', be it that this theory is understood by the Court in a very broad manner as indicated in its decision in Cases 5, 7 and 13 to 24/66 *Kampffmeyer* [1967] ECR 245.

[44] See Schermers, *art. cit., Legal Issues of European Integration*, 1975, pp. 136ff.

2

The International Scope of the Community Provisions Concerning Free Movement of Workers

(With Special Reference to the Law of the United Kingdom)

T.C. HARTLEY

There are two aspects to this problem which, though interrelated, are quite distinct. The first is the *territorial scope* of the Community provisions, i.e. within what territory is free movement permitted? The second aspect is the *personal scope*: which persons may benefit from the Community rights? These two aspects will be considered separately; but they do interact since one would *prima facie* expect the beneficiaries of the right of free movement to be the persons living in the territory to which the right applies. This is a matter of reciprocity: if workers from territory X are allowed to take up employment in territory Y, it would be reasonable to imagine that the inhabitants of territory Y would enjoy a like right to seek work in territory X. However, this interdependence between the territorial and the personal scope, though fairly obvious from the point of view of theory, is not always expressly stated in the relevant texts; the difficulties that result from this will be considered below.

I. Territorial Scope

It is stated in Article 48(1) EEC that freedom of movement must be secured "within the Community" and Article 48(3) speaks of the right to move freely "within the territory of Member States".[1] It seems fairly clear, therefore, that the territorial scope of the provisions is the "territory of the Member States" and this is expressly stated in Reg. 1612/68, Articles 1

F.G. Jacobs, ed. European Law and the Individual © 1976, North-Holland Publishing Company

and 47.[2] Two problems remain: first, what exactly are these territories? Secondly, when is a person employed "within" a particular territory? The first problem is simply one of geographical definition: the second involves questions of localisation similar to those encountered in private international law.

Geographical Definition

As a general principle, the territory within which the right of free movement applies is the same as the territory to which the Treaty as a whole applies. Paragraph 1 of Article 227 EEC (as amended by the Treaty of Accession) states that this is the nine Member States. This seems to exclude dependencies and other associated territories that are not actually part of one of the Nine. However, a number of qualifications to this appear in paragraphs 2 to 5. Paragraph 2 deals with Algeria (originally part of France) and the French overseas departments. It gives the Council (acting on a proposal from the Commission) the power to decide the extent to which the free movement provisions will apply to these territories. The Council has exercised this power and the four French overseas departments – Guadeloupe, French Guyana, Martinique and Réunion – are now included in the area to which free movement applies.[3] Algeria, now an independent country, is not included.

Paragraph 3 states that the special arrangements for association set out in Part Four of the Treaty apply to the overseas countries and territories listed in Annex IV to the Treaty. This list contains a number of territories including some associated with Britain. To discover the status of these territories, one must look at Part Four where it is stated, in Article 135:

> ...freedom of movement within Member States for workers from the countries and territories, and within the countries and territories for workers from Member States, shall be governed by agreements to be concluded subsequently with the unanimous approval of Member States.[4]

No such agreements have in fact been concluded and it would seem a fair inference from Article 135 that freedom of movement is not to extend to these territories unless and until such agreements are concluded. It follows, therefore, that the overseas countries and territories listed in Annex IV are outside the territorial scope of the free movement provisions.

What of the associated and dependent territories not included in Annex

IV? As far as the United Kingdom is concerned the answer is simple. The second sentence of paragraph 3 of Article 227 (as amended) provides:

> This Treaty shall not apply to those overseas countries and territories having special relations with the United Kingdom of Great Britain and Northern Ireland which are not included in the aforementioned list.

They are consequently excluded.

This does not, however, end the matter. The fourth paragraph of Article 227 provides:

> The provisions of this Treaty shall apply to the European territories for whose external relations a Member State is responsible.

There is thus a distinction between associated and dependent territories *in* Europe (which come under paragraph 4) and those *outside* Europe (which come under paragraph 3).

Gibraltar clearly comes under paragraph 4 and is therefore included.[5] A number of other British territories would also be included but for the provisions of paragraph 5 (added by the Accession Treaty) which makes certain exceptions to paragraph 4. Sub-paragraph (b) of this excludes the Sovereign Base Areas in Cyprus from the Treaty altogether[6] and sub-paragraph (c) provides that the Channel Islands and the Isle of Man are included to the extent necessary to ensure the implementation of the arrangements for those islands set out in the Treaty of Accession. These arrangements, which are set out in Protocol No. 3, do not bring these islands within the scope of the free movement provisions of the Treaty. It follows, therefore, that the only British territories to which the free movement provisions apply are the United Kingdom (i.e. England, Scotland, Wales and Northern Ireland[7]) and Gibraltar.[8]

The position regarding the overseas territories of the Netherlands is rather complicated. Under Dutch constitutional law the term, "The Kingdom of the Netherlands" (*Het Koninkrijk der Nederlanden*), includes both the European territory of the Netherlands and the overseas territories.[9] Until recently the latter were two in number: Surinam (Dutch Guyana) which became independent in November 1975, and the Netherlands Antilles. Under a protocol to the EEC Treaty, it was agreed by the signatories that the Government of the Netherlands was entitled to ratify the Treaty on behalf of the European territory of the Netherlands and Netherlands New Guinea only.[10] In this way Surinam and the Netherlands Antilles were excluded from the scope of the Treaty. (Netherlands

New Guinea is now no longer associated with the Netherlands and is therefore also excluded.)

When the EEC Treaty was signed, the Six also made a Declaration[11] expressing their readiness to conclude an association agreement with Surinam and the Netherlands Antilles. Such an agreement has been concluded but it did not bring these territories within the scope of the free movement provisions.[12]

When Regulation 1612/68 was enacted the Governments of the Member States, meeting in the Council, expressed their willingness to conclude a convention for the extension of the free movement provisions to workers from Surinam and the Netherlands Antilles. However, these territories did not take advantage of this offer because they did not want to allow free immigration from the neighbouring territory of French Guyana, which, as a French overseas department, was already within the scope of the free movement provisions.[13] The result is that the Dutch overseas territories remained outside the territorial scope of the provisions.

Localisation

The question of localisation is unlikely to cause problems as far as the right of entry is concerned. It could, however, cause difficulties with regard to some of the other provisions such as the prohibition against discrimination contained in Article 48(2) EEC. This prohibition would obviously apply whenever the work was done in the Community. The European Court has held that it is applicable to employment on board merchant ships of a Member State,[14] and no doubt it would apply also to employment on oil rigs under the jurisdiction of a Member State[15] or to the employment of crew on aircraft of a Member State.

A recent ruling of the European Court suggests, however, that the scope of Community Law could extend further and might apply to employment outside the Community if the contract of employment was entered into within the Community. This was the case of *Walrave & Koch* which was a reference from the Netherlands under Article 177 EEC.[16] The Court defined the international scope of the prohibition against discrimination in the following paragraph of its ruling:

> The rule on non-discrimination applies in judging all legal relationships in so far as these relationships, by reason either of the place where they are entered into or of the place where they take effect, can be located within the territory of the Community.

It is not entirely clear what is meant by this, especially by the phrase "take effect", but it seems that the prohibition would apply *either* if the contract of employment is made within the Community *or* if it is carried out within the Community. It should also be mentioned that the Court held that the prohibition against discrimination was binding not only on public authorities but also on associations and other bodies of a private nature. Moreover, it is clear from the judgment that the prohibition can bind bodies which have their head office outside the Community.

The case itself concerned motor-paced cycle racing, which is a sport in which the cyclist rides behind a pacemaker on a motor cycle and is able to attain speeds of up to 100 k.p.h. as a result of the slipstream created by the pacemaker. The pacemakers are professionals, employed by the cyclist or by a national cycling association or a sponsor, and the Court had to decide whether the prohibition against discrimination could apply to them. The international body controlling the sport, the *Association Union Cycliste Internationale* (the UCI), had adopted a rule that pacemaker and cyclist had to be of the same nationality and they proposed to apply the rule in the world championships to be held in Spain. The plaintiffs were two professional pacemakers of Dutch nationality and they had asked the Dutch court for a declaration that the rule of the UCI was void and for an order against the UCI that they should be allowed to ride in the world championships for cyclists who were nationals not only of the Netherlands but of any Community country.

The case raised many issues, not least whether cyclist and pacemaker constitute a team so that the rule requiring them to be of the same nationality could be justified on the ground that they represented their country, but it seems clear from the judgment that the application of the prohibition was not to be ruled out by the fact that the championships were to be held outside the Community nor by the fact that the UCI had its headquarters outside the Community. In this respect the European Court seems to have extended the scope of Community law to its limits; in fact it is hard to see how it could be proper for the courts of one country to attempt to interfere in the conduct of an international sporting event held in another country.

The importance of the case is that it could entail the application of the prohibition against discrimination to companies – whether Community or foreign – that recruit workers in the Community for employment outside it.[17] It is also conceivable that a body operating outside the Community, for example a trade union, might be 'guilty' of a breach of

Community law if it tried to prevent such a company recruiting workers who were nationals of a particular Member State. Here again, however, it is doubtful whether the granting of a remedy against such a body would be either proper or, since it might be impossible to enforce, practicable.[18]

II. Personal Scope

The principal provisions in the Treaty, Articles 48, 49 and 51 are unclear as to the personal scope of the rights they grant. Article 48(1) speaks simply of "workers"; Article 48(2) refers to "workers of the Member States"; and these phrases are repeated in the following Articles. Article 51 also speaks simply of "workers".

Obviously the Treaty was not intended to grant immigration rights to workers from the whole world; so there must be some limitation on the word "workers". Two criteria spring to mind: nationality and residence. These are not the only possible criteria, but even if we limit ourselves to these two, there are four possible solutions to the scope of the Treaty: it could apply to all nationals of Member States irrespective of their residence; secondly, it could apply to all residents irrespective of their nationality; thirdly, it could apply only to those who are both nationals and residents; or finally it could apply to those who are either nationals or residents. The Treaty gives no clue as to which of these is correct.

The Council, however, appears to be of the opinion that the first of the above solutions is right and the implementing legislation under both Article 49 and Article 51 is based on the concept of nationality.[19] This, however, is not the end of the matter. The European Court has held that Article 48 is directly applicable;[20] consequently if its scope is wider than that of the implementing legislation all those persons included within its scope could avail themselves of the Community rights even if they were not covered by the implementing legislation.[21] It is also possible, on the other hand, that the implementing legislation is too wide in scope. If Article 49 were interpreted as applying only to workers resident in a Member State, then Regulation 1612/68 would be *ultra vires* in so far as it purports to grant rights to non-residents. It is possible that one day these questions will be raised in the courts of a Member State and will be referred to the European Court under Article 177. Since, however, this has not so far occurred, it will be assumed from now on that nationality is the proper criterion.

Before considering what exactly is meant by a "national" of a Member

State, two subsidiary matters must be considered. First, there is the question of stateless persons and refugees. Reg. 1408/71 (which makes social security provisions for migrant workers) provides that stateless persons and refugees resident within the territory of a Member State are included within its scope.[22] No such provision is found in Reg. 1612/68. The Council was in fact pressed by the Economic and Social Committee to include these categories of persons[23] but instead the Governments of the Member States, meeting in the Council, made a declaration to the effect that they would view with "particular favour" the entry of refugees settled in another Member State.[24] This does not of course give the refugees any legal rights of entry. The result is that refugees and stateless persons have no right of free movement within the Community but if they are in fact admitted into another Member State they are entitled to the social security benefits provided by Reg. 1408/71.

Secondly, there is the question of the families of workers. Since the status of the *worker* is the main criterion, the nationality of his family is irrelevant so long as the worker himself comes within the scope of the provision. This is the case as regards both the right of entry[25] and social security.[26] However, there is an additional provision in the case of social security. Under Reg. 1408/71 the survivor of a deceased worker is included within the scope of the Regulation, irrespective of the national status of the worker, so long as the survivor is a national of a Member State or a stateless person or refugee resident in a Member State.[27]

The next question to consider is what exactly is meant by "nationality" in this context. It might seem at first sight that this would present no problems. Under international law the question whether a person is a national of a particular country is decided by the law of that country. One assumes, therefore, that Community law refers to the national law of each Member State to define this term and that, once one has discovered who the nationals of the nine Member States are, one would know exactly who were the beneficiaries of the rights granted under Community law. The problem is not, however, so simple.

The difficulty arises from the fact that, in the case of at least some Member States (Britain included), citizenship is bestowed not only on the inhabitants (to use a deliberately vague word) of the states themselves, but also on the inhabitants of overseas dependencies or former dependencies. Thus, in the case of the United Kingdom, there is no such thing as citizenship of the United Kingdom alone, but only citizenship of the United Kingdom *and Colonies*. The question is whether inhabitants or former inhabitants of such overseas territories are, or should be, included within the scope of the Community provisions. The United Kingdom Government has, of course, made a Declaration which excludes most citizens of the United Kingdom and Colonies who are in this category. However, as the legality of this Declaration has been questioned, it is desirable to consider first the position apart from it.

At first sight, it might seem that under the Treaty provisions all citizens of a Member State should be included, irrespective of whether they obtained that citizenship through a connection with that Member State itself or with a dependency or former dependency. However, on further consideration, this seems less certain. It should be remembered that the Treaty is concerned only with free movement *within* the Community. This would clearly exclude immigration from territories outside the Community, even if the persons concerned were citizens of a Member State. Thus, for example, a person wanting to immigrate into the Community from Hong Kong or Kenya would not be able to benefit from the Community provisions.

What is the position if someone from one of these territories immigrates first to a Community country, say Britain, and then claims that he is entitled under Community law to free entry into another Member State? This would of course be movement *within* the Community so it might be thought that the Community provisions would apply. Article 135 EEC provides, however, not only that the countries and territories listed in Annex IV are outside the territorial scope of the Treaty but also that workers "from" these territories are outside the personal scope of the provisions. The exact words of Article 135 are:

> ...freedom of movement within Member States for workers from the countries and territories...shall be governed by agreements to be concluded...

As already mentioned, it seems that this excludes these workers since no such agreements have as yet been concluded.[28]

The position of workers from overseas territories connected with Britain that are not included in the list in Annex IV is probably the same. It will be remembered that under Article 227(3) EEC these territories are excluded entirely from the territorial scope of the Treaty. The Treaty does not say whether workers from these territories are excluded from the personal scope of the Community provisions but this might be a fairly reasonable inference. It would be strange if workers from territories completely outside the scope of the Treaties were in a better position than those from associated territories.

It will be seen that Community law appears to exclude from the personal scope of the free movement provisions those workers who are "from" the overseas territories.[29] Unfortunately, it is nowhere made clear exactly which workers are regarded as being "from" these territories. However, it might be logical to suppose that the framers of the Treaties intended that the link between the territorial and the personal scope of the provisions should be maintained. The arguments in favour of such a link were given at the beginning of this paper. If this is correct, one might infer that the personal scope of the provisions should cover only those nationals of the Member States who possess that nationality by reason of their connection with the European territory of the state in question. Consequently, persons who possess the nationality of a Member State by virtue of, for example, their birth in an overseas territory would be regarded as as being "from" that territory and therefore excluded.

The United Kingdom Declaration

The Declaration by the United Kingdom Government defining the term "national" with reference to the United Kingdom was made at the time of the signature of the Treaty of Accession. Under this definition, the following three categories of persons are United Kingdom nationals:

1. Citizens of the United Kingdom and Colonies who are patrials;
2. British subjects who are citizens neither of the United Kingdom and Colonies nor of any other Commonwealth country who are patrials;
3. Persons who are citizens of the United Kingdom and Colonies by birth, registration or naturalisation in Gibraltar or whose father was so born, registered or naturalised.

In addition, it is provided in Article 2 of Protocol 3 to the Accession Treaty[30] that Channel Islanders and Manxmen do not benefit from the Community provisions relating to free movement of persons and services. Article 6 of the Protocol contains a definition of such persons. These islands were excluded at their own request.

In order to understand the scope and effect of the United Kingdom declaration, it is desirable to consider separately each of the three categories of persons covered by it.

Category 1

This is by far the most important category since the vast majority of persons who qualify as United Kingdom nationals for Community purposes will do so under it. It consists of those persons who are both citizens of the United Kingdom and Colonies and patrials. To discover who these persons are it is necessary to consider the concepts of *citizenship of the United Kingdom and Colonies* and *patriality*.

Originally, British nationality was based on the concept of allegiance and all those born in the King's dominions were regarded (except in special cases such as ambassadors) as owing allegiance to the King. They were British subjects. In principle[31] the status of British subject was uniform throughout the British Empire and there was no separate nationality for the inhabitants of individual colonies or the Mother Country. However, when the Dominions (as the self-governing colonies began to be called after the First World War) moved towards complete independence they naturally desired to have a separate nationality to complement their separate statehood.

The decisive step was taken by Canada when it enacted the Canadian Citizenship Act 1946 and thus created the status of a Canadian citizen. Other countries followed suit and from the common status of British subject each carved out its own citizenship. Each country adopted its own criteria of citizenship, and they were not always the same; however, there was a general similarity between the rules adopted by most of the countries. Thus, one might expect some or all of the following categories of persons to have citizenship: those born in the country; those whose fathers were born there (possibly subject to a requirement of registration); those naturalized there; and the wives of any of the foregoing (again possibly subject to registration).

How was Britain to react to this development? Britain could have done likewise and carved out her own citizenship according to the same criteria. Two difficulties would, however, have resulted if this course had been followed. First, what would have been the status of the inhabitants of the remaining colonies? Secondly, what would have happened to those British subjects who had obtained that status through a connection with an independent Commonwealth country but who were not claimed as citizens by the country concerned (or who had no desire to be citizens of it)?

The solution adopted was not to create a citizenship of the United Kingdom but of the United Kingdom *and Colonies*. This citizenship, which was established by the British Nationality Act 1948, contains three basic categories of persons. The first was those persons who, under the normal criteria (i.e. those adopted by most other Commonwealth countries), would be citizens of the United Kingdom as such. Secondly, there were those who, under the same criteria, would be citizens of one of the remaining colonies. Thirdly, any other British subjects who were not claimed as citizens (or, in some cases, did not wish to be citizens) of the independent Commonwealth country in which they lived were also made citizens of the United Kingdom and Colonies. This meant that in theory everyone who was previously a British subject would become a citizen of some country.[32] Moreover, the common status of British subject was retained but put on a new basis. It no longer depended on British law alone but on the citizenship laws of all the Commonwealth countries: the rule was that the citizens of each Commonwealth country automatically became British subjects. And since the term "British subject" offended the republican sentiments of some countries, an alternative term, "Commonwealth citizen", was adopted which could be used instead. In British law these two terms have exactly the same meaning.[33]

The other concept that must be considered is *patriality*. This concept is of recent origin, having been created by the Immigration Act 1971 for the purposes of immigration law. It is not possible to discuss the history of British immigration law, but it may be said that originally all Commonwealth citizens had a free right of entry into the United Kingdom, but restrictions were progressively applied as a result of popular feeling against the coloured immigrants who had come to Britain in large numbers after the Second World War. The purpose of the Immigration Act was to limit the right of entry to those persons who have a connection with the United Kingdom. The term "patrial" was coined to refer to such persons.

A definition of patriality is given in section 2 of the Act. It is rather complicated, but may be summarized (with some loss of accuracy) by saying that the following categories of persons are patrials:

1. Citizens of the United Kingdom and Colonies who obtained that citizenship by birth, adoption, naturalization or registration in the United Kingdom or Islands. (By "Islands" is meant the Channel Islands or the Isle of Man.)
2. Citizens of the United Kingdom and Colonies whose father or mother falls into *Category 1* (above).
3. Citizens of the United Kingdom and Colonies whose father or mother falls into *Category 2* (above).

4. Citizens of the United Kingdom and Colonies who have been lawfully resident in the United Kingdom or Islands for a period of at least five years and who were free of any immigration restrictions at the end of that period.
5. Commonwealth citizens whose father or mother was a citizen of the United Kingdom and Colonies by birth in the United Kingdom or Islands.
6. Commonwealth citizens who are the wives of any of the above.

It is now possible to return to the definition of a United Kingdom national for Community purposes. It will be remembered that the first category under this definition consisted of persons who are both citizens of the United Kingdom and Colonies and patrials. The persons who satisfy this requirement are those who fall into categories 1 to 4 of the definition of patriality together with those persons in category 6 (wives) who are citizens of the United Kingdom and Colonies.[34] The only exception to this is that Channel Islanders and Manxmen are excluded.[35]

This may seem all rather complicated. However, the essential point about the first category of the definition of a United Kingdom national for Community purposes is that it corresponds almost exactly to what the definition of a United Kingdom citizen would be if it had been decided to create such a citizenship on the basis of the same criteria as were adopted by other Commonwealth countries when they framed their citizenship laws. In other words, it excludes those persons who are citizens of the United Kingdom and Colonies on the basis of a connection with a colony or former colony. It is, therefore, by no means an unreasonable definition of the concept of a United Kingdom national.

Category 2

This category consists of British subjects who are citizens neither of the United Kingdom and Colonies nor of any other Commonwealth country and who are patrials. Since, as was stated above, it was a basic principle of the United Kingdom and Commonwealth nationality law that everyone who was previously a British subject would obtain the citizenship of either the United Kingdom and Colonies or of some other Commonwealth country, it might seem that nobody could fall into this category. In fact, however, the principle never operated perfectly and there is a small anomalous group of persons who do come within it. This group is made up of two classes of person: certain citizens of the Irish Republic, and persons falling under certain transitional provisions.[36]

The first class consists of persons coming within the provisions of section 2(1) of the British Nationality Act 1948. This allows citizens of the Irish Republic who were British subjects immediately before the 1948 Act to remain British subjects if they claim the right to do so by notice to the Home Secretary.[37] The grounds on which the claim may be made are set out in the Act. As citizens of the Irish Republic, these persons will, anyway, be able to benefit from the Community provisions concerning free movement. So their inclusion in the definition of a United Kingdom national for Community purposes does not give them any additional rights.

The second class of persons are those coming within section 13 of the British Nationality Act 1948. This transitional provision was designed to deal with the fact that when the 1948 Act came into force not all the independent Commonwealth countries had adopted their own citizenship laws. It was therefore provided in section 13 that persons who were potentially citizens of such countries would have the status of British subjects without citizenship.[38] The idea was that such a status would be temporary; as soon as the country in question adopted its own citizenship law, these persons would either become citizens of that country or, if they did not come within the scope of the new law, they would automatically become citizens of the United Kingdom and Colonies.[39]

In order to come within the second category of United Kingdom nationals for Community purposes such persons must, of course, also be patrials. If reference is made to the definition of patriality given above, it will be remembered that categories 1-4 of that definition consisted of persons who are citizens of the United Kingdom and Colonies. British subjects without citizenship are by definition not citizens of the United Kingdom and Colonies. They are, of course, Commonwealth citizens, since it is provided by section 1(2) of the British Nationality Act 1948 that the terms "British subject" and "Commonwealth citizen" mean the same thing. It is therefore possible for them to come within categories 5 and 6 of the definition of patriality. Whether significant numbers of them do is another question.

It might be thought wrong to include British subjects without citizenship in the definition of a United Kingdom national for Community purposes since they are by definition not citizens of the United Kingdom and Colonies. However, they are potentially such citizens because if their own country adopts a citizenship law under which they do not obtain citizenship they automatically become citizens of the United Kingdom and Colonies. This is provided by section 13(2) of the British Nationality Act

1948. If they do obtain the citizenship of the Commonwealth country in which they live, they will, of course, cease to be United Kingdom nationals for Community purposes.

Category 3

This consists of Gibraltarians, that is citizens of the United Kingdom and Colonies who obtained that citizenship by birth, registration or naturalization in Gibraltar, or whose father so obtained it. If there was a separate citizenship of the colony of Gibraltar, these persons would have that citizenship. They need not be patrials in order to be United Kingdom nationals for Community purposes. The reason why Gibraltarians are included in the definition of United Kingdom nationality for Community purposes while the "citizens" of all other British colonies are excluded is that Gibraltar is the only British colony within the territorial scope of the free movement provisions of the Treaty.[40]

Is the United Kingdom Declaration Legally Valid?

It is necessary to consider this question since it has been argued by Böhning in an article in the Common Market Law Review[41] that the Declaration is illegal because "it is incompatible with the Treaty of Rome and its derivative legislation to have one nationality definition for domestic purposes but to exclude from it certain sections of the population for EEC purposes". However, as has been pointed out, this is precisely what Community law itself requires under Article 135 EEC. Even if the Declaration had not been made it is likely that most non-patrials would have been excluded anyway under the Treaties (just as Netherlands citizens from Surinam and the Netherlands Antilles are excluded). In view of the lack of clarity of the Community provisions, however, a Declaration from the United Kingdom Government was certainly much to be desired.

Is the Declaration Justifiable?

Finally, it is desirable to consider whether the Declaration is morally justifiable. The fact that citizens of independent Commonwealth countries are not included is no ground for criticism: they are obviously not United Kingdom nationals.[42] Nor is there any reason for concern over the exclusion of patrials who are not citizens of the United Kingdom and Colonies: they, too, cannot be regarded as United Kingdom nationals.

There is a stronger case for criticising the Declaration on the ground that it excludes non-patrial citizens of the United Kingdom and Colonies. These are persons who obtained the citizenship of the United Kingdom and Colonies either by a connection with a colony or by a connection with a former colony which has since become independent. In the latter case there will usually be some special reason why they did not become citizens of that country. The justification for excluding such persons from the definition of a United Kingdom national for Community purposes is that their country of origin is outside the territorial scope of the Treaty. Their exclusion is, therefore, justified on the basis of the principle of reciprocity: if Community workers have no right to work in their country, why should they be given the right to work within the Community?

It might, however, be objected that this principle does not apply if they settle in the United Kingdom, especially if, as is the case with the "Kenya Asians", they are unable to return to their native country. The answer to this is that any citizen of the United Kingdom and Colonies who settles in the United Kingdom will automatically become a patrial after five years: he will fall under category 4 of the definition of patriality given above.[43] Consequently, all citizens of the United Kingdom and Colonies who settle in the United Kingdom may, after a relatively short period, benefit from the Community provisions.[44]

Perhaps the best way of summing up the personal scope of the free movement provisions is to draw a comparison with the ways in which the free movement of goods may be brought about. As is well known, there are basically two ways of doing this – a free trade area and a common market. The former is more restrictive: only goods originating in a Member State are allowed free entry into the other States. In a common market, on the other hand, goods imported into one Member State from the outside world are allowed free entry into the other States. The difference, of course, between the two is that a common market has a common set of rules for imports from third countries; a free trade area does not.

If we draw on this analogy, we can say that the Community provisions concerning the free movement of persons are equivalent to a free trade area, not a common market. Workers "originating" in a Member State can move freely to other Member States; but immigrants from outside cannot. This is really quite understandable, since the Community has no common immigration policy. Until this is achieved, it is unlikely that immigrants from third countries will be fully included in the free movement provisions.

[1] See also Articles 48(3) (d) and 51 ((b) EEC.

[2] JO 1968, L 257/2. See also Directive 68/360, JO 1968, L 257/13, Art. 2; Reg. 1251/70, JO 1970, L 142/24, Art. 1; and Reg. 1408/71, JO 1971, L 149/2, Art. 3(1).

[3] See the Council Decision of 15 October 1968, Dec. 68/359, JO 1968, L 257/1.

[4] The phrase "countries and territories" is defined in Article 131 as those listed in Annex IV.

[5] Special provisions applicable to Gibraltar with regard to certain products and to turnover taxes are found in Article 28 of the Treaty of Accession. Annex I excludes Gibraltar from the customs union. It is not entirely clear what territories besides Gibraltar fall under Article 227(4) EEC. For the view that Monaco, San Marino and Andorra are excluded, see Maestripier, *La Libre Circulation des Personnes et des Services dans la CEE* (1971), pp. 119-120; see also Mégret. *Le Droit de la Communauté Économique Européenne*, vol. 3, p. 132 (concerned with the right of establishment, but the same argument would seem to apply to the free movement of workers). For the contrary view as regards Monaco and San Marino, see Campbell, *Common Market Law*, vol. III, p. 433, and Bathurst (et al.), *Legal Problems of an Enlarged European Community* (1972), p. 162 (Marshall and Simmonds). West Berlin is within the scope of the Treaty: at the time of the signature of the EEC Treaty the German Government made a Declaration allowing it to declare, prior to the ratification of the Treaty, that the Treaty applied to West Berlin. Such a Declaration was made.

[6] See also the Joint Declaration on the Sovereign Base Areas made in connection with the signing of the Treaty of Accession.

[7] However, Annex VII to the Act of Accession, Part VII, allows the United Kingdom and the Republic of Ireland to maintain until 31 December 1977 their provisions requiring prior authorisation for immigration into Northern Ireland and the Republic respectively.

[8] An interesting question is how the right of free movement could be enforced with regard to Gibraltar. If Community workers were not allowed entry to Gibraltar, no doubt the Commission or another Member State could bring proceedings against the United Kingdom under Articles 169 or 170 EEC, but if a Community worker brought proceedings in the courts of Gibraltar could a reference be made from those courts to the European Court? Article 177 EEC speaks of a court "of a Member State" and it might be argued that Gibraltar is not truly a Member State.

However, under Article 227(4) EEC, the "provisions" of the Treaty apply to Gibraltar. Since Article 177 is such a provision, it could be argued that it applies to Gibraltar and a reference from the courts of that territory could be made. This seems a preferable solution, since otherwise the enforcement of the Treaty would be less effective.

[9]   See C.W. Van der Pot, *Handboek van het Nederlandse Staatsrecht* (8th ed. 1968), pp. 201 *et seq.*

[10]   Protocol on the Application of the Treaty Establishing the EEC to the Non-European Parts of the Kingdom of the Netherlands, Cmnd. 4864 (1972), p. 133.

[11]   *Ibid.* p. 167.

[12]   See now Art. 38 and Annex VIII of Council Decision 70/549, JO 1970, L 282/83.

[13]   See Edens and Patijn, "The Scope of the EEC System of Free Movement of Workers" (1972) 9 C.M.L. Rev. 322 at 325-326.

[14]   Case 167/73 *Commission v. French Republic* [1974] ECR 359.

[15]   See Maestripieri, (*op. cit.*, note 5), pp. 114-119.

[16]   *Walrave & Koch v. Association Union Cycliste Internationale et al.* (case 36/74) [1974] ECR 1405.

[17]   The Court held that it was unnecessary to decide whether the pacemaker was an employee (in which case Article 48 would be applicable) or the provider of a service (in which case the relevant provision would be Article 59) since the rule against discrimination applies in the same way in both cases.

[18]   It would of course depend on the rules of private international law of the country where the proceedings were brought whether the court would have jurisdiction over such a body.

[19]   For measures under Article 49 (free movement) see: Reg. 1612/68, JO 1968, L 257/2, preamble (6th "whereas"), Art. 1(1) "Any national of a Member State, irrespective of his place of residence, shall have the right..." and Art. 47; Directive 68/360, JO 1968, L 257/13, Art. 1; Directive 64/221, JO 1964, No. 56, p. 850, Art. 1; Reg. 1251/70, JO 1970, L 142/24, Art. 1. For social security (Article 51 EEC), see Reg. 1408/71, JO 1971, L 149/2, Art. 2(1).

[20]   Case 167/73 *Commission v. French Republic* [1974] ECR 359; Case 41/74 *Van Duyn v. Home Office* [1974] ECR 1337.

[21]   See W.R. Böhning, "The Scope of the EEC System of Free Movement of Workers: A Rejoinder" (1973) 10 C.M.L. Rev. 81 at 83.

[22]   Reg. 1408/71, JO 1971, L 149/2, Art. 2(1). Art. 1(d) provides that "refugee" has the meaning assigned to it in Art. 1 of the Geneva Convention on the Status of Refugees of 28 July 1951; Art. 1(e) says that "stateless persons" has the meaning assigned to it in Art. 1 of the New York Convention on the Status of Stateless Persons of 28 September 1954; and Art. 1(h) states that "residence" means habitual residence.

[23] See opinions of 25 March 1964 and of 25-26 October 1967, referred to in Mégret, *Le Droit de la CEE*, vol. 3, p. 2.

[24] Declaration of 25 March 1964, JO 1964, No. 78, p. 1225. Refugees are defined as in the Geneva Convention (above). There is no mention of stateless persons.

[25] See Reg. 1612/68, Articles 10 and 11. Art. 10(1) allows the worker's family (as there defined) to reside with him and Art. 11 allows his spouse and children under 21 to work in the country in question.

[26] See Reg. 1408/71, Art. 2(1) which provides that the Regulation applies also to the worker's family (defined in Art. 1(f)) and to his survivors (defined in Art. 1(g)).

[27] Art. 2(2).

[28] See Edens and Patijn, "The Scope of the EEC System of Free Movement of Workers" (1972) 9 C.M.L. Rev. 322. (This article was criticised by Böhning in (1973) 10 C.M.L. Rev. 81 but the conclusions of Edens and Patijn as regards Community law still seem sound. For a reply by Edens and Patijn, see *ibid* at p. 84.) See also Maestripieri, *op. cit.* note 5, pp. 21-22.

[29] See also Art. 42(3) of Reg. 1612/68, which provides that the Regulation does not apply to workers from non-European countries or territories having institutional ties with a Member State who immigrate to such Member State on the basis of a special relationship or agreement between the territory and the Member State. For comments on this, see Edens and Patijn, (1972) 9 C.M.L. Rev. at 324.

[30] See also Article 227(5)(c) EEC as added by the Accession Treaty, Art. 26(1).

[31] There were certain exceptions to this: for example locally naturalized persons.

[32] The exceptions to this are considered below.

[33] British Nationality Act 1948, s. 1(2).

[34] Persons in category 5 are excluded for the following reason: if they are citizens of the United Kingdom and Colonies they will fall under category 2; if not, they cannot come within the first category of the definition of a United Kingdom national for Community purposes. It should also be mentioned that the wife of a citizen of the United Kingdom and Colonies has the option of obtaining that citizenship by registration: British Nationality Act 1948, s. 6(2).

[35] See Articles 2 and 6 of Protocol 3 to the Accession Treaty (discussed above).

[36] There is also a third class: the wives of persons in the two other classes, provided they (the wives) register under the provisions of s. 1 of the British Nationality Act 1965. Approximately 200 have done so (information supplied by the Home Office) but it is doubtful if many of these are patrials and thus United Kingdom nationals for Community purposes.

[37] Just over 123,000 have done so (information supplied by the Home Office).

[38] For a definition of who is "potentially" a citizen of a Commonwealth country, see s. 32(7) and (8) of the British Nationality Act, 1948.

[39]   At the present time there are several hundred thousand persons who are British subjects under s. 13 (information supplied by the Home Office). They are persons who, before 1949, were British subjects by virtue of a connection with India or Pakistan. It is unlikely that many of them are patrials and thus United Kingdom nationals for Community purposes.

[40]   It is asserted by W.R. Böhning, *The Migration of Workers in the United Kingdom and the European Community* (1972), p. 154 that the Declaration is racialist because it includes non-patrial citizens of the United Kingdom and Colonies from Gibraltar (who are mainly white) and excludes other non-patrial citizens of the United Kindom and Colonies (who are mainly coloured). This contention is obviously misconceived for the reason stated in the text. If Community workers from e.g. France or Germany have the right to work in Gibraltar but not in Hong Kong, it is only reasonable that workers from Gibraltar should be allowed to work in France or Germany but that workers from Hong Kong should not.

[41]   (1973) 10 C.M.L. Rev. 81 at 83-84.

[42]   It is suggested by Böhning that British subjects who are not citizens should (even if non-patrial) be regarded as United Kingdom nationals if they are settled in the United Kingdom. The foundation of his argument is the fact that they have political rights in the United Kingdom (e.g. voting rights). (See W.R. Böhning, *The Migration of Workers in the United Kingdom and the European Community* (1972), p. 158.) It may be unusual for a country to grant such rights to persons who are not its nationals, but this does not alter the fact that such persons do not have British nationality; it is merely a hang-over from the days of a united British-ruled Empire. To suggest that the status of being a British subject, i.e. a Commonwealth citizen, is equivalent to United Kingdom nationality is to deny the separate nationhood of the independent Commonwealth countries.

[43]   See the Immigration Act 1971, s. 2(1)(c).

[44]   The only qualification to this is that the provisions of the Joint Declaration on the Free Movement of Workers (made at the time of the signing of the Treaty of Accession) might be invoked.

3

"An Incipient Form of European Citizenship"

RICHARD PLENDER

In the progressive interpretation of constitutional documents it not infrequently happens that provisions acquire over a period of time a significance radically different from any which might have been contemplated by their draftsmen. In the case of the Magna Carta of 1215, the prohibition on imprisonment and outlawry *nisi per judicium parium* was designed to ensure that in a very limited class of cases suitors of the court might themselves give the court's judgment without royal control; but that passage was later interpreted as a guarantee of the right to trial by jury.[1] Likewise, an article in the Magna Carta which stipulated that alien merchants should be free to enter and leave England "in accordance with ancient and lawful customs" was almost certainly intended to prohibit the levying of certain tolls on certain traders; but it came to be regarded as evidence of a right enjoyed by aliens to enter British territory.[2]

In the case of the European Economic Community, the articles in the founding treaty which provide for the free movement of labour were conceived in economic terms. The authors of the Spaak Report wrote of the need to make rational use of the "factors of production" in the Member States, and identified those factors as capital and manpower.[3] They contemplated that the programme to establish freedom of movement would stimulate an increase in the volume of migration between the territories of the Members.[4]

In the event, the establishment of freedom of movement has been accompanied by a fall in the volume of intra-Community migration, at least in

F.G. Jacobs, ed. European Law and the Individual © *1976, North-Holland Publishing Company*

relative terms. In 1959, when the programme had barely begun, some three quarters of the migrant workers in the original Community of six came from the Member States, but in 1973, when the programme was said to have reached fruition, three quarters of the migrant workers within the enlarged Community of nine came from Third States, and only the remainder from the territories of the Members.[5] In the year following the enlargement of the Communities, the volume of migration of workers from the United Kingdom to the original Member States fell significantly, as did the number of workers from those States migrating in the opposite direction.[6] There is reason to believe that this is not mere coincidence. In ensuring that nationals of the several Member States, employed within the same enterprise in the Communities, will enjoy equally with nationals of the State in which the enterprise is situated the same pay, the same social security entitlements and the same conditions of employment the organs of the Communities seem to have made nationals of the Member States less attractive to employers within the Communities than are nationals of Third Countries, to whom those rights have not yet been applied.[7]

In any event, the demographic consequence that was envisaged when the founders of the Community drafted the articles on freedom of movement has by no means materialised; but those articles have been invested with a constitutional significance instead. Only twelve years after the conclusion of the Treaty of Rome, the Vice-President of the Commission discerned in the articles governing free movement of labour not merely an economic purpose but "an incipient form...of European citizenship".[8] More recently, the Commission has envisaged the creation of a Passport Union, "as a natural extension of the principles of free movement" set out in these articles, adding "that the introduction of such a passport would have a psychological effect, one which would emphasize the feeling of nationals of the nine Member States of belonging to the Community".[9]

These developments prompt us to ask to what extent the programme to establish freedom of movement for labour in the European Communities has already developed characteristics, however embryonic and immature, of a law governing the status and rights of citizens. If any European citizenship is indeed to be discerned, even in incipient form, there should be reason to expect the development of at least three features: first, a class of persons exclusively defined by a common (European) criterion; second, the enjoyment of some consequential privileges by those persons, including the right of movement throughout the common European territory; and third, the abolition of discrimination between those persons on the ground of some other nationality in cases in which they seek to assert their consequential privileges or rights.[10]

I. A Common Definition

At first sight the Treaty establishing the European Economic Community appears to provide the basis for a common European definition of a class of persons akin to citizens. Articles 48 to 50 of that Treaty refer to "workers" as the persons who are entitled to the freedoms set out in that document, and it is well established that this term falls to be defined by Community law. In *Hoekstra (née Unger)* v. *Bestuur der Bedrijfsvereniging voor Detailhandel en Ambachten* a Dutch pensions authority asserted, to the contrary, that the word "worker" in this context fell to be defined by domestic law, and in advancing this contention it was supported by no less an authority than Advocate-General Lagrange. The argument was, however, roundly rejected by the Court of Justice of the European Communities in terms remarkably forthright:

> Articles 48 to 51 of the Treaty, by the very fact of establishing freedom of movement for 'workers', have given Community scope to this term. If the definition of this term were a matter within the competence of national law, it would therefore be possible for each Member State to modify the meaning of the concept of 'migrant worker' and to eliminate at will the protection afforded by the Treaty to certain categories of person.[11]

Unger's Case has been followed in a series of decisions of the same Court having the collective tendency to expand the category of persons qualifying for the protection given to "workers". In *Vaassen-Goebbels* v. *Beambtenfonds voor het Mijnbedrijf* the Court extended that protection to the widow of a worker, who herself had never worked, and who had migrated for reasons wholly unconnected with employment.[12] In *Caisse de maladie des C.F.L. "Entr'aide Médicale" et al.* v. *Compagnie belge d'assurances générales sur la vie et contre les accidents* the Court held that the expression applied in relation to an injury sustained in circumstances not connected with employment.[13] In *Hessische Knappschaft* v. *Maison Singer et fils* it held that the term "migrant worker" was not limited to persons moving their locations in order to fulfill their obligations to their current or prospective employers.[14] In reaching this conclusion the Court expressly stated that the term formed one of the foundations of the Treaty and was thus to be construed with generosity. With a few exceptions of marginal importance[15] the domestic courts have followed the lead of the Court of Justice in interpreting the expression widely, and in accordance with common criteria.

However, the principal Regulations giving effect to the programme for freedom of movement have imposed on the term "worker" a limitation neither expressed in the Treaty nor discussed by the Court of Justice: the right to freedom of movement is extended under those Regulations only to workers who are nationals of the Member States.[16] From the earliest days it has been accepted in most quarters that in this context, as in general international law, it is for each state to determine who is and who is not one of its nationals – even though the state by so doing might modify the concept "migrant worker" precisely contrary to the words of the Court of Justice in *Unger's Case*.[17] The point is not academic. When the European Communities were enlarged there was appended to the Act of Accession a Declaration by the United Kingdom to the effect that in relation to that country, and for the purposes of free movement of labour, the term "national" means a citizen of the United Kingdom and Colonies or a British subject without citizenship having in either case the right of abode in the United Kingdom, or a citizen of the United Kingdom and Colonies by birth or naturalization or registration in Gibraltar, or by descent from such a citizen.[18]

Granted that freedom of movement was to be enjoyed only by nationals of the Member States, there was a need for some guidance on the application of that principle to the United Kingdom. There is no definition of a national of the United Kingdom in domestic law; and to apply the meaning most commonly ascribed to the expression in the conduct of international relations[19] would have entailed extending freedom of movement to persons who do not enjoy the right of abode in the United Kingdom.[20] The Declaration has nevertheless proved controversial,[21] and one commentator at least has argued that it is ineffective, since it contravenes a principle whereby Community law and not domestic law must identify the beneficiaries of the programme for free movement of labour.[22] In order to test his argument it is necessary to ask two questions: first, whether in limiting the right of free movement to the nationals of the Member States the principal Regulations purport to impose an unwarranted restriction on the founding Treaty; second, whether Community law might impose any restriction on the capacity of a state to define its own nationals for the purposes of a Regulation in which the reference to nationals of the Member States is assumed to be impeccable.

A careful reading of the Treaty suggests that the draftsmen did not necessarily intend to restrict to nationals of the several Member States enjoyment of the freedom of movement. Articles 48 to 51 provide that the freedom shall be enjoyed by "workers" or "workers of the Member States" – any mention of nationality is excluded; conversely the following articles stipulate that freedom of establishment is to be enjoyed by "nationals of the Member States". The contrast appears to be deliberate[23] and rational: in the case of workers the paramount economic consideration is mobility, and the freedom of an unemployed worker in France to take employment in Germany will be beneficial both to the country of immigration and to that of emigration even if the migrant is a Moroccan; but in the case of establishment the economic arguments connected with mobility weigh less heavily whereas a number of problems arise which are peculiarly susceptible of resolution on national grounds.[24] Secondly, the draftsmen of the Treaty may well have foreseen a possibility that appears to have materialised, that is, that if nationals of the Member States were to be the sole recipients of the expensive privileges given to migrant workers they would become less attractive to prospective employers than nationals of third countries, whereas this consideration does not apply in the case of establishment, where the beneficiaries are by definition self-employed.[25] Thirdly, the term "workers" is used elsewhere in Community law without an implied reference to nationality[26] and it might be assumed at first sight that a single term has a single meaning in a single body of law. Indeed, the implementing regulations on social security expressly include within the term "worker" refugees protected by the Geneva Convention of 1951: such persons are by definition not nationals of the states in which they live. Fourthly, the use of nationality as one of the criteria for determining whether an individual qualifies as a worker involves attributing to Member States the capacity to modify the content of the expression, contrary to the words of the Court in *Unger's Case*.[27] Finally, the Commission is now working on a proposed Regulation to govern the condition of migrant workers who have taken employment in the Communities but are nationals of Third Countries.[28] It would be difficult to find authority for such a Regulation other than in article 49 of the Treaty.[29]

All of this is not to assert that the term "workers", still less the expression "workers of the Member States", applies indiscriminately to all employees whatever, without regard to residence, place of work or personal or national status. The draftsmen unquestionably contemplated that some limitation would be imposed on the categories of persons eligible to assert the freedom of movement. But it appears reasonable to suggest that the limitation contemplated by the founders of the Treaty might have been one based on the worker's status in immigration or employment law rather than in the law of nationality of the country of emigration. Had the Council employed some such limitation in place of nationality, the programme for free movement would have entailed some approximation of immigration laws among the Member States so as to ensure that nationals of Third Countries could not again admission to a Member State with strict immigration controls by the mere device of qualifying as a worker in a Member State where controls are more relaxed.[30]

When the Council adopted Regulation 1612 of 1968 (which contains the principal provisions for giving effect to the programme for freedom of movement) the definition of the nationals of the Member States presented little serious difficulty.[31] Some elucidation of the term was required in the cases of Germany and France[32] and this was provided by way of Declaration. When therefore the need arose for the term "national" to be defined in relation to the United Kingdom the problem was met by use of a Declaration once more.[33]

The legal effect of Declarations annexed to the founding treaties, and to the Act of Accession, has received insufficient scholastic attention. It is possible only to offer some propositions on the subject with a modicum of confidence.[34] Where a Declaration amounts to a Member State's objective statement of its own law on a point from which there is a remission from the Communities' legal order it will be conclusive in the absence of very persuasive evidence to the contrary. Where it amounts to a Member State's description of a point of Community law it is of lesser value. Where it amounts to a reservation it is ineffective.

The Declaration on United Kingdom nationality does not amount to an objective statement of domestic nationality law:[35] it adapts to the United Kingdom part of a Regulation which was adopted without regard to the particular circumstances of that country. The Act of Accession does not expressly authorise and the Treaty establishing the European Economic Community does not expressly envisage the adaptation of Regulations by this means. Formal legal principle thus might lead to the conclusion that the Declaration is not necessarily binding in Community law, and may be reviewed by any Court of appropriate jurisdiction.

Experience and practical considerations indicate, however, that no court will readily avoid the Declaration in the present state of development of Community law.[36] To do so would entail reclaiming for the judiciary, or for the central Community institutions, the capacity to determine the beneficiaries of the programme for freedom of movement, and would risk upsetting the plans laid by the Council in the development of this area of Community legislation. So long as the judiciary or central institutions remain unlikely to reclaim from Member States the capacity to make that determination, we can scarcely expect the development of a common definition of the persons entitled to the rights of freedom of movement.

II. Consequential Rights

A search for the consequential rights or privileges of migrant workers leads in the first instance to the Treaty and thence to Regulation 1612/68, which expressly articulates the content of free movement.[37] For instance, in *Re Residence Permits* the Berlin Verwaltungsgericht stated as early as 1962 that a national of a Member State must be issued with a residence permit where he has already been issued with a work permit and no objection can be found on grounds of public order or health to his remaining in the Federal Republic.[38] It is however noteworthy that the right to which the Regulation refers is the right to move to "other" Member States: there is no express statement of a right to move to or reside or work in one's own country, and since the programme for freedom of movement does not appear applicable in the case of immigration into the territory of the Communities of a person working outside it, the cases in which Community law will guarantee an individual's right to reside or work in his own country are likely to be very exceptional and few.

Further, the provisions for derogating from freedom of movement, set out in the Treaty[39] and in the Regulation[40] and Directive[41] continue to be vague and undefined. The public policy exception has given rise to a massive volume of litigation[42] but the case-law provides little basis for the deduction of general principles, and the Directive on public policy gives negative rather than positive guidance. Likewise, the expression "employment in the public service" is imprecise.[43] Late in 1975 the Commission published a report on the establishment of a Passport Union within the EEC. If that report were implemented it would constitute a significant step towards abolition of documentary controls on the movement of persons within the Community.[44] However, the view has not yet been taken that the right to freedom of movement is incompatible with the maintenance of documentary controls on the migration of eligible workers between the territories of the several Member States. Indeed, progress towards the abolition of such controls has been made more rapidly and visibly in western European organizations other than the Communities. The Council of Europe provided the forum in 1957 for the conclusion of the European Agreement on Regulations governing the Movement of Persons between the Member States of the Council of Europe[45] which has enjoyed a real if modest success in extending to nationals of contracting parties the facility of using national identity cards rather than passports in visits of less than three months' duration. The Council also provided the forum for conclusion of the European Agreement on Travel by Young Persons on Collective Passports...[46] which is useful to organizers and members of parties, even though the Member States on ratifying the Treaty imposed many and varied reservations. The Organization for European Economic Cooperation, which functioned on the basis of a Convention that specifically envisaged the progressive reduction of obstacles to the free movement of persons,[47] adopted a number of recommendations on the subject, including that of December 20, 1955 on the movement and employment of foreign manpower.[48] Some of these provided the initiative for conclusion of bilateral agreements between the Member States, and these in turn have made possible the use of new and cheaper kinds of passports, such as British Visitors' Passports or Visitors' Cards.[49]

The European Communities, on the other hand, made until very recently a relatively modest contribution to the abolition of documentary controls. Although Article 69(1) of the Treaty instituting the European Coal and Steel Community envisaged that Member States would renounce "any restriction based on nationality upon the employment in the coal and steel industries of workers" of proven qualifications,[50] although in pursuance of that article the Council adopted an administrative agreement which provided for the issuance of Community Labour Cards to such workers,[51] and although these cards were said in the same arrangement to "enable their holders to travel freely in response to an offer of work",[52] a Decision of the Council of Ministers expressly provided that the Community Labour Card would not itself be sufficient to enable the holder to cross national frontiers. Passports or national identity cards would be required in addition.[53] Likewise, in the case of the European Communities, the right to move from one country to another continues to be contingent on production of a national identity card or passport;[54] and although work permits are not required by Community nationals seeking employment in a Member State other than their own, a new form of residence permit continues to be required,[55] and although these are said to be available by right, their issuance is contingent on production of a certificate from an employer, just as the issuance of work permits was in most of the Member States contingent on production of such a document.[56] A truly integrated community of labour, such as exists within the Benelux countries, finds it unnecessary to construct such novel forms of residence permits or identity cards, since it permits migrant workers to travel without any formality other than production of a personal identity card or national passport.[57]

This is not to deny that the European Communities have enjoyed some real success in reducing the formal and documentary requirements that apply in the case of the movement of nationals of one Member State to the territory of another. It is not insignificant that the Communities have made possible the more widespread use of national identity cards for the purpose of movement between different parts of the Communities. Nor is it insignificant that Member States are required by Directive to issue passports or identity documents to their own nationals who wish to look for work in a part of the Communities other than their own country.[58] This last requirement appears to destroy, within its limited field of application, a conspicuously outdated principle of English law to the effect that the issuance of passports is entirely a matter of prerogative and beyond the purview of the domestic courts.[59] These changes are to be welcomed, and they go a long way towards atoning for the fact that much of the documentary system governing migration in the European Communities is a bureaucrat's not a migrant's paradise. Only the Commission's report on the Passport Union, itself a tentative document, awaiting approval, provides rational basis for hope that there will develop in the Communities a right to free movement enjoyed by all workers without significant limitation.

III. Abolition of Discrimination

In attempting to abolish discrimination between the nationals of the several Member States, the organs of the European Communities have met with more visible success. The courts have held that it is now unlawful to discriminate on grounds of nationality between locals and migrant workers from other Member States by denying to the latter aggregation of income and benefits during a period of compulsory military service abroad.[60] They have held that unlawful discrimination is entailed when a Member State requires a minimum proportion of the crews of its merchant vessels to consist of its own nationals.[61] They have detected unlawful discrimination in limitations imposed on the issuance of television operating licences,[62] and in several instances involving the provision of schooling[63] and social security benefits.[64] The French Court of Appeal, however, has found that no unlawful discrimination is entailed when a national rail network provides concessionary fares to large families only when the latter consist of citizens of the operating state.[65]

An account of the success of the Communities' efforts to abolish discrimination between the nationals of the Member States must, however, remain qualified. In the first place, such discrimination is to be avoided only in cases which do not fall within the exceptions set out in the Treaty, and those exceptions appear inadequately defined.[66] In the second place, the process of ensuring that nationals of the several Member States will be treated equally appears to have contributed to the fall in intra-Community migration.[67] In the third, it remains uncertain to what extent the Communities will extend to nationals of Third States the right to be treated equally with nationals of the Members. In 1974 the Commission submitted to the Council an action programme on migrant workers, the tenor of which was to abolish distinctions between Community nationals and citizens of other countries. On this theme it contains a number of specific proposals for the amendment of Community law. It envisages implementation of voting rights by 1980 for all migrant workers, regardless of nationality, in local elections in the Member States. It contemplates improvements in the social security situation of migrants from non-Member States, aimed at the progressive realization of equality of treatment for all people who live and work in the Community.[68]

If those proposals are adopted, and if significant progress is made towards realizing the principle of priority of the Community labour market, and if the courts rise to the challenge presented by Articles 48 to 51 of the EEC Treaty, and if the Commission's proposals on the Passport Union are adopted by the Council it will then be possible to justify the Vice-President's claim that the programme to establish freedom of movement contains an incipient form of European citizenship. But if those conditions remain unfulfilled it will be easier to discern a basis for that citizenship in such sources as the proposed "European Company". In that event, the attempt to invest articles 48 to 51 with the significance of a citizen's charter will prove to be an exercise in legal mythology.

¹   Art. 39; Radcliffe and Cross, *The English Legal System* (1971), p. 50; Holt, *Magna Carta* (1965), p. 224.

²   Art. 41 of the Magna Carta of 1215; formally repealed, Statute Law (Repeals) Act 1969, s. 1, sched. 1, pt. 1. See Craies, "The Right of Aliens to Enter British Territory", 6 L.Q.R. (1890) 27, 29. During the debate on the Aliens Bill in 1792 Lord Grenville cited this article of Magna Carta as evidence of such a right: XXX Cobbett's *Parliamentary History*, col. 146. Further sources are cited in the author's *International Migration Law* (1972), p. 40.

³   *Comité intergouvernmental créé par la Conférence de Messine: Rapport des Chefs de Délégation aux Ministres des Affaires Etrangères*, Brussels, 21 April 1956 (Secretariat), p. 15.

⁴   The authors of the Spaak Report anticipated that the rise in intra-Community migration would be limited by such perennial factors as linguistic problems and natural conservatism of workers: *Supra*, n. 3 at, p. 80. The Treaty itself provides that Member States shall actively encourage the exchange of young workers: art. 50. Member States had already made arrangements to this effect; see Cmnd. 8478. A programme of exchanges was set up by a Declaration on May 8, 1964 (64/307, JO 1964 1226). The Commission has made a Recommendation setting out the conditions under which young persons are to be employed: January 31, 1967 (67/123, JO 1967 405).

⁵   *Action Programme in Favour of Migrant Workers and their Families,* Com. (74) 2250, p. 1. See *Report on the Development of the Social Situation in the Community in 1974,* Brussels/Luxembourg, March 1975; Bouvard, *Labour Movements in the Common Market* (1972), preface (by Hoffman); Böhning, *The Migration of Workers in the European Community* (1972), statistics at p. 81.

⁶   Reply to Question in the European Parliament by Lord O'Hagan, Qu. 571/74.

⁷   The statistical correlation between the development of the programme and the change in national composition of migrant workers in the Communities is so marked that coincidence appears an insufficient explanation. Research to disclose the precise effects of the programme would however be costly and has not yet been undertaken. For commentaries on equal entitlements to pay, social security benefits and conditions of employment, see Jett, "Free Movement of Labour in the EEC", 8 Tex Int. L.J.(1973) 375; Simmonds, "Immigration Control and the Free Movement of Labour: A Problem of Harmonisation", 21 I.C.L.Q. (1972) 307; Poole, "Mobility of Labour and Job Opportunities", 122 New L.J. (1972) 1147;

Turack, "Freedom of Movement and Travel Documents in Community Law", 17 Buffalo L.J. (1968) 435; Fitzgerald, *The Common Market's Labor Programs* (1966); EEC Publication 1862/1966; Bernstein, "Labour and the European Communities" in Shimm, Baade and Everett, *European Regional Communities: A New Era on the Old Continent* (1961); ter Heide, "The Free Movement of Workers in the Final Phase", 6 C.M.L. Rev. (1970) 466; Seché, "The Revision of Regs. Nos. 3 and 4 (Social Security of Migrant Workers) in the Light of their Interpretation by the Court of Justice", 6 C.M.L. Rev. (1970) 170; "Improvement of the System of Social Security for Migrant Workers", 3 *Bulletin of the EEC* (1970) 30; Rodière, "L'arrêt Bentzinger et la jurisprudence de la C.J.E.C. relative aux conflits des lois de sécurité sociale", X(3) Rev. trim. de dr. eur. (1974) 431 and the papers by Lipstein and Hartley in this volume.

[8]   *Bulletin of the European Communities,* Vol. I, No. 11 (1968) 5-6.

[9]   *Implementation of Point 10 of the Final Communiqué Issued at the European Summit Held in Paris on 9 and 10 December 1974 Concerning a Passport Union,* COM (75)322 Final, pp. 7, 23.

[10]   Consensus is lacking on the definition of nationality in general international law,but the three features set out in the text are normal characteristics of nationality statuses known in the modern Western world. See Oppenheim, *International Law* (1952), Vol. I, p. 508; Lauterpacht, *International Law and Human Rights* (1950), p. 347; Batiffol, *Droit international privé* (1967), pp. 8-10. British subjecthood does not meet these three conditions, and is not to be classified as a form of nationality in the strict sense of that term. It denotes an individual's status in relation to a group of countries known as the Commonwealth rather than his status in relation to any one. Under English law a British subject is a person who is a citizen of the United Kingdom and Colonies or of any Commonwealth country having its own citizenship law or exceptionally a person having neither of those citizenships (but being a British subject without citizenship) or having both of them (being a dual citizen). The meaning of the term "British subject" is not uniform throughout the Commonwealth, and in most Commonwealth countries the expression "Commonwealth citizen" is used in preference to the term "British subject".

[11]   Case 75/63 [1964] ECR 177.

[12]   Case 61/65 [1966] ECR 261.

[13]   Case 27/69, XV *Recueil* 405.

[14]   Case 44/65 [1965] ECR 965.

[15]   In one case a German court refused to accept that an Italian qualified as a migrant worker on the commendably forthright ground that he was an "idle layabout": *City of Wiesbaden v. Barulli,* [1968] C.M.L.R. 239. Similar reasoning was employed by the Metropolitan Magistrate in *R.* v. *Secchi,* [1975] 1 C.M.L.R. 383, 392: "Not every such national who in the course of his life may at different times have done a few hours, a few days or even a few weeks work can be regarded as someone whose freedom of movement is necessary". In each of those cases the same

result could have been reached by application of the public order exception set out in art. 48(3) of the Treaty.

[16] Reg. 1612/68 of October 15, 1968, J.O. 295/12(L), art. 1; formerly Reg. 15/61 of August 15, 1961, J.O. 1073/1961, art. 1 and Reg. 38/64 of March 25, 1964, J.O. 965/1964, art. 1.

[17] *Supra*, n. 11.

[18] Cmnd. 4862, p. 118.

[19] The *Foreign Service Instructions* of the United Kingdom Government record as follows:

"The term "national" is a term of international law connoting a person who is connected with a state by a special legal tie entitling that State to protect the person in its relation with other states. The term "United Kingdom national" includes the following categories:

(i) citizens of the United Kingdom and Colonies;

(ii) the three surviving original classes of British subjects [viz: citizens of Eire who were British subjects before 1949 and have connexions with the United Kingdom, British subjects without citizenship and wives of the foregoing];

(iii) British protected persons; and

(iv) Citizens of Southern Rhodesia."

[20] Immigration Act 1971, ss. 1, 2.

[21] See Simmonds, *supra* n. 9 and Edens and Patijn, "The Scope of the EEC System of Free Movement of Workers", 9 C.M.L. Rev. (1972) 322.

[22] Böhning, *supra* n. 9 and "The Scope of the EEC System of Free Movement: A Rejoinder", 10 C.M.L. Rev. (1973) 81. See also Parry and Hardy, *EEC Law* (1974) para. 23-03.

[23] This is the view taken by Campbell in *Common Market Law* Supp. 2 (1971), p. 226; it is also taken by Böhning, *supra*, n. 21.

[24] E.g. problems concerning mutual recognition of qualifications and admission to professional organizations. See McMahon, "Ireland and the Right of Establishment in the Treaty of Rome", 6 Ir. Jur. (1971) 217; Scarman, "Law of Establishment in the European Economic Community", 24 N. Ir. L.Q. (1973) 61; Mitchell, "Lawyers and the European Communities", 22 N. Ir. L.Q. (1971) 149; Kramer, "Liberal Professions in the EEC", 122 New L.J. (1972) 648.

[25] *Supra*, n. 7.

[26] E.g. the proposed Directive on Collective Dismissals.

[27] *Supra*, n. 11.

[28] *Supra*, n. 5.

[29] Article 235 provides a basis for adoption of Regulations not expressly authorised elsewhere, but the parameters of that article are not unlimited. See Marenco, "Les conditions d'applicabilite de l'art 235 CEE", 131 Rev. Fr. du Marché Commun, 147-157.

[30] See Reisner, "National Regulation of the Movement of Workers in the

European Communities", 13 A.J. Comp. L. (1964) 361.

[31]   See the paper by Hartley in this collection, at n. 14.

[32]   See MacDonald, *The New Immigration Law* (1972) para. 330.

[33]   *Supra,* n. 18.

[34]   See Reuter, *La Communauté Européenne de Charbon et de l'Acier* (1953), p. 30; Wortley, *An Introduction to the Law of the European Economic Community* (1972), p. 96 and Lasok and Bridge, *Introduction to the Law and Institutions of the European Communities* (1973), p. 86.

[35]   *Supra,* n. 19 and text.

[36]   See Scheingold, *The Law Relating to Political Integration: the Evolution and Integrative Implications of Regional Legal Processes in the European Community* (1971).

[37]   See generally *Nonnenmacher* v. *Bestuur der Sociale Verzekeringsbank* [1964] ECR 281 and *Caisse de Companestion pour allocations familiales des charbonnages du Couchant de Mons* v. *Di Bella,* 3/70, XVI *Recueil* 415; *Van Duyn* v. *Home Office,* 41/74, [1974] ECR 1337; Simmonds, "Van Duyn v. Home Office: the Direct Effectiveness of Directives", 24 I.C.L.Q. (1975) 419.

[38]   [1964] C.M.L.R. 5.

[39]   Art. 48(3): "public policy, public security or public health"; art. 48(4): "public service".

[40]   Reg. 1612/68, art. 8.

[41]   Directive 68/360, J.O. 1968 L 257/13, art. 2. *Reyners* v. *Belgian State,* 2/74 [1974] ECR 631.

[42]   *Re Deportation of a Belgian National,* Munster Oberverwaltungsgericht, Case No. IV A 542/71 [1974] C.M.L.R. 107; *Re Deportation of an Italian National,* Gættingen Landgericht, Case No. I T 114/63; *Re Deportation of an Italian National,* Munster Oberverwaltungsgericht, Case No. II A 483/63; *Bonsignore v. City of Cologne* 67/74, [1975] *ECR* 297; *Rutili,* 36/75, [1975] ECR 1219; *Public Prosecutor* v. *Royer,* 48/75 (not yet reported); see further Chesné, *L'établissement des étrangers en France et la Communauté Européenne Economique* (1962); Macheret, *L'immigration étrangère en Suisse à l'heure de l'intégration européenne* (1969).

[43]   In Case 2/74 *Reyners* v. *Belgian State* [1974] ECR 631 that phrase was interpreted, for the purpose of applying Article 51 of the EEC Treaty, so as to exclude the practice of trial advocacy. See also *Sotgiu v. Bundespost,* 152/73, [1974] ECR 153.

[44]   *Implementation of Point 10 of the Final Communiqué Issued at the European Summit Held in Paris on 9 and 10 December 1974 Concerning a Passport Union,* COM (75)322 Final.

[45]   E.T.S. 25.

[46]   E.T.S. 37. See also the European Convention on Establishment, E.T.S. 19. For the çontribution of the Council of Europe to liberalising of passport controls generally, see Turack, *The Passport in International Law* (1974) 67-80.

[47]   Convention on European Economic Cooperation, art. 8; 43 A.J.I.L.

(Supp.)(1949) 94.

48   *European Yearbook* 1 (1955) 231. For the contribution of the O.E.E.C. (now the O.E.C.D.) to liberalising passport controls generally, see Turack, *supra* n. 44 at 53-66.

49   British Visitors Passport and Visitors Cards have grown in popularity in recent years, and now outnumber ordinary British passports, although they have a shorter period of validity.

50   Fot the interpretation and application of this article see Bernstein, *supra* n. 7 at 226, 242.

51   E.C.S.C. Report on *Arrangement en exécution de la Décision relative à l'application de l'article 69 du Traité instituant la C.E.C.A.* (1956).

52   (1957) E.C.S.C. *Official Journal*, p. 367, art. 12(2).

53   Turack, *supra* n. 44 at 101.

54   Directive 68/360, J.O. (L) 257/13, arts. 2, 3.

55   Reg. 1612/68, J.O. (L) 257/2, art. 1.

56   Reisner, *supra* n. 29; E.E.C. Survey V/702/59-D (1959).

57   Turack, *supra* n. 44 at 89-100.

58   Directive 68/360, J.O. (L) 257/13, art. 4.

59   *R.* v. *Brailsford*, (1905) 2 K.B. 730, 745; *R.* v. *Home Secretary ex p. Schadeo Bhurosah*, (1968) 1 Q.B. 266, 274; Street, *Freedom, The Individual and the law* (1965) 271; cf. *Kent* v. *Dulles*, (1957) 357 U.S. 116; *Schachtman* v. *Dulles*, (1955) 96 App. D.C. 287; Parker, "The Right to go Abroad" 40 Virginia L.R. (1954) 853; *Satwant Singh Sawhney* v. *Assistant Passport Officer, New Delhi*, (1967) A.I.R. 1035; Nambiar, "Right to a Passport", 7 *Ind. J. Int. Law* (1967) 526.

60   *Württemburgische Milchverwertung-Südmilch A.G.* v. *Ugliola*, 15/69, XV *Recueil* 363.

61   *Commission* v. *French Republic*, 167/73 [1974] ECR 359.

62   *Sacchi*, 155/73 [1974] ECR 409.

63   *Casagrande* v. *Landeshauptstadt Munich*, 9/74 [1974] ECR 773; *Alaimo* v. *Prefect of the Rhone*, [1975] ECR 109.

64   *Nonnenmacher* v. *Bestuur der Sociale Verzekeringsbank*, 92/63 [1964] ECR 281; *Caisse Régionale d'Assurance Médicale Paris* v. *Biason*, 24/74 [1974] ECR 999; *Bestuur der Sociale Verzekeringsbank* v. *Smieja*, 51/73, [1973] ECR 1213.

65   *Fiorini* v. *S.N.C.F.*, Cour d'Appel (1975) C.M.L.R. 459.

66   *Supra*, p. 45.

67   *Supra*, n. 7.

68   *Supra*, n. 5.

4

Conflicts of Laws in Matters of Social Security Under the EEC Treaty[1]

K. LIPSTEIN

The mobility of labour is not assured, unless a worker can be certain that the benefits of social security which he has acquired or to which he can look forward in the future in the first member state accompany him to the second member state into which he moves, and that while he is in the second member state his benefits and expectations will continue to run and to be maintained. At the same time care must be taken that such a worker is not subject to compulsory social security charges in more than one country, for such a double imposition might itself act as a deterrent against migration.

The situation is complicated by a number of factors. Firstly, the types of social security benefits differ considerably in their nature and their conditions of application. Secondly, social security legislation, being concerned with relations between an individual and the State, is unilateral in character, like all rules of so-called public law, and touches only persons and events inside its own geographical sphere of operation. It can thus be described as territorial and closed to the application of foreign social security legislation.[2] Thirdly, even where the local legislation applies, it refuses to acknowledge claims by dependent persons, such as widows and children, who reside permanently outside its territorial spheres.

1. The Purpose and Extent of EEC Social Security Provisions

In the absence of any precepts of uniform social security legislation

F.G. Jacobs, ed. European Law and the Individual © 1976, North-Holland Publishing Company

within the EEC, the normal techniques of approximation,[3] coordination[4] and harmonization[5] offer the best solution. Since these techniques serve usually to approximate laws, to coordinate activities and policies and to harmonize contributions or aids[6] and since the diversity and technicality of the national systems of social security make it practically impossible to adjust them to each other by approximation, the coordination of social security activities offered a way out.[7] It was achieved by establishing a single competent jurisdiction which, having regard to the nature of social security legislation described above, always applies its own law in cases involving certain types of claims brought by certain types of persons.[8] Thus the solution assumes the form of a rule of the conflict of laws in which operative facts (type of claim, person of claimant) are linked to a certain system of laws by connecting factors (place of employment, residence of claimant, etc.).

In devising the appropriate rules care had to be taken to observe the provisions of Article 51 of the Treaty according to which migrant workers and their dependants were to be assured that

(a) all periods recognized by the domestic law of the countries concerned as qualifying periods for acquiring and retaining rights to benefits and for calculating these benefits are to be added together; and
(b) any such benefits will be paid even if the beneficiaries are resident in another country of the Community.

The Community Court has expressed the intention of Article 51 in these words: "...the Treaty has...placed upon the Council the duty to lay down rules preventing those concerned, in the absence of legislation applying to them, from remaining without protection in the matter of social security...[or from being placed] in an unfavourable legal position".[9] Its purpose is to abolish the territorial limits of application of the various social security schemes.[10] "The aim of this provision is to allow the migrant worker to acquire the right to benefit for all periods of work completed by him in various Member States, without discrimination. . .".[11] Article 51 "... deals essentially with the case in which the laws of one Member State do not by themselves allow the person concerned the right to benefits by reason of the insufficient number of periods completed under its laws, or only allow him benefits which are less than the maximum":[12] *pro rata*-ing presupposes aggregation.[13] Most important, Article 51 does not serve to equalise the benefits, but to exclude loss of benefits by aggregation; aggregation and *pro rata*-ing are linked, but the Treaty does not require *pro rata*-ing as such.[14]

To remedy this situation [Article 51 of the Treaty and Reg. 3 art. 27] provide, for the benefit of the worker who has been subject *successively* or *alternately* to the legislation of two or more Member States, for the aggregation of periods of insurance completed under the legislation of each of these States...but not when in a State the object sought by Article 51 is attained under the national legislation alone...apportionment of benefits may not be made, unless it has been necessary, in order to give rise to entitlement, to aggregate beforehand the periods completed under different legislations, but it may not be used to reduce the benefits which the person concerned can claim *under the legislation of a single State.* . . . A different interpretation would lead to a discrimination at the expense of the migrant worker by giving him, in the same legal circumstances, smaller rights than those accorded to the worker who completes the whole of his occupational career in a single Member State. If this interpretation is capable of leading in certain cases to an *accumulation of pensions,* this consequence follows *not from the interpretation of Community law but from the system at present in force,* which, in the absence of a common social security scheme, rests on a simple coordination of national legislations which have not yet been harmonized.[15]

Aggregation and apportionment...cannot therefore be carried out if their effect is to diminish the benefits which the person concerned may claim by virtue of the laws of a single Member State on the basis solely of the insurance periods completed under those laws, always provided that this method *cannot lead to a duplication of benefits for one and the same period.* Aggregation is not applied even in cases where insurance periods completed in the State concerned coincide with insurance periods completed in another Member State. In fact, if the laws of one Member State allow such a double affiliation, there are no grounds based on the objectives of Article 51 which make it permissible to refuse to a worker who does not need to have recourse to Regulations 3 and 4 the advantages of the application *in toto* of the laws of that State.[16]

However, a cumulation of benefits, while not prohibited by Article 51 of the Treaty, may be frowned upon by the law of a member state which is applicable. Reg. 3 art. 11(2)[17] seeks to provide some guidance by leaving it in the discretion of the law applicable, except where old age, death and invalidity benefits are concerned, and Reg. 1408/71 seeks to improve on this provision. In this connection the Community Court has said:

Under art. 11(2) the provisions for the reduction or the suspension laid down by the legislation of a member state for cases of cumulation of benefits with other social security benefits may be invoked against a beneficiary, even in respect of benefits acquired under the scheme of another member state. In order to determine the meaning and the scope of this provision, it must be interpreted in the light of art. 48-51 of the Treaty. . . . As these articles are designed to ensure the free movement of workers by conferring certain rights on them, it would be acting outside the purpose and the framework of these provisions to impose on workers a reduction of their rights without, as a counterpart, any of the advantages provided for in the regulations. *In cases where the regulations grant workers the advantage of social security benefits which they could not obtain except by application of these regulations, limitations may be imposed as a counterpart to the advantages which they thereby enjoy.* In the absence of any such counterpart, such limitations cannot be justified, since their effect would be to place a worker in a less favourable position than that in which he would be placed, in the absence of these regulations, by the application of domestic law or of specific conventions concluded by member states. Consequently, *restrictions* such as those provided or allowed by art. 11(2) of Reg. 3 with regard to certain social security benefits *cannot apply to insured persons, unless they enjoy benefits acquired on the strength of this Regulation.*[18]

Apart from this licence given to the law applicable to take into account benefits of the same kind received elsewhere, the choice of jurisdiction and law expressed in general terms by Reg. 3 is not to be regarded as excluding cumulation altogether.

Article 12 (of Reg. 3) includes no provision prohibiting the simultaneous application of several systems of legislation...such a restriction on the freedom of the national legislature should be presumed only to the extent that such simultaneous application is clearly contrary to the spirit of the Treaty...these provisions are not opposed to legislation by the Member States designed to bring about additional protection by way of social security for the benefit of migrant workers.[19]

2. Technical Execution – Rules of the Conflict of Laws by EEC Regulation: The Problems

It was left to the Council to elaborate suitable provisions of the Conflict of Laws. Given the territorial character of social security legislation, such rules had to establish the competent jurisdiction on the implied understanding that the authorities in the competent member state will apply their own law and should not be called upon to apply more than one legal system.[20] In addition the following considerations applied:

Firstly, in order not to deprive migrant workers of previous acquired rights, the facts which gave rise to any such rights abroad are to be taken into account by the competent authorities, even if they cannot administer the foreign social security legislation, at least to the extent that benefits in the country having jurisdiction are affected by such facts and that failure to take these facts into account would deprive the migrant worker of some benefits which he would have enjoyed, if all the facts had taken place in the same country.

Secondly, the existence of rights to benefits acquired successively or alternatively required a solution. This involved, on the one hand, the *right* of the competent country to take into account rights acquired previously abroad; on the other hand it involved the question of a right or duty of member states other than that which has primary jurisdiction, to confer concurrent or additional benefits on the claimant migrant worker or his dependant, given previous employment in that state or any other connection.[21] As will be shown below, the second question has not been answered so far.

3. *The Solutions – Connecting Factors*

The general connecting factor is the place where the worker is employed (*lex laboris*), even if he is permanently resident in the territory of another member state or if the employer resides or the registered office of the enterprise by which he is employed is situated in the territory of another member state.[22] The authorities of that country have jurisdiction, and the law of that country applies.[23] The flag of a vessel on which a worker is employed determines the law to be applied to him.[24] Civil servants and persons treated as such are governed by the law of their administration.[25] The *lex laboris* is not affected by a call up for military service in the home country.[26] However, the general principle establishing the pre-eminence of the place of employment, in determining the competent country and the applicable law is subject to a number of far-reaching exceptions.[27]

In the first place, and most important, a worker whose permanent residence is in country *A* but who is sent to country *B* by an undertaking which has an establishment in country *A* to which the worker is normally attached, in order to carry out some work on behalf of that enterprise, remains subject to the laws of country *A* as if he continued to work there, provided that the likely duration of the work to be carried out in country *B* does not exceed twelve months and that the worker has not been sent as a replacement of another who has come to the end of his stay abroad on behalf of his enterprise.[28] If for unforeseen reasons the stay exceeds twelve months, the law of country *A* continues to apply until the job is completed, provided that the competent authority[29] consents.[30] This rule applies, and not the general principle referring to the place of emplyment, if the employee has been engaged for the exclusive purpose of carrying out a job abroad. It is not necessary that the execution of the work abroad is merely incidental to an engagement of a longer duration in the country of the worker's permanent residence by an enterprise established there, where the worker carries out his functions normally.[31] It applies equally if the worker is engaged in the country of his permanent residence by an enterprise established there which supplies enterprises abroad with qualified workers who are needed for a short period to execute particular tasks. The test is not whether during his stay abroad the worker is subject to instruction by the enterprise situated there, but whether he remains subordinate to the enterprise which engaged him and whether the latter continues to be his employer, pays his wages and can dismiss him.[32] Since the aim of this provision is to regulate the position of wage-earning workers who enjoy stable employment by an enterprise in a member state and who are sent abroad for a limited period, it could apply to the very different case of commercial travellers until Reg. 24/64, art. 1 amended Reg. 3, art. 13(c).[33]

In the second place, employees of an international transport undertaking with a registered office in one member state who are employed as travelling personnel in another or in several member states are subject to a series of special rules. Generally they are subject to the law of the member state where the registered office is situated; if they are engaged by a branch of the enterprise in one member state while the registered office is in another, the law of the state applies where the branch is situated; if exclusively employed in the member state of their permanent residence where the enterprise has neither its registered office nor a branch, the law of the country of their permanent residence applies.[34]

In the third place, a worker other than an employee of an international transport undertaking who normally performs his duties in several member states is subject to the law of the country of his residence, if he operates partly there or if he is attached to several undertakings or several employees having their registered offices or places of business in different member states.[35] This rule applies irrespective of whether the worker is employed by one or by several employers acting in agreement,[36] and, since Reg. 3, art. 13(1)(c) was amended by Reg. 24/64, art. 1, also to commercial travellers.[37] If the worker does not reside in any of them, he is subject to the law of the country where the employer is established or where the enter-

prise which employs him has his seat.[38] Special rules deal with workers
employed in one member state by an enterprise having its seat in another
member state, if the two states have a common frontier;[39] with workers
who are either normally employed by an enterprise in one member state or
on board vessels flying the flag of a member state and who are sent on
board a vessel flying the flag of another member state in order to carry out
work there;[40] with workers who, without being habitually employed on the
high seas, are employed in the territorial waters or in a part of a member
state on board a vessel flying the flag of another member state[41] and to
workers who are employed on board a vessel flying the flag of one member
state but have their residence in another state and receive their wages from
an employer in the latter member state.[42] Further provisions deal with
service personnel employed by diplomatic missions or in the personal
service of officials of such posts.[43] In principle the place of employment
determines jurisdiction and the applicable law, but workers who are
nationals of the sending or the receiving member state may exercise an
option in favour of the law of their country of origin,[44] and a similar option,
both a little broader and a little narrower, is open to *subordinate personnel*
employed by the European Communities.[45]

Naturally the interpretation of the connecting factor of residence in
Reg. 3 and 1408/71[46] defined in Reg. 3 as *"séjour habituel"* (translated as
habitual residence, better habitual sojourn, see also Reg. 1408/71 art.1(h))
as distinct from sojourn as such which is temporary caused difficulties:
see Reg. 1408/71 art. 1(i). Factors other than mere professional must be
considered. Consequently an itinerant activity of seeking out clients, being
unstable in nature, does not render the country where these activities are
carried on a country of residence, while a domicile in the technical sense
constitutes such a residence for a commercial traveller, the more so if he is a
national of the latter country since it is "the permanent centre of his interests to which he returns in the intervals between his tours".[47]

4. *Operative Facts – Ratione Personae*

The original Reg. 3 applied to wage earners or assimilated workers who
are or have been subject to the legislation of one or more of the member
states and are nationals of a member state or are stateless persons or
refugees permanently resident in the territory of a member state, including
members of their families and their survivors, including those survivors

subject to the legislation of a member state, irrespective of their nationality, if they are nationals of a member state or stateless persons or refugees
permanently resident in the territory of a member state.[48] Here again
questions of characterization arose. In particular the meaning and extent
of the term "wage earners or assimilated workers" gave rise to litigation in
which the law of the member states was called upon to determine in the
particular case whether a claimant was qualified to receive social security
benefits because he possessed all the attributes of a worker[49] and whether
his qualification had been maintained because he was likely to resume this
activity.[50] Nevertheless it was held that the notion itself of a "wage earner
or assimilated worker" was one of Community law, the uniform interpretation of which could not be modified by the laws of the member states.[51] For
the purpose of this characterization the Community Court appears to have
relied on the law of the last permanent residence, which was also the
national law of the worker.

The requirement that the wage earners must be or have been *subject to the
legislation* of one or more of the member states has also caused difficulties.[52]
Reg. 3, art. 1(b) stated that legislation included all laws, regulations, and
other *dispositions statutaires* present and future of each member state relating
to the social security schemes and branches of social security set out in Reg.
3.[53] The meaning of laws, regulations and dispositions will be discussed
below. *Ratione personae,* the workers must be "subject" to this legislation
which has been held, negatively, to mean in relation to Reg. 3, art. 42(6) in
the version of Reg. 1/64, art. 1 that legislation under which no benefit is
conferred must be disregarded as being legislation to which the worker
concerned is *not subject,*[54] although in principle it applies to him.

The difficulties and uncertainties created by the notion of workers in
Reg. 3 led to the inclusion of a definition in Reg. 1408/71.[55] Once again
the Regulation extends to nationals of member states, stateless persons[56]
and refugees[57] who reside in one of the member states.[58] The notion of
worker has now been given as objective a content as possible and comprises
persons who qualify under one of three headings. The basic tests are
whether the person concerned is:

(a) covered by an obligatory or optional insurance against one or several
    risks envisaged by social secutiry provisions through a scheme which is
    applicable to employed persons

or:

(b) covered by an obligatory insurance against one or several risks envisaged by a scheme falling within Reg. 1408/71 through a general system of social insurance for all residents or persons of working age, provided that the manner of administering or of financing the scheme makes it possible to classify the insured as a worker or, if this should be impossible, that the claimant is insured by an obligatory or optional insurance which covers certain risks set out in Annex V of Reg. 1408/71 as part of a scheme for employed persons

or:

(c) covered by a voluntary insurance against one or several risks enumerated in Reg. 1408/71 by a scheme applicable either to employed persons or to all residents or to certain categories of residents, provided that the claimant was previously compulsorily insured against the same risks under a scheme for employed persons in the same state.[59]

As in the old Reg. 3,[60] the new Regulation applies to workers who are or were subject to the law of one or more member states.[61] The term "subject" (*soumis*) clearly relates to the choice of law resulting from the reference to the place of employment, the seat of an enterprise or the residence of a worker and does not attract the meaning given to it by the Community Court in relation to Reg. 3, art. 42(6).[62]

A nice problem involving a preliminary question arises from the fact that the Regulation applies to families of wage earners falling within the ambit of the Regulation and their survivors.[63] Under Reg. 3 the term "members of the family" was to be construed according to the law of the country of their permanent residence.[64] Thus the strange situation could arise that the wage earner was subject to the laws of member state *A* according to which the claimant was not regarded as a member of his family, while according to the laws of member state *B* enjoyed this status and was to be treated as such in member state *A*.

Regulation 1408/71, art. 1(f) now provides that the qualification of being a member of the family is to be determined by the law under which the benefits accrue. It must be assumed that this is the law which applies to the benefits of the worker himself.[65] However, Reg. 1408/71 once again relies on the law of the place of residence of the dependant in two cases. The first concerns benefits in kind for illness or confinement during a temporary stay[66] (*sojourn*) abroad;[67] the second, in connection with invalidity pensions, applies if the worker is subject exclusively to regimes according to which the amount of invalidity benefits is independent of the periods of insurance.[68] Going still further, Reg. 1408/71, art. 1(f), formerly Reg. 3, art. 1(n) does not only provide a choice of law rule, but supplies an overriding rule of Community law as well. If according to the laws of the member states where the benefits accrue or where in the two cases set out above a claimant who alleges to be a member of the family resides permanently only those persons living under the same roof as the worker are regarded as members of the family, such persons are deemed for the purposes of the Regulations to be members of the household, if they are primarily dependent on the workers concerned.[69]

The notion of "survivors", on the other hand, is interpreted somewhat differently. Under the old Reg. 3 it was determined according to the legislation applicable,[70] which probably meant that which applied according to Reg. 3, arts. 12 and 13[71] to the insured himself. Thus a conflict between the law applicable to the insured and the claimant was eliminated. The new Reg. 1408/71[72] replaces the reference to the law applicable by one to the law on the strength of which the benefits are provided, thus giving the rule governing survivors the same range as that dealing with members of the family, except that the reference to arts. 22(1)(a) and 39 is omitted since the latter are inapplicable in the circumstances. In substance Reg. 1408/71 has not changed the beneficial solution first provided by Reg. 3.[73] It must be noted that the same overriding rule of Community law as in the case of a "member of the family" (Reg. 1408/71, art. 1(f)) is provided here as well. If according to the law applicable only those persons who were living under the same roof as the deceased worker are regarded as survivors such persons are deemed to be survivors if they were primarily dependent upon the deceased.[74] Such survivors enjoy an additional advantage. If the wage earner was subject to the legislation of one or more member states but was not a national of a member state (as the Regulation requires in principle),[75] his survivors as defined here[76] are entitled to the benefit of the Regulation if they themselves are nationals of a member state, or stateless persons or refugees permanently resident in the territory of a member state.[77]

Regulation 3 stated expressly that it did not apply to established members of the diplomatic and consular services or to persons who form part of the staff of an administrative branch of government of a member state who are sent into the territory of another member state.[78] In a somewhat obscurely worded provision, Reg. 1408/71 appears to have reversed this rule in so far as officials of a member state are concerned and may, possibly, include diplomats as well.[79]

5. Operative Facts – Ratione Materiae

Reg. 3 as well as Reg. 1408/71 envisage social security provisions of a certain substance and of a certain form:

(i) In substance they apply to all legislation which deals with social security benefits of the following types:[80] sickness and maternity; invalidity, including grants for the purpose of maintaining or improving earning capacity,[81] old age and survivors' pension, industrial accidents or occupational diseases, death grants, unemployment and family allowances. The sphere of operation of the Regulations does not extend to social and medical assistance, war pensions and to special schemes for officials.[82]

Naturally difficulties of interpretation or characterization have occurred. These are all the greater since the Community Court cannot even characterize domestic law.[83] However, an abstract test has been found in the criterion whether the benefit is based on an individual appreciation of the needs of the claimant – in which case it must be characterized as pertaining to assistance – or whether the benefit accrues on the strength of legal provisions and is an entitlement – in which case it falls within the ambit of social security, even if the benefit displays certain features of social or medical assistance.[84]

Within the categories of social security, social security benefits have been held to include (in the case of tuberculosis) prophylactic aids for establishing the claimant in professional life, economic aid and preventive assistance not related to his earning capacity,[85] payments to handicapped persons, and minimum guaranteed sums for old age pensions, even if it should not always be easy to draw the line between social security benefits and social or medical assistance since such benefits may fulfil a dual function.[86] On the other hand benefits in kind (*prestations en nature*), being the concomitant of a concrete loss, as all benefits are, do not include supplementary benefits outside the range expressed to be covered by the Regulation, such as payments to assist the holder of a pension covered by the Regulation in financing the conclusion and maintenance of a subsequent sickness insurance for the future.[87]

(ii) In form, legislation concerning social security in the meaning of Reg. 3, art. 2(1), now Reg. 1408/71, art. 4(1), includes all laws, regulation, *dispositions statutaires* and all other implementing measures, present and future, excluding, in general, existing or future industrial agreements, even if they have been rendered compulsory or extended in scope by the authorities. As an exception, they are included after a declaration by the member state concerned, if they put a compulsory scheme into operation or set up a scheme to be administered by the same authorities which administer a compulsory scheme.[88]

The Community Court, applying Reg. 3, held that as used in the Regulation, *dispositions statutaires* included schemes laid down by institutions other than public authorities who exercise delegated or supplementary powers.[89] Thus the present definition is more restrictive.

Exceeding its professed aim not to interfere in domestic law, the Regulation establishes the principle of equality,[90] excludes the requirement of residence for entering a voluntary or optional continued insurance, if the claimant was previously subject to the legislation of the country concerned[91] and required that periods of insurance elsewhere in accordance with the Regulation are to be taken into account.[92]

6. Conflict of Applicable Laws – Cumulation – The Problem

Conceived in terms of rules of the conflict of laws, the Regulation indicates the competent jurisdiction and the law applicable there. If this is its only function within Community law, it leaves the question unsolved as to how the courts and administrative authorities in the other member countries – namely in the states where the claimant is not employed or resident or where the enterprise has its seat – are to deal with a claim which is raised either additional to or in the absence of a similar claim in the competent jurisdiction under the Regulation. Here only overriding rules of the conflict of laws on a Community or semi-international level can assist which not only confer jurisdiction, but also exclude jurisdiction, not only indicate the law applicable, but also rule out any other law as applicable. In addition any such division of jurisdictional and legislative competences must be considered on two different levels – *firstly* of space, where the same claim covers the same period of insurance and *secondly*, where the periods are successive, thus raising a conflict of laws in time. No such overriding rules of the conflict of laws have come into existence in the EEC, and thus member states other than that competent under the regulation are free to accord benefits on their own, with or without taking into account benefits accruing under the regulation.

7. Conflict of Laws – Guiding Principles

It will be remembered that in matters of social security the Community Court has adhered to the following principles. The purpose of the Treaty, and thus of the Regulation

(i)   is to prevent a migrant worker being without protection or being placed in an unfavourable position compared with the worker who stays at home;

(ii) is not to interfere if this purpose is achieved on the basis of a particular member state's legislation alone, without any help from the Treaty and the Regulation;

(iii) is not to exclude a cumulation of benefits which might ensue from the existence, side by side, of the various social security systems at present in force in the member states, which are not yet harmonized and may thus not be sufficiently coordinated;

(iv) is to aggregate periods of insurance in several countries in order to preserve acquired rights and to *pro-rata* the ensuing benefit between the member states;

(v) is to save a worker from being rendered liable to dual charges contemporaneously;

(vi) possibly, however, to exclude a cumulation of benefits for the same period,[93] *sed quaere,* if no dual charges are involved.

The problem is thus two-fold:

Firstly, to what extent can or must the competent authorities applying their own law, take into account rights to benefits accrued elsewhere;

Secondly, to what extent can authorities in other member states under whose laws a benefit has accrued, reduce or suspend such a benefit on the ground that in another jurisdiction, under another law, applicable under the Regulation, the claimant has acquired a benefit of *the same kind.*

It is proper to keep in mind the general principle enunciated by the Community Court that even if the cumulation of benefits is not the purpose of the Treaty, such cumulation is allowed because it is not expressly prohibited. While Reg. 3 was naturally inspired by the principle of non-discrimination[94] and professed *not* to *confer* or *maintain* entitlement under the legislation of the member states, *to more than one benefit for the same kind or more than one benefit in respect of any one insurance period or assimilated period,*[95] Reg. 1408/71, treating the principle of non-discrimination as identical with equality,[96] proclaims that a worker to whom Reg. 1408/71 applies *is to be subject to* the legislation of a single member state only.[97]

However, for the benefit of the insured the principle of non-cumulation was breached from the beginning for old age, death and invalidity insurance[98] and extended now to occupational disease;[99] on the other hand, subject to the same exceptions, the right of national legislation to reduce, suspend or withdraw benefits in cases of overlapping can be invoked even though the right to such benefits was acquired under the legislation of another member state.[100]

Although the choice of jurisdiction and of the applicable law according to the Regulation only concerned compulsory social insurance and did not under Reg. 4[101] and does not under Reg. 1408 cover insurance periods by way of voluntary or optional continued insurance under the legislation of another member state,[102] Reg. 1408/71 following Reg. 3, art. 28(3) goes further[103] by stating that if the legislations of two or more member states overlap – which seems to refer to a conflict of laws in space, but possibly also in time – involving a system of compulsory insurance and a continued voluntary or optional scheme, the beneficiary is thrown by operation of law upon that system which is compulsory. If the cumulation of laws and benefits involves two or more voluntary or optional continued insurance, the beneficiary must opt.[104] Once again in the case of invalidity, old age and death pensions a cumulation is permitted, this time between a voluntary or optional and a compulsory scheme, but only if the state where the voluntary or facultative scheme operates allows the cumulation.[105]

8. *Effect of the Regulations Upon National Law and Benefits*

Before considering the limits set by Regulation 1408/71 upon cumulation of benefits, it is well to remember that according to the principles announced by the Community Court, any amount of cumulation should be allowed and should not be curtailed by the Regulation, unless the Regulation itself has regulated the subject matter by conferring rights upon the beneficiary. In short, any restriction imposed upon member states not to grant benefits irrespective of any other benefits conferred elsewhere is the concomitant of a grant of benefits by the Regulation which would not have been available to the claimant otherwise;[106] workers are not to be deprived of their nationally acquired rights as such.

Thus, when Reg. 3, art. 28(3) required the competent authority in granting an invalidity pension not to take into account any voluntary insurance, a German worker who was first employed for a full qualifying period in Germany and a smaller period in France, but had retained a voluntary insurance in Germany during his employment in France, was denied a full pension in Germany available to him through the combined operation of a German compulsory and a voluntary insurance and was thrown back on aggregation and *pro-rata*-ing under Regulation 3 his German and French compulsory insurance benefits which gave him less. In the Community Court he succeeded.[107] The benefits under the Regulation accrue, and the restriction imposed by it apply only if equal or better benefits do not accrue on the strength of a single system of domestic law. To this extent Reg. 3, art. 28(3) and Reg. 4, art. 13(1)(b) and (5) were *ultra vires.* If no aggregation is necessary because the benefits accrue according to the law of one member state alone applying a compulsory system of insurance, *pro-rata*-ing is similarly excluded.[108] If, however, the qualifying periods do not overlap, a full entitlement according to the domestic law of one country can be combined with a benefit in another country according to the domestic law of the latter without relying on the Regulation for a justification and without offending against the Treaty (art. 51) or Reg. 3 (art. 11(1)).[109]

However, as the Community Court, pointed out in *Guissart v. Belgium*[110] the complexity of the problem which is posed by the attemps to coordinate domestic social security legislation makes it impossible to attribute absolute validity to the interpretation set out here, seeing that in certain circumstances it may lead to the concession of unjustified benefits. Such is the case where actual qualifying periods in one member state overlap with fictitious periods in another. In these circumstances, the actual periods served abroad may be discounted in favour of the local fictitious periods (see note 110).

In terms of the Conflict of Laws: the choice of law rule (i.e. the Regulation) operates and a particular member state exercises jurisdiction and applies its own law within the limits of the choice of law rule (Regulation) only if the lex fori does not, by itself, offer greater satisfaction.

9. *Instances of Prohibited Cumulation Under the Regulations*

The scheme of the Regulations requires not infrequently that not only facts and rights which arose within the jurisdiction designated by the Regulation are to be considered alone, but also that facts, such as periods of insurance in other member states are to be aggregated[111] and benefits accruing in other member states are then to be *pro-rata*-ed,[112] or that upon a change of employment or of residence continued provision of benefits in kind or in money, other than a pension should be made,[113] subject to a right of recourse by the paying institution.[114] These are required cumulations.

Such situations occur *either* because the competent jurisdiction and legislation is that of the place of employment or that of the seat of an enterprise, while the worker resides in another member state or because the relevant fact (accident, birth) occurred while the claimant was subject to the jurisdiction of another member state – and concerns thus a social security benefit effective contemporaneously in space *or* because the worker has successively or alternately been subject to the legislation of two or more member states.[115]

The first concerns the physical continuation of benefits; the second concerns the combination of facts or rights which have arisen independently in two member states, either successively or alternately, and thus alone involves a problem of cumulation.

Regulation 1408/71 seems to have attempted a break with the system as it was evolved by the Community Court in the course of applying Reg. 3, to the effect that when the Regulation does not apply, cumulation is allowed. The new principle appears to be expressed in the general provision (art. 44(2)) that where a claim for an old age pension is introduced, all payments due under the laws which applied at one time or another must be liquidated simultaneously and brought into hotchpotch.[116] Upon the express demand of the interested party the realization of payments due under the laws of other member states may be postponed, provided that the periods completed under the laws of other member states are not aggregated in other member states.[117] Formerly, under Reg. 3, no such restriction was imposed.

Nevertheless, any possibility of cumulating benefits by virtue of this option is excluded by the overriding provisions of arts. 46(1) and (2), 49(2). According to these provisions, if no aggregation is required in order to qualify, the competent institution in each member state, the law of which has applied to the worker at some time and according to which the necessary conditions have been fulfilled in order to qualify for an old age or death pension, calculates the amount of the benefits to which he is entitled by reference to its own law, taking into account all those periods of insurance which that law requires to be counted.[118] By a second operation the same competent institution completes a process of aggregation and *pro-rata*-

ing as it is prescribed by the Regulation in order to preserve for the worker benefits which he would not receive if the applicable law were considered alone.[119] The higher figure reached by either of these processes represents the benefit due by the institution of the member state concerned.[120]

Thus, by compelling the authorities in each member state (and several may be involved by virtue of their own domestic law – see art. 49(1)) to take into consideration the periods served in all other member states, even where no aggregation is necessary either because the necessary period of insurance has been completed or because no such completion is required, and by establishing a maximum entitlement, which is then *pro-rata*-ed, the Regulation has created a general scheme which excludes any serious cumulation of alternate or successive benefits.

According to the principles set out above on the strength of the previous practice of the court with regard to Reg. 3 but also to Reg. 1408/71,[121] any such interference with rights acquired under one or several systems of laws for purposes other than to improve the position of the worker is incompatible with art. 51 of the Treaty. The latter seeks to protect the migrant worker against loss of rights and discrimination. Equality not egalitarianism is the guiding principle, and a reduction of rights acquired under various systems of social security is not intended. The principle of non-cumulation may inspire the scope, the interpretation and the application of Regulations 3 and 1408/71, but when benefits have accrued cumulatively without the help of Regulations 3 or 1408/71 by virtue of national law alone, it is not within the ambit of art. 51 of the Treaty to reduce these benefits. The legality of Reg. 3, art. 28(3), since it attempted to do so, was questioned by this writer[122] and it was subsequently held to be invalid by the Community Court.[123] The legality of Reg. 1408/71, arts. 46(1), (2), 49 is open to attack for the same reason. It may even be asked whether the charge of illegality is not confined to the situation where the benefits arise, independently of the Regulations, not only successively, but also alternately.[124]

Notes

1   Lyon-Caen, *Droit Social International et Européen* (3 ed. 1974) p. 222 no. 288ff;
Seché 1968 *Rev. trim dr. eur.* 475 with lit.; (1969) 6 C.M.L.Rev. 170; Tantaroudas,
1972 *Rev. trim dr. eur.* 36; Freyia, *Rev. crit. d.i.p.* 1956, 446; Duperyoux, *J.C.P.* 1959
I. 1504; Ribas and Creffard (1973) *Rev. M.C.* 103; Ribettes-Tilhet and Bonnet in
Dalloz, *Répertoire de droit international* II (1969) 803-842.

2   Gothot and Holleaux, note to Cass. 18 Febr. 1971, *Methfessel and Saud Bin
Jalwi, Rev. crit. d.i.p.* 1973, 673, 681.

3   EEC Treaty, arts. 3(h), 27, 100(1); 117, 2nd para.

4   Arts. 6(1), 40(2)(b); 54(3)(g); 56(2); 57(2), (3); 66; 70(1); 105(1), 111(1).

5   Arts. 99, 112(1); 117, 1st and 2nd paras.

6   See Lipstein, *The Law of the EEC* (1974) 268 and notes 4-6.

7   *Direction régionale de la Sec. sociale...Parisienne* v. *Mancuso* [1973] ECR 1449,
1456(17).

8   Council Reg. 3 of 25 September 1958, O.J. 1958, 561 as amended; supplemented in technical details by Council Reg. 4 of 3 December 1958, O.J. 1958, 597 as
amended; *replaced* by Council Reg. 1408/71, O.J. 1971, L 149/2 as amended;
supplemented in technical details by Council Reg. 574/72 O.J. 1972 L 74 as
amended.

9   *Nonnenmacher* v. *Bestuur der Sociale Verzekeringsbank* [1964] ECR 281 at 287, 288;
Allowed Reg. 3, art. 12; deceased worker employed in France – habitually
resident in the Netherlands where he worked previously; widow claims widow's
pension under Dutch law, since the deceased husband had been insured under that
Law from its inception on 1 October 1959; *Caisse d'Assurance de Vieillesse des Travail-
leurs salariés de Paris* v. *Duffy (Jeanne)* (1969) 15 Rec. 597, 603(6)(9); 1971 CMLR 391;
Reg. 3, art. 11(2); Belgian widow, French by marriage to deceased worker in
France – Old Age Pension in Belgium; Widow's pension in France – allowed; *De
Cicco* v. *Landesversicherungsanstalt Schwaben* [1968] ECR 473, 479; *Niemann* v. *Bundes-
versicherungsanstalt f. Angestellte* [1974] ECR 571, 579(4)-(7).

10   *Hessische Knappschaft* v. *Singer* [1965] ECR 965, 971; *Vaassen-Goebbels* v. *Beambtenfonds voor het Mijnbedrijf* [1966] ECR 261, 277; *De Moor* v. *Caisse de Pensions des
Employés privés* [1967] ECR 197, 206.

11   *Hagenbeek* v. *Raad van Arbeid* [1966] ECR 425, 430, 599 weeks for invalidity
/death in Netherlands (1926-); 7 years 2 months in Belgium. Widow claims
Widow's Pension in the Netherlands. Allowed.

12   *Niemann* v. *Bundesversicherungsanstalt f. Angestellte* [1974] ECR 571, 579(6) Old
age pension; 437 periods of insurance in Germany; 138 in France; voluntary insur-

ance in Germany at the same time, disregarded; reduction of German pension in view of French pension illegal.

[13]   *Caisse régionale de securité sociale du Nord-Est* v. *Goffart* [1967] ECR 321, 327; *Guissart* v. *Belgium* [1967] ECR 425, 433; *Sécurité Sociale-Paris* v. *Mancuso* [1973] ECR 1449, 1454(7)-1455(8).

[14]   *Caisse régionale etc.* v. *Goffart* (above n. 13) at p. 327.

[15]   *Sécurité Sociale Paris* v. *Mancuso* [1973] ECR 1449, 1455(8)-(11); 1456(16), (17): French invalidity pension independent of periods of contribution (1955) converted into old age pension (1965); Italian pension based on number of contributions (1957-1964): allowed: *Niemann* v. *Bundesversicherungsanstalt f. Angestellte* [1974] ECR 571, 579(6).

[16]   *Niemann* v. *Bundesversicherungsanstalt f. Angestellte* [1974] ECR 571, 580(6)-(7) holding Reg. 3, art. 28(3) to be incompatible with Article 51 of the Treaty, if the global sum after aggregation and *pro rata*-ing is lower than that to which the worker is entitled by virtue of the law of a single member state; but see *Hagenbeek* v. *Raad van Arbeid* [1966] ECR 425, 430: "it does not by any means follow from this that he must of necessity succeed, by the mere interplay of various national legislative systems in succession to one another, in obtaining a higher aggregate sum in benefits than would accrue to him under Article 28(3)".

[17]   Now Reg. 1408/71, art. 12(2); Lipstein 98 and n. 11.

[18]   *Caisse d'Assurance Vieillesse des Travailleurs salariés de Paris* v. *Duffy (Jeanne)* (1969) 15 Rec. 597, 603(4)-(10); [1971] CMLR 391, 399, 401.

[19]   See *Nonnenmacher* v. *Bestuur der Sociale Verzekeringsbank* [1964] ECR 281, 288; *Bestuur van de Nieuwe Alg. Bedrijfsvereniging* v. *Kaufman* [1974] ECR 517, 525(10).

[20]   *Sociale Verzekeringsbank* v. *van der Vecht* [1967] ECR 345, 353; *Bentzinger* v. *Steinbruchsberufsgenossenschaft* [1973] ECR 283, 288(4).

[21]   *Sociale Verzekeringsbank* v. *van der Vecht* [1967] ECR 345, 353; if additional charges for the worker or the employer are involved which are not balanced by a counterpart of Social Protection.

[22]   Reg. 1408/71, art. 13(2)(a); formerly Reg. 3, art. 12(1).

[23]   *Bentzinger* v. *Steinbruchsberufsgenossenschaft* [1973] ECR 283, 288(4).

[24]   Reg. 1408/71, art. 13(2)(b): formerly Reg. 3, art. 12(2) inserted by Reg. 47/67, art. 2.

[25]   Reg. 1408/71, art. 13(2)(c).

[26]   Reg. 1408/71, art. 13(2)(d) reproducing the decision of the Community Court in *Württembergische Milchverwertung-Südmilch A.G.* v. *Ugliola* (1969) 15 Rec. 363; [1970] CMLR 194.

[27]   *Bentzinger* v. *Steinbruchsberufsgenossenschaft* [1973] ECR 283, 288(3); *Angenieux* v. *Hakenberg* [1973] ECR 935, 947(9)-(12).

[28]   Reg. 1408/71, art. 14(1)(a)(i); formerly Reg. 3, art. 13(1)(d) first para. as amended by Reg. 24/64, art. 1 and by Reg. 47/67, art. 2.

[29]   For the meaning of this term see Reg. 1408/71, art. 1(b).

[30]   Reg. 1408/71, art. 14(1)(a)(ii), formerly Reg. 3, art. 13(1)(a) 2nd para. as

amended by Reg. 24/64, art. 1 and Reg. 47/67, art. 2.

[31]   *Sociale Verzekeringsbank* v. *van der Vecht* [1967] ECR 345, 354.

[32]   *Manpower SARL* v. *Caisse Primaire d'Assurance Maladie de Strasbourg*(1970) 16 Rec. 1251, 1257(9)-(13); [1971] CMLR 222.

[33]   *Angenieux* v. *Hakenberg* [1973] ECR 935, 947(12)-(22): art. Reg. 3 art. 12 applied and the test was where the employment was concentrated; this was the state where the enterprises represented by the commercial traveller had their seat.

[34]   Reg. 1408/71, art. 14(1)(b); formerly Reg. 3, art. 13(1)(b).

[35]   Reg. 1408/71, art. 14(1)(c)(i) formerly Reg. 3, art. 13(1)(c) first para. as amended by Reg. 24/64, art. 1.

[36]   *Bentzinger* v. *Steinbruchsberufsgenossenschaft* [1973] ECR 283, 288(3)-(5).

[37]   *Angenieux* v. *Hakenberg* [1973] ECR 935, 949(25)-(28).

[38]   Reg. 1408/71, art. 14(1)(c)(ii), formerly Reg. 3, art. 13(1)(c) second para., first sentence.

[39]   Reg. 1408/71, art. 14(1)(d), formerly Reg. 3, art. 13(1)(d).

[40]   Reg. 1408/71, art. 14(2)(a), formerly Reg. 3, art. 13(2)(a) added by Reg. 47/67 art. 2.

[41]   Reg. 1408/71, art. 14(2)(b) formerly Reg. 3, art. 13(2)(b) added by Reg. 47/67, art. 2.

[42]   Reg. 1408/71, art. 14(2)(c), formerly Reg. 3, art. 13(2)(c) added by Reg. 47/67, art. 2.

[43]   Reg. 1408/71, art. 16(1); formerly Reg. 3, art. 14(1). See Admin. Dec. 89, O.J. 1974 C 86/7.

[44]   Reg. 1408/71, art. 16(2); formerly Reg. 3, art. 14(2).

[45]   Reg. 1408/71, art. 16(3), formerly Reg. 3, art. 14 bis, added by Reg. 80/64, art. 1.

[46]   See e.g. above note 35.

[47]   *Angenieux* v. *Hakenberg* [1973] ECR 935, 950(29)-(32).

[48]   Reg. 3, art. 4(1), (2) now Reg. 1408/71, art. 2(1), (2).

[49]   *de Cicco* v. *Landesversicherungsanstalt Schwaben* [1968] ECR 473 at 480; *Janssen* v. *Alliance Nationale* (1971) 17 Rec. 859, 864(7); [1971] CMLR 13.

[50]   *Unger* v. *Bestuur der Bedrijfsvereniging voor Detailhandel* [1964] ECR 177, 186; *Angenieux* v. *Hakenberg* [1973] ECR 935, 946(3)-(4).

[51]   *Unger,* above note 50, at pp. 184, 185; *Janssen* v. *Alliance Nationale* (1971) 17 Rec. 859, 964(6), (8), (9); *Angenieux* v. *Hakenberg* (above note 50) at 946(5).

[52]   Reg. 1408/71, art. 2(1).

[53]   See now Reg. 1408/71, art. 1(g) as amended by the Treaty of Accession, Pt. II, Annex I, IX, 1.

[54]   *Caisse de Compensation etc. de Mons* v. *Di Bella* (1970) 16 Rec. 415, 421(14)-(15); [1970] CMLR 232; the question is whether the same meaning attaches to Reg. 3, art. 4: for the meaning of the term "who have been subject..." see *Janssen* v. *Alliance Nationale* (1971) 17 Rec. 859, 865(12).

[55] Art. 1(a); 2(1).

[56] For the definition see Reg. 1408/71, art. 1(e).

[57] For the definition see Reg. 1408/71, art. 1(d).

[58] Reg. 1408/71, art. 2(1).

[59] Reg. 1408/71, art. 1(a).

[60] Reg. 3, art. 4(1).

[61] Reg. 1408/71, art. 2(1).

[62] Above note 47.

[63] Reg. 3, art. 4(a); Reg. 1408/71, art. 2(1); Reg. 3, art. 17(1); Reg. 1408/71, art. 19.

[64] Reg. 3, art. 1(n).

[65] I.e., Reg. 1408/71, arts. 13-16.

[66] Defined in Reg. 1408/71, art. 1(i).

[67] Reg. 1408/71, art. 22(1)(a).

[68] Reg. 1408/71, art. 39(4).

[69] Reg. 1408/71, art. 1(f), formerly Reg. 3, art. 1(n).

[70] Reg. 3, art. 1(o).

[71] See above p. 59.

[72] Reg. 1408/71, art. 1(g).

[73] Reg. 3, art. 1(o).

[74] Reg. 1408/71, art. 1(g); formerly Reg. 3, art. 1(o).

[75] Reg. 1408/71, art. 2(1) formerly Reg. 3, art. 4(1), art. 1(a) and Annex A.

[76] Reg. 1408/71, art. 1(g), formerly Reg. 3, art. 1(o).

[77] Reg. 1408/71, art. 2(2), formerly Reg. 3, art. 4(2).

[78] Reg. 3, art. 4(5).

[79] Reg. 1408/71, art. 2(3).

[80] Reg. 3, art. 2(1); Reg. 1408/71, art. 4(1).

[81] Reg. 1408/71, art. 4(1) omits the exception of the latter in cases arising from industrial accidents or occupational diseases, as expressed formerly by Reg. 3, art. 2(1)(b); cf. *Caisse régionale d'assurance maladie* v. *Biason* [1974] ECR 999, 1007(13)-(16); *Dingemans* v. *Bestuur der Sociale Verzekeringsbank* [1964] ECR 647, 653.

[82] Once again Reg. 1408/71, art. 1(1)(d) omits the exception, expressed formerly in Reg. 3, art. 2(1)(d), of benefits arising from an industrial accident or an occupational disease.

[83] Lipstein, p. 330 n. 6; *Caisse régionale d'assurance maladie* v. *Biason* [1974] ECR 999, 1006(6); *Frilli* v. *Belgium* (1972) 18 Rec. 457, 465(10).

[84] *Caisse régionale etc.* v. *Biason* [1974] ECR 999, 1007(9)-(12); *Callemeyn* v. *Belgium* [1974] ECR 553, 561(5)-562(13).

[85] *Heinze* v. *Landesversicherungsanstalt Rheinprovinz* [1972] 18 Rec. 1105, 1114(5), (6), 1115(8); *Land Niedersachsen* v. *Landesversicherungsanstalt* [1972] 18 Rec. 1127, 1137(5), (6), (8). *Allgemeine O K K Hamburg* v. *Landesversicherungsanstalt Schleswig Holstein* (1972) 18 Rec. 1141, 1151(5), 1152(6), (8) involving Reg. 3, art. 26 (invalid-

ity benefits).

⁸⁶   *Callemeyn* v. *Belgium* [1974] ECR 553, 561(6), (7); *Costa or Mazzier* v. *Belgium* [1974] ECR 1251, 1260(6)-1261(11); *Frilli* v. *Belgium* (1972) 18 Rec. 457, 465(13), 466(8).

⁸⁷   *Dekker* v. *Bundesversicherungsanstalt für Angestellte* [1965] ECR 901, 905; cf. *Vaasen-Goebbels* v. *Beambtenfonds voor het Mijnbedrijf* [1966] ECR 261, 277.

⁸⁸   Reg. 1408/71, art. 1(g) as amended by the Treaty of Accession Pt. II Annex I(ix)1 enlarging Reg. 3, art. 1(b).

⁸⁹   *Vaassen-Goebbels* v. *Beambtenfonds voor het Mijnbedrijf* [1966] ECR 261, 274.

⁹⁰   Reg. 1408/71, art. 3; formely Reg. 3, art. 8.

⁹¹   Reg. 1408/71, art. 9(1).

⁹²   Reg. 1408/71, art. 9(2); Reg. 3, art. 9.

⁹³   See above n. 16: *Niemann* v. *Bundesversicherungsanstalt für Angestellte* [1974] ECR 571 at 580(6). But see below p. 69.

⁹⁴   Reg. 3, arts. 9, 10; Reg. 1408/71, art. 9, 10.

⁹⁵   Reg. 3, art. 11(1); reproduced with modifications by Reg. 1408/71, art. 12(1): compulsory insurance only; benefits in respect of invalidity, old age, death (pensions), occupational disease. See *De Moor* v. *Caisse de Pension des Employées Privés.* [1967] ECR 197, 206.

⁹⁶   Reg. 1408/71, art. 3; Reg. 3, art. 8.

⁹⁷   Reg. 1408/71, art. 13(1).

⁹⁸   Reg. 3, art. 11(1) – see in particular Reg. 3, art. 26, 27.

⁹⁹   Reg. 1408/71, art. 12.

¹⁰⁰   Reg. 1408/71, art. 12(2); Reg. 3 art. 11(2).

¹⁰¹   Reg. 4, art. 13(1)(b) – subject to a saving in respect of contributions; see Reg. 4, art. 13(5); *Niemann* v. *Bundesversicherungsanstalt f. Angestellte* [1974] ECR 571, 580(9).

¹⁰²   Limited to completed periods by Reg. 3, art. 13(1)(b).

¹⁰³   Reg. 1408/71, art. 15(2), first alternative.

¹⁰⁴   Reg. 1408/71, art. 15(2), second alternative.

¹⁰⁵   Reg. 1408/71, art. 15(3).

¹⁰⁶   See above and below n. 107.

¹⁰⁷   *Niemann* v. *Bundesversicherungsanstalt f. Angestellte* [1974] ECR 571, 579(6)-580(9); Lipstein 124; cp. *Sécurité Sociale – Paris* v. *Mancuso* [1973] ECR 1449, 1454(6)-1455(11); if aggregation produces a better result, the claimant may rely on it; *Gross* v. *Caisse d'Assurance Vieillesse de Strasbourg* [1971] 17 Rec. 871, 877(9), 10(12); *The same ibid* 893.

¹⁰⁸   *Ciechelski* v. *Caisse Régionale de Sécurité Sociale du Centre d'Orléans* [1967] ECR 181, 188-190; *De Moor* v. *Caisse de Pensions des Employés Privés* [1967] ECR 197, 206; *Office National des Pensions* v. *Couture* [1967] ECR 379, 388.

¹⁰⁹   *Ciechelski* v. *Caisse régionale* etc. (note 108) at p. 188; *Caisse régionale de Sécurité Sociale du Nord-Est* v. *Goffart* [1967] ECR 321, 327; *Colditz* v. *Caisse d'Assurance Vieil-*

lesse des Travailleurs Salariés de Paris [1967] ECR 229, 234; *Guissart* v. *Belgium* [1967] ECR 425, 433; *Caisse d'Assurance Vieillesse des Travailleurs Salariés de Paris* v. *Duffy (Jeanne)* (1969) 15 Rec. 597, 602(2)-604(9); *Keller* v. *Caisse Assurance Vieillesse de Strasbourg* (1971) 17 Rec. 475, 495, 501.

[110] *Guissart* v. *Belgium* (note 109) at 434.

[111] Sickness and maternity: Reg. 1408/71, art. 18(1), 25(1); Invalidity, art. 38(1); Old Age and Death (Pensions), art. 44,including non-contributory schemes: *Hagenbeek* v. *Raad van Arbeid* [1966] ECR 425, 430; Reg. 3, Annex G. Pt. III; *van der Veen* v. *Bestuur der Sociale Verzekeringsbank* [1964] ECR 565, 575.

[112] See Reg. 1408/71, arts. 40(1), 46(1), (2); Reg. 3, art. 28(1)(b).

[113] Sickness and Maternity: Reg. 1408/71, arts. 21, 22, 24, 25(1).

[114] Sickness and Maternity: Reg. 1408/71, arts. 28, 29(1), 36; Old Age and Death Pensions: art. 49(1); Invalidity Pensions converted: art. 43(2).

[115] Invalidity: Reg. 1408/71, art. 37, 41(1)(b), (c), 43(2); Old Age and Death (Pensions): Reg. 1408/71, art. 44(1).

[116] Thus overriding the cases cited above note 109.

[117] Reg. 1408/71 art. 44(2) Exception.

[118] Reg. 1408/71, art. 46(1) first para. as amended by the Treaty of Accession, Pt. II Annex I(ix)1, Cmnd. 4862 II p. 96.

[119] Reg. 1408/71, art. 46(1) second para. as amended.

[120] Reg. 1408/71, art. 46(1) second para. as amended.

[121] *Sociale Verzekeringsbank* v. *Smieja* [1973] ECR 1213, 1222(18) suggests, however, that the term "legislation of one or more Member States" includes Reg. 1408/71 – wrongly, it is believed.

[122] Lipstein p. 124.

[123] *Niemann* v. *Bundesversicherungsanstalt f. Angestellte* [1974] ECR 571, 580(9).

[124] But see *Niemann* v. *Bundesversicherungsanstalt f. Angestellte* (above n. 123) at 580(6); *Ciechelski* v. *Caisse régionale de Sécurité Sociale du Centre d'Orléans* [1967] ECR 181, 189. *Petroni* v. *ONPTS* [1975] ECR 1149.

5

Recent Decisions of the Court of Justice
in the Field of Free Movement of
Persons and Free Supply of Services

P. LELEUX

1. The Concept of "Restrictions" in Articles 48 and 52

It is important to determine what obstacles to the free movement of persons have been eliminated under Articles 48 and 52 and what obstacles are to be eliminated by the approximation of laws, since the first can no longer, *as of law*, hinder the beneficiaries.[1]

(a) The first and most important restriction is *any discriminatory treatment on grounds of nationality* as far as the taking up and exercise of economic activities are concerned.

Already in *Costa* v. *ENEL*[2] the Court ruled on discrimination in relation to Article 53:

Article 53 is therefore satisfied so long as no new measure subjects the establishment of nationals of other Member States to more severe rules than those prescribed for nationals of the country of establishment, whatever the legal system governing the undertaking.

This was strongly reaffirmed in 1974 in *Reyners*:[3]

The rule on equal treatment with nationals is one of the fundamental legal provisions of the Community.

The prohibition of any discrimination is absolute and, as far as workers are concerned, also serves the purpose of protecting nationals against the conse-

F.G. Jacobs, ed. European Law and the Individual © 1976, North-Holland Publishing Company

quences of unfavourable conditions for migrant workers – *Commission* v. *French Republic*:[4]

> The absolute nature of this prohibition, moreover, has the effect of not only allowing in each State equal access to employment to the nationals of other Member States, but also, in accordance with the aim of Article 177 of the Treaty, of guaranteeing to the State's own nationals that they shall not suffer the unfavourable consequences which could result from the offer or acceptance by nationals of other Member States of conditions of employment or remuneration less advantageous than those obtaining under national law, since such acceptance is prohibited.

(b) By discrimination *on grounds of nationality* is to be understood not only overt discrimination, but also covert discrimination; for example, under the disguise of a requirement of residence, the result may in fact be a discrimination against nationals of other Member States. This was clearly held by the Court in *Sotgiu*:[5]

> It may therefore be that criteria such as place of origin or residence of a worker may, according to circumstances, be tantamount, as regards their practical effect, to discrimination on the grounds of nationality, such as is prohibited by the Treaty and the Regulation.

(c) Can the requirement of residence, irrespective of the nationality of the beneficiary, be of itself an obstacle to the free movement of persons? Even if this requirement creates an obstacle for nationals of the host country?

The general wording of Article 48 would allow for such a construction. It is more difficult with Article 52.

The reasoning could be that, beyond the prohibition of discrimination on grounds of nationality, the basic purpose of the free movement of persons is that the whole territory of the Community be open to *any* citizen of one of the Member States for exercising an economic activity irrespective of boundaries and whatever the place whence he comes; and it would be paradoxical that a national of a Member State is "off limit" in his own country. This is not an academic question, with the great number of migrant workers whose children would like to return to their country of origin. A case is presently pending in the Court, concerning an insurance broker of Dutch nationality, economically established in the Netherlands but resident in Belgium, to whom is opposed a rule of Dutch law which imposes as a condition of registration as an insurance broker, residence in the Netherlands (Case 39/75, *Coenen*).[6]

(d) Discriminations do not fall under the Treaty and are not prohibited if they concern non-economic activities or non-economic facts. In Case 36/74 *Walrave and Koch*,[7] the Court applied this principle to the practice of sport:

> (1) Having regard to the objectives of the Community, the practice of sport is subject to Community law only in so far as it constitutes an economic activity within the meaning of Article 2 of the Treaty.

Furthermore, the Court added that:

> (2) The prohibition on discrimination based on nationality contained in Articles 7, 48 and 59 of the Treaty does not affect the composition of sport teams, in particular national teams, the formation of which is a question of purely sporting interest and as such has nothing to do with economic activity.

The decision is not at all clear: the second ruling is understandable only if it deals with *professional* practice of sport, subject to Community law. But it is a case where the process of composing a sport team is separable from the professional activity of the members of such a team. If the team is to appear in a competition as a *national* one, it is understandable that the requirement of nationality is not regarded as a discrimination under the Treaty because, says the Court, it is "a question of purely sporting interest". But why the words "in particular national teams" which seem to mean that a rule prohibiting foreigners from being members of a professional team without a *national* connotation would not be contrary to the rule of non-discrimination. That cannot be so, and I prefer to take, as a clue for deciphering that ruling, what the Advocate-General said in his Opinion:

> The crucial test is whether the provision in the rules is aimed at the constitution of national teams. If it is, I do not think that the nature of the event in which they are to compete – whether it be for a world title or for some more local title, for instance the European – matters, provided of course that it is an international event. But even the concept of "international event" must be interpreted flexibly. Thus I believe that the international rugby championships are between England, France, Ireland (the whole of it), Scotland and Wales.

After this paper was delivered the Court added an important contribution to the construction of the exception of public order, in case 36/75 Rutili (Judgment of 28.10.75). In this decision the Court strongly reaffirms the necessity of a strict interpretation of the exception and insists on the procedural guarantees for the protection of the individual against the discretionaly power of the national authorities. Quite remarkably the Court refers to the Convention for the Protection of Human Rights and Fundamental Freedoms to support its point of view (par. 32). On the other hand the Court, unlike in *Van Duyn*, clearly insists on the principle of non-discrimination in the application of restrictive measures,in the instant case where the residence is limited to part only of the national territory (par. 50 and 53).

(e) The discriminatory restrictions which are prohibited are not only those originating in statutes, regulations or administrative action by the public authorities, but also "rules of any other nature aimed at collectively regulating gainful employment and services" (Case 36/74, *Walrave and Koch*).

Although this ruling expressly applies to Articles 48 and 59, it is obvious that the same applies to Article 52, since the Court explained it by saying that "Articles 7, 48 and 59 have in common the prohibition in their respective spheres of application, of any discrimination on grounds of nationality", and Article 52 has the same aim.

As to Article 48, it was already accepted that the prohibition of discrimination was also binding on employers, and this has been confirmed by relevant provisions of the implementing regulation 1612/68,[8] since wage-earning activity implies a working contract between private persons. As to Articles 52 and 59 it was generally believed that they only covered the action of public authorities. Articles 53 and 62, and also Article 60(3), seemed an indication in that direction, but the Court rejects that argument by referring to "the general nature of the terms of Article 59, which makes no distinction between the source of the restrictions to be abolished"; this applies similarly to Article 52.

The Court argues:

> The abolition as between Member States of obstacles to freedom of movement of persons and to freedom to provide services, which are fundamental objectives of the Community contained in Article 3(c) of the Treaty, would be compromised if the abolition of barriers of national origin could be neutralized by obstacles resulting from the exercise of their legal autonomy by associations or organizations which do not come under public law.

and

Since, moreover, working conditions in the various Member States are governed sometimes by means of provisions laid down by law or regulation and sometimes by agreements and other acts concluded or adopted by private persons, to limit the prohibitions in question to acts of a public authority would risk creating inequality in their application.

Nevertheless, the Court does not, at least in this judgment, go as far as its Advocate-General, Mr Warner, who proposed to say that Article 59 binds private persons, without making any distinction as to whether they act individually or collectively.

Taken as it is, this ruling is most important as it fills an apparent gap, and a wide one, by prohibiting discriminatory clauses in, *inter alia*, rules of membership in professional organisations, articles of association, etc.

2. *The "Second Function" of Directives: Implementation of Article 57 (Mutual Recognition of Diplomas and Approximation of Laws)*

The Court explained for the first time in *Reyners* that:

...in the system of the Chapter on the right of establishment the "general programme" and the directives provided for by the Treaty are intended to accomplish two functions, the first being to eliminate obstacles in the way of attaining freedom of establishment during the transitional period, the second being to introduce into the law of Member States a set of provisions intended to facilitate the effective exercise of this freedom for the purpose of assisting economic and social interpenetration within the Community in the sphere of activities as self-employed persons.

(a) Drawing the line between both functions presupposes that one can determine whether a given rule appears of such a nature as to fall under the prohibition of discrimination, or is part of the regulation of the activity concerned which binds everyone, nationals and non-nationals, residents and non-residents alike. That is not easy to decide when confronted with requirements which can be covert discriminations, or which "although applicable irrespective of nationality [have as their effect], exclusively or principally, to hinder the taking up or pursuit of such activity by foreign nationals".[9] For example: the requirement of a previous training period in the host country, or the rules governing the use of a national professional title.

But normally, one can say that the whole set of rules which may exist and regulate a given activity in a Member State are binding on everybody, and the foreigner cannot escape abiding by them; if that prevents the foreigner *de facto* from enjoying the right of establishment, the elimination of this obstacle is a matter for application of Article 57.

(b) What is clear is that measures under Article 57 can no longer be a condition precedent for the prohibition of discriminatory restrictions. This is also true for Article 57(3) concerning the medical and allied and pharmaceutical profession. This conclusion clearly follows from the Court's ruling in *Reyners'* case. The Court's judgment does not expressly state that this provision can no longer be relied upon after the end of the transitional period. However, the very fact that, although the Court was fully aware of the problem, it expressed itself in very general terms (particularly in points 22, 29, 30 and 31 of the Grounds of Judgment), implies that the rule on equal treatment with nationals has also applied without reservation to those professions since the end of the transitional period, notwithstanding the absence of directives on coordination of the conditions for their exercise. This is the only conclusion which is compatible with the absolute and unconditional nature of the rule on equal treatment with nationals ("one of the fundamental legal provisions of the Community") and there seems to be no good reason for refusing to apply it, for instance, to a doctor who fulfils all the conditions as to diploma, training and professional qualifications required by a Member State of its nationals for the sole reason that he is not a national of the State in question.

3. The Concept of "Restriction" on the Free Supply of Services in Article 59

(a) In contrast with the right of establishment, the *main* restriction prohibited by Article 59 is any specific requirement of residence in the Member State in which the service is provided. Of course discrimination on grounds of nationality is also prohibited, but Article 59 is based on the idea of the necessity to liberate transactions involving a supply of services *across the border* and it does not mention the nationality of the beneficiary. In this respect it can be compared with the provisions on free movemnet of goods.

In Case 33/74, *Van Binsbergen*,[10] the court clearly mentioned both grounds: residence and nationality. The case was clear, and involved only a question of residence, since the person who provided the service in the

Netherlands was a Dutch citizen, but resident in Belgium:

> In particular, a requirement that the person providing the service must be habit-
> ually resident within the territory of the State where the service is to be provided
> may, according to the circumstances, have the result of depriving Article 59 of
> all useful effect, in view of the fact that the precise object of that Article is to
> abolish restrictions on freedom to provide services imposed on persons who are
> not established in the State where the service is to be provided.

(b) But which border must be crossed in order for the supply of services to
be within the scope of Article 59? The Court seems to have ignored the
somewhat awkward condition in the text of Article 59, that the supplier of
services should be established in a State "other than that of the person for
whom the services are intended". This would exclude the many cases in
which a person provides abroad a service for a person resident in the same
country. Examples: an architect in country *A* building for a client also
resident in country *A* a home in country *B*; a lawyer established in country
A goes to plead before a court in country *B* to present the case of a client
also established in country *A*. Those services must clearly be covered
because such restrictions as may exist are based not on the residence of the
person for whom the service is intended, but on the residence of the
supplier. Article 60 giving a definition of services under the Treaty as a
residuary notion, it is this chapter which has to govern the matter.

The Court seems to share this view as it has repeatedly referred, in the
grounds as well as in the tenor of its judgment, to "the establishment of the
person providing a service in a Member State other than that in which the
service is to be provided" and never to the Member State "other than that
where the person for whom the service is intended is resident".

4. *Difficulties Specific to the Supply of Services in Determining What is a Restriction*

(a) In contrast with the *Reyners* case for Article 52, the Court has slightly
qualified its ruling about the direct effect of Article 59 in *Van Binsbergen*: "at
least in so far as they [Articles 59 and 60] seek to abolish any discrimination
against a person providing a service by reason of his nationality or of the
fact that he resides in a Member State other than that in which the service
is to be provided".

Does this mean that the Court would discover other "restrictions" as to
the requirement of nationality or residence, without at this stage deciding

whether their prohibition is apt to have direct effect? One might think of requirements of the local law which are obviously linked to a stable and permanent activity in the country, and are such a hindrance for persons only providing occasional services that they are to be treated as restrictions. Another hint of "other" restrictions is contained in paragraph 10 of the judgment, where the Court says that "The restrictions to be abolished pursuant to Articles 59 and 60 include all requirements...which do not apply to persons established within the national country or *which may prevent or otherwise obstruct the activities of the person providing the service*". One might think of the compulsory membership of local professional organisations.

However, for the sake of legal security, the exemption from this requirement has been introduced in the directives under Article 57, as a measure to facilitate services coming under the scope of the "second function" of the directives (for example, Article 16 of directive 75/362 on doctors).

(b) There is a second qualification in the ruling of the Court in *Van Binsbergen,* about the actual meaning of "restrictions" when the activity concerned is subject to special conditions under the local law of the country in which the service is provided, applicable also to persons established in that country. It is elaborated in paragraphs 12, 13 and 14.

The Court accepts that the host country may, without infringing the Treaty, impose "specific requirements" on the person providing the service. Two grounds are given:

the necessity that this person be subject to the professional rules that may exist justified by the general good "in particular rules relating to organisation, qualification, professional ethics, supervision and liability";[11]

the need to prevent a misuse of the right to provide services in order to escape the rules applicable to persons established in the host State.[12]

The Court in paragraph 14 goes so far as accepting a requirement of a permanent professional establishment in the host country, which obviously results in denying the right to provide services, when, but only when it is *"objectively justified"*.[13] To be sure, the Court seems to limit that requirement to persons "whose functions are to assist the administration of justice".

This sophisticated reasoning is all the more remarkable in that it was not necessary for the Court in order to give its judgment, since the activity involved in the case is *not* regulated in the Netherlands. It raises as many questions as it answers. Does it imply the complete application of the local professional rules, which is apparently the meaning of paragraph 12? But from paragraph 13 it appears that those rules are not as such applicable to a person providing a service ("which would be applicable to him if he were established within that State"). Do the *specific* requirements referred to in paragraph 12 imply that rules applicable *only* to persons providing services and not applicable to persons established would be compatible with the Treaty?

5.

In fact, these difficulties turn around the basic problem of Articles 59 and 60: two legal orders are necessarily and simultaneously involved in any supply of service across the border; how and to what extent to reconcile the freedom to provide services with the respect for the law of the country where the service is provided?

It is no great use to refer to principles of private international law to decide which of the legal orders is to be applied to various categories of rules: professional qualifications, requirements for the physical performance of the service, legal effect of the performed act, and so on. Private international law essentially deals with matters of private law, and the application of foreign law is rejected only when this foreign law is contrary to very fundamental principles of the domestic law. This does not work properly as far as public, administrative law is concerned, the principle of territorial application being prevalent, and we are here confronted with this category of law.

Article 60, paragraph 3, of the Treaty seemed to give a clue by imposing respect for the local law *only* on persons *moving into* the country in which the service is to be provided, and "temporarily" pursing this activity in that country. Does this rule still obtain after *Van Binsbergen*? To be sure the case referred to the Court involved a physical movement of the person providing the service, so that no clear indication can be drawn from the judgment, but the general terms used by the Court could mean that the principle of "equal treatment" prevails in all circumstances, and that even when the person who provides the services does not leave his home country, the law of the place in which the service is provided applies whatever the difficulties this might entail. That cannot fail to have consequences in economic sectors as important as insurance and banking activities.

6. *Construction of Article 55, Paragraph 1*

Before *Reyners* a controversy raged concerning the interpretation of this provision. The difficulties arose from its wording:

the first argument in favour of a broad interpretation of this exception rested on the fact that the article refers to activities *connected* with the exercise of official authority. Some argued therefrom that not only activities which by themselves entail the exercise of official authority fall under Article 55, but also those activities which are ancillary to such an exercise; this argument was used in relation to the profession of practising lawyer, considered as assisting in the proper functioning of the judiciary.

The second argument rested on the words *"even occasionally"*, to contend that if, in the exercise of a profession, some isolated and occasional activities imply the exercise of official authority, the whole profession should be excluded from the right of establishment.

Without bothering to discuss the literal interpretation, the Court has wiped out these arguments by its usual method of looking at the spirit and system of the Treaty, and more particularly of the chapter on the right of establishment.

Taking into consideration the fundamental principle of the free movement of persons and of equal treatment, the Court said that "Article 55 "cannot be given a scope which would exceed the objective for which this exemption clause was inserted" (43)." Those were the same words as the Court had used in relation to Article 48(4) in *Sotgiu*.

Thus looking at this scope, the Court holds that Article 55 has as its sole purpose "to exclude non-nationals from taking up functions involving the exercise of official authority" (44); hence the Court concludes that "this need is fully satisfied when the exclusion of nationals is limited to those activities which, taken on their own, constitute a direct and specific connection with the exercise of official authority" (45).

The Court thus refuses the extension of the exemption to a whole profession, except "in cases where such activities were linked with that profession in such a way that freedom of establishment would result in imposing on the Member State concerned theobligation to allow the exercise, even occasionally, by non-nationals of functions appertaining to official authority" (46); this is not the case when "the activities connected with the exercise of official authority are separable from the professional activity in question taken as a whole" (47).

On the other hand, although the application of Article 55 can vary from State to State in accordance with the organisation and the practice of a given profession, it is necessary that the Community character of the limits imposed by Article 55 on the exception so permitted be taken into account "in order to avoid the effectiveness of the Treaty being defeated by unilateral provisions of Member States". This is tantamount to an affirmation that the exercise of official authority is a *concept of Community law,* the substance of which cannot vary from State to State; only its application can vary according to the fact that privilege of official authority is bestowed or not upon the professional.

Applying this interpretation to the legal profession, the Court denies that the cooperation, even compulsory, in the functioning of the courts constitutes, as such, connection with the exercise of official authority.

7. *Exception of Public Order and Public Security*[14]
(Article 48(3); Article 56; Directive 64/221 of 25.2.1964)

This exception has recently opened a new field in the case-law of the Court, as a result of references by national courts under Article 177. Two judgments have been delivered, and two more cases are presently pending.

(a) The first case raising questions of that sort is also the first one referred to the Court by an English Court, *Van Duyn* v. *Home Office* (Case 41/74[15]).

In this case, apart from the question of direct effect of provisions of a directive not dealt with in this paper, the Court was first called on to state whether public order and public security are concepts of Community law. The Commission, in its observations, had argued that they were. The Court, following the opinion of the Advocate-General Mr Mayras, implicitly but clearly rejected this view: "the particular circumstances justifying recourse to the concept of public policy may vary from one country to another and from one period to another, and it is therefore necessary in this matter to allow the competent national authorities an area of discretion within the limits imposed by the Treaty" (18). However the Court insists that the Member States do not have a completely free hand, because the concept of public policy, "where, in particular, it is used as a justification for derogating from the fundamental principle of freedom of movement for workers, must be interpreted strictly, so that its scope cannot be determined unilaterally by each Member State without being subject to control by institutions of the Community" (18).

(b) In the exercise by the national authorities of the discretion thus left to them, does the rule of non-discrimination have a bearing?

The facts in *Van Duyn* were that the ground for refusing entry into the United Kingdom was the declared intention of this Dutch citizen to take an employment with a "pseudo philosophical cult" (the Church of Scientologists) not unlawful and open to membership by nationals but nevertheless considered to be "socially harmful".

The Court accepts that a Member State has the right, under the exception of public order, to impose on a foreigner restrictions which have no parallel as far as nationals are concerned, so that the principle of non-discrimination does not apply:

> ...a Member State, in imposing restrictions justified on grounds of public policy, is entitled to take into account as a matter of personal conduct of the individual concerned, the fact that the individual is associated with some body or organisation the activities of which the Member State considers socially harmful but which are not unlawful in that State, despite the fact that no restriction is placed upon nationals of the said Member State who wish to take similar employment with the same body or organisation. (judgment, point 3.)

The reasoning is that "where the competent authorities of a Member State have clearly defined their standpoint as regards the activities of a particular organisation and where, considering it to be socially harmful, they have taken administrative measures to counteract these activities, the Member State cannot be required, before it can rely on the concept of public policy, to make such activities unlawful, if recourse to such a measure is not thought appropriate in the circumstances". But the Court further adds a ground on international law, the principle "that a State is precluded from refusing its own nationals the right of entry or residence", to justify the proposition that leave to enter the territory of a Member State may be refused to a national of another Member State. It is hard to see the relevance of this argument. To be sure, this principle obtains in all the Member States, and it is clear that the Treaty, by the exception of Articles 48(3) and 56, accepts a discrimination on this precise point, in that a national, *even if and when he constitutes an immediate and clear danger for the public order or public security,* may *not* be refused entry or residence. The question in *Van Duyn* is totally different: if a given form of conduct by a national is *not* a threat to public order and public security, can the *same* conduct become such a threat when a foreigner is involved?

The answer given by the Court can be accepted in the particular circumstance of the case, if one bears in mind the fact that in the United Kingdom there was and is no power under national law to prohibit the establishment of an organisation like the Church of Scientology, and that the national authorities should not pay the price of such a liberal legal regime by being unable to invoke the exception of public order against foreigners.

It remains that a breach in the fundamental principle of non-discrimination cannot fail to cause some concern, because it seems to open a gap through which arbitrary decisions of the national competent authorities ("police des étrangers") could easily sweep in.

(c) It is well known that Article 3 of Directive 64/221 prohibits measures taken on grounds of public order or public security which are not based exclusively on the *personal conduct* of the person concerned.

This concept of personal conduct was involved in *Van Duyn*, the question being whether association with an organisation can in itself constitute such personal conduct. The Court held that:

> Although a person's past association cannot, in general, justify a decision refusing him the right to move freely within the Community, it is nevertheless the case that present association, which reflects participation in the activities of the body or of the organisation as well as identification with its aims and its designs, may be considered a voluntary act of the person concerned and, consequently, as part of his personal conduct within the meaning of the provision cited. (17)

It is clear from this ruling that "personal conduct" is to be established in each specific case. This was strongly confirmed by the Court in Case 67/74 *Bonsignore,*[16] in connection with the other rule in Directive 64/221 that "previous criminal convictons shall not in themselves constitute grounds for the taking of such measures".

The Court held that "a deportation order may only be made for breaches of the peace and public security which might be committed by the individual affected". The reference was made to the Court by the administrative tribunal of Cologne because the justification, invoked by the authorities for the deportation order, was of a general preventive nature, with the purpose of creating a deterrent effect in immigrant circles having regard to the resurgence of violence in the large urban centres. The Court ruled that Article 3(1) and (2) of Directive 64/221 preclude deportation if it is based on such reasoning.

[1]   I do not discuss in this paper the "direct effect" of these articles; see the contribution of Professor van Gerven.

[2]   Case 6/64, *Costa* v. *ENEL* [1964] ECR 585, 597.

[3]   Case 2/74, *Reyners* v. *Belgian State* [1974] ECR 631, 651.

[4]   Case 167/73, *Commission* v. *French Republic* [1974] ECR 359, 373.

[5]   Case 152/73, *Sotgiu* [1974] ECR 153, 164.

[6]   The Court, in deciding this case on 26.11.75, avoided dealing with this question, limiting the scope of the judgement to the aspect of supply of services.

[7]   Case 36/74, *Walrave and Koch* [1974] ECR 1405.

[8]   J.O. L 257 of 19.10.68.

[9]   General Programme – title III, B – O.J. Special Edition IX, January 1974, p. 7.

[10]   Case 33/74, *Van Binsbergen* [1974] ECR 1299.

[11]   "However, taking into account the particular nature of the services to be provided, specific requirements imposed on the person providing the service cannot be considered incompatible with the Treaty where they have as their purpose the application of professional rules justified by the general good – in particular rules relating to organisation, qualifications, professional ethics, supervision and liability – which are binding upon any person established in the State in which the service is provided, where the person providing the service would escape from the ambit of those rules by being established in another Member State."

[12]   "Likewise, a Member State cannot be denied the right to take measures to prevent the exercise by a person providing services whose activity is entirely or principally directed towards its territory of the freedom guaranteed by Article 59 for the purpose of avoiding the professional rules of conduct which would be applicable to him if he were established within that State; such a situation may be subject to judicial control under the provisions of the chapter relating to the right of establishment and not of that on the provision of services." (Paragraph 14.)

[13]   "In accordance with these principles, the requirement that persons whose functions are to assist the administration of justice must be permanently established for professional purposes within the jurisdiction of certain courts or tribunals cannot be considered incompatible with the provisions of Articles 59 and 60, where such requirement is objectively justified by the need to ensure observance of professional rules of conduct connected, in particular, with the administration of justice and with respect for professional ethics." (Paragraph 14.)

[14]   I prefer to use the term "public *order*" instead of public *policy*, the latter

involving in my view other aspects of governmental action which are not relevant to the exception.

15   Case 41/74 *Van Duyn v. Home Office* [1974] ECR 1337.

16   Case 67/74 *Bonsignore* [1975] ECR 297 (an Italian citizen ordered to be deported from Germany).

6

The Mutual Recognition of Qualifications in the EEC

R. WÄGENBAUR

From its inception the European Economic Community was not meant simply to create the Europe of bankers and big bosses – as people sometimes allege – but everybody's Europe, with just as much "Community" as is necessary in order to allow every citizen to take advantage of the wider economic and social opportunities available. The recognition of professional qualifications is of interest to employed as well as self employed people. It is a good example of how the Community can benefit its 250 million inhabitants – far beyond any business consideration. Undoubtedly, this matter belongs to the "social face" of the Community on which, fairly enough, much emphasis is laid nowadays. A short time ago the Council agreed on the recognition of doctors' qualifications. In 18 months – the time allowed to Member States for implementing the directives – freedom of movement will come into being for doctors. Other professions will follow.

This paper is divided into four major parts: the principle of freedom of movement for persons, which constitutes the background of recognition of qualifications (I); the principle of mutual recognition of qualifications, its implications and the numerous difficulties involved in its application (II); the present situation in the various fields where proposals have been made (III); and finally, some particular problems encountered during the discussion in the Council of the doctors' directives but moreover likely to be of general interest (IV).

The "mutual recognition of qualifications" is in fact a very wide subject. This paper is therefore limited to the broad outlines of the topic.

F.G. Jacobs, ed. European Law and the Individual © 1976, North-Holland Publishing Company

I. The Principle of Freedom of Movement for Persons

Free movement for persons, as postulated by the EEC Treaty,[1] is one of the four fundamental principles on which the Treaty is based. It involves freedom of movement for employed people ("workers" in the phraseology of the Treaty[2]), and the right of establishment for the self-employed.[3] For both categories of people, recognition by the host Member State of any professional qualifications obtained in the State of origin appears essential. Recognition of qualifications is also important for self-employed persons who wish to provide cross-frontier services within the Community.[4] The word "freedom" should not be misunderstood: it means "the abolition of any discrimination based on nationality"[5] and residence, in other words, "the rule of equal treatment with nationals",[6] and signifies therefore the implementation of the general provision of Article 7 of the EEC Treaty under which "any discrimination on grounds of nationality shall be prohibited". As to the fulfilment of this objective, it is well known that the Community for a long period has not had equal success in all fields: whilst freedom of movement for employed people was reached at a rather early stage,[7] the institutions of the Community, until the middle of 1974, still had to deal with what the Treaty calls "abolition of restrictions" for some remaining types of activities of self-employed persons. In particular, discriminations had not yet been removed for the whole range of liberal professions.

Things changed when the Court of Justice was asked by the Belgian Conseil d'Etat, in the famour _Reyners_ case,[8] whether Article 52 was a directly applicable provision, despite the absence of directives as normally required under Articles 54, paragraph 2, and 57, paragraph 1. Bearing in mind previous statements of the Court on direct applicability, and the fact that all discriminations in the field of establishment and services were to be abolished before the end of the transitional period (31 December 1969), the question submitted to the Court is not at all surprising – nor is the positive response given by the Court. In its subsequent judgment in the _Van Binsbergen_ case[9] the Court ruled that Article 59 concerning the freedom to provide services is also directly applicable.

These two judgments signify, consequently, that for nationals of Member States the right of establishment and the freedom to provide services within the Community are now effectively guaranteed, all national legislation providing restrictions on grounds of nationality being effectively abolished in application of the Treaty.[10]

The rule of equal treatment with nationals of the Member States does not change anything as to the qualifications required under national legislation for certain activities. The very case of Mr Reyners is a good illustration of the limited effect of the Judgment of the Court: Mr Reyners, of Dutch nationality, happens to possess the Belgian qualifications required in Belgium for a person wanting to become an "avocat". The application of Mr Reyners for admission to the Brussels bar was refused solely on grounds of nationality.

But these circumstances are, of course, quite exceptional. The mere removal of obstacles resulting from nationality would have remained without practical effect if Mr Reyners, being of Dutch nationality, had obtained his law degree in Holland, as Dutch people normally do.

II. *The Principle of Mutual Recognition of Diplomas under the EEC Treaty*

In order to complete the provisions of the Treaty on the abolition of discrimination, Article 57, paragraph 1, requires that the Council shall, on a proposal from the Commission and after consulting the "European Parliament", issue directives for the mutual recognition of diplomas, certificates and other evidence of formal qualifications. This is a big step forward. One has to bear in mind that until now it was the Member States who decided, either under their own rules or under bilateral arrangements, whether or not a foreign diploma was equivalent to a national diploma. This usually meant that the foreigner had no right to claim equivalence, and, under the narrow quotas at times provided for in bilateral arrangements, very often even discretionary measures of the administration in favour of foreigners had to be set aside.[11]

The provision on recognition of qualifications has been inserted in the chapter on "Right of Establishment". It applies to services as well,[12] but there is no corresponding provision in the chapter on workers.[13] Consequently, the proposals sent by the Commission to the Council on the recognition of qualifications applied to self-employed persons only. Plainly, this situation was not at all satisfactory. It may be that non-self-employed professional persons have a greater interest in having their qualifications recognized in other Member States than do the self-employed. The problem might have been solved by taking into consideration the very nature of "recognition" of qualifications. One must admit[14] that recognition always and necessarily applies to a qualification as such, regardless of whether it is being used by its holder for a self-employed or a non-self-employed activity. There is some precedent in this field: Council directive No. 64/221/EEC on the co-ordination of special measures concerning foreign nationals which are justified on grounds of public policy, public security or public health,[15] of 25 February 1964, is based on Article 56, paragraph 2, of the Treaty, but it applies equally to self-employed and employed persons. Yet another possibility would have been to consider Article 49 as the relevant legal basis and to have listed it as such. The Council – after some hesitations – finally agreed on the necessity of extending the scope of all directives on mutual recognition to employed persons.[16] But unfortunately there was no unanimity as to the appropriate legal basis.

A typical – and rather bad – compromise settled the question. As the example of the doctors' directive on recognition shows, the Council deemed it necessary to invoke not only Article 57 and Article 49, but also Article 235. A statement by the Commission on the contradiction thereby involved has been entered in the minutes of the Council meeting at which the Directive was adopted.

The scope of the "recognition" postulated by the EEC Treaty needs some comment. Article 57 opens with the words: "In order to make it easier for persons to take up and pursue activities...". This is not just an introduction in order to show the motivation of the provision. Nor are these words a mere guideline. They stress that recognition has essentially practical value in so far as the qualification is required for the access to, and exercise of, certain activities.

This has two consequences. First, recognition of qualifications is not considered as an aim in itself. It needs to be stressed that, under Article 57, the Community does not intervene in the academic side of recognition. It is only the practical side of qualifications which is taken into consideration. The value of a certain qualification for the purpose of further University training in another Member State, for instance, does not fall within the scope of Article 57. This provision is concerned only with the professional aspect of the subject.[17]

Secondly, Article 57 paragraph 1 deals with recognition only in so far as a qualification is a condition, under national law, for taking up or pursuing an activity. It has always been understood that, under Article 57, it is out of the question to provide recognition for qualifications which are not legally required in at least one country. If no special qualification is required in Member States for becoming a self-employed piano teacher, then there is no room for recognition of qualifications even if issued by the most famous Academy of Music.

This interpretation of Article 57 may seem rather narrow. A wider interpretation may prevail one day – but probably not before recognition has been obtained for qualifications falling under this narrow interpretation.

In an ideal world, recognition might be envisaged as a global action: it would be sufficient to list the qualifications concerned in a Community directive and to state that henceforth these national qualifications are to be recognised everywhere in the Community. Unfortunately, this seems for the moment to be quite out of the question. Recognition of qualifications, as they stand, would easily be feasible if two conditions were fulfilled: that the national qualifications for a certain activity are of a roughly equivalent level, and that Member States trust each other that this level is maintained in the future. These two conditions are to some extent connected and interdependent: the less one insists on the equivalence of training, the more mutual trust is required from the Member States concerned.

In fact, attempts have been made in the Community towards "global recognition". It is not surprising that, up to now, such an approach on the basis of mutual trust has mainly been desired by Member States already practising a very open-minded system in according equivalence to foreign qualifications.[18]

The authors of the EEC Treaty, it seems, were fully aware of the sometimes appreciable differences in the level of national qualifications. It is for this reason that the Treaty provides not only for mutual recognition of qualifications (Article 57, paragraph 1), but also "for the coordination of the provisions laid down by law, regulation or administrative action in Member States concerning the taking up and pursuit of activities..." (Article 57, paragraph 2). What the Treaty calls "coordination" in Article 57, paragraph 2, is roughly the same as what is listed elsewhere under the more general denomination of "approximation" of the laws of the Member States (Article 100). In modifying national regulations, "coordination" serves the purpose of making national qualifications more or less "equivalent" or "comparable" in standard. Under this system, "recognition" is only the final act by which the Council declares that certain determined national qualifications are subject to recognition in the entire Community – the main difficulty lying in the previous "coordination" of national law.

Following this understanding of "recognition" and "coordination", it would appear that the extent to which "coordination" is necessary is subject to political appreciation. Coordination like recognition is not, and can never be, an end in itself. The only objective of coordination must be to render recognition possible and politically acceptable. It should therefore be restricted to essentials and handled with great care. Experience shows that the delay in adopting the directives concerning liberal professions is mainly due to the differing views Member States hold on the necessary extent of coordinating training requirements. This restrictive understanding of the need for "coordination" also has the advantage of less interference with national education policies.

Prob not true anymore

Bearing this in mind, however, does not prevent a lot of time-consuming blundering around. The Commission's proposals – at least some of them – originally contained very detailed prescriptions as to the course of University studies, going as far as listing not only the various subjects to be taught, but also the number of hours to be spent on each subject. It is only fair to add that this was not due to the "Eurocrat's" understanding of a perfectly harmonised Community, but rather to the determined wishes of the majority of the Member States participating in the elaboration of the proposals.

Owing to experience, and also to a slightly different approach taken after the enlargement of the Community, matters are about to change. In an effort to seek a somewhat modified political approach, the Commission – on the initiative of Commissioner Dahrendorf – proposed guidelines to the Council for its future work in this field. These were based on "flexibility" as to coordination and on "comparability" in respect of the final results of the training process. The resolution adopted by the Council on 6 June 1974[19] stresses that "despite the differences existing between one Member State and another in training courses, the final qualifications giving access to similar fields of activity are in practice broadly comparable". For this reason, directives "should resort as little as possible to the prescription of detailed training requirements". The Resolution therefore recommends the method of listing the qualifications "recognised as being equivalent" and the setting up of "Advisory Committees".

In fact, there is some room for doubt as to the starting point of this Resolution ("broad comparability" of the end-product), and it is unlikely that Member States will easily abandon the system of training requirements as a part of coordination. Still, it is certainly a step in the right direction, and hopes can be entertained for quicker progress in this field in the future.

III. The Present Situation

It would hardly be possible, without breaking all time-limits, to enter into a detailed discussion of the various proposals put forward to date in the field of mutual recognition of qualifications. On the other hand, one can hardly omit all reference to the present situation. Let me therefore describe briefly the stage which has now been reached.

Doctors

At a Council meeting in February 1975, eight governments agreed on a series of proposals in this field which the Commission had made several years before. The Danish Government, however, made a reservation.[20] This reservation was lifted at the beginning of June. For this reason the proposals on doctors were formally adopted on 16 June 1975.[21] The texts the Council agreed upon comprise a directive on mutual recognition concerning both the qualifications of medical practitioners and qualifications in specialised fields of medicine. This directive also includes measures to facilitate the effective exercise of the right of establishment and freedom to provide services. The package also comprises a directive concerning the coordination of national provisions in the field concerned. Furthermore, there is a decision setting up an Advisory Committee on Medical Training, a statement on hospital doctors (with regard to the legal situation of these doctors in France and Italy) and a decision setting up a Committee of Senior Officials on Public Health.

The agreement reached on the doctors' directives is, in public opinion, generally considered as a great break-through. This is certainly true, but it should be remembered that agreement was already imminent at the end of 1972.[22] The ensuing delay of more than two years was due to the normal implications of the enlargement of the Community and the modified approach to coordination which has prevailed since British membership. The value of this agreement as a pattern for other professions should not, however, be over-estimated, each profession having, to varying degrees, its own particular aspects.

Some details of the doctors' directives are reserved for the final section of this paper.

Nurses

The proposals on nurses were sent to the Council during the same year – 1969 – as the doctors' directives. They were under discussion in the competent working group of the Council from the beginning of 1975. This dossier seems to be rather easy to handle and it is hoped to get it adopted in the

near future. There will be one directive on coordination – limited to the
extent required by recognition – and another on recognition itself. Following the precedent provided by the doctors' directives, there will probably
also be an Advisory Committee on the training of nurses.

Architects

As to architects – one of the oldest dossiers in this field – seeing that the
proposals of the Commission bear the date of 1967 –, much work has
already been done at the level of the working group of the Council, but
many difficulties are still ahead. Matters in this field are rather complicated because of the considerable differences existing between the
Member States. Access to the activities of an architect is regulated in some
Member States, in others it is not; in some Member States the right to the
title of "architect" is protected, but not in all. There is no uniform definition of the activities of an architect valid in all the Member States. Not
only do the training requirements leading to access to these activities differ
widely from one country to another, there are also different forms of training within the various Member States. Considerable progress has recently
been made in discussing the remaining points, but full achievement of the
task is not yet in sight. It is worth mentioning, however, that it is envisaged
now to insert quantitative and qualitative training requirements in the
directive on recognition. For a long time, the Commission strongly
opposed such a procedure. It now however seems acceptable, in the light of
the new "flexibility" upon which the Council and the Commission agreed
under the Resolution of June 1974 – with the hope that the training
requirements will nevertheless be introduced in all Member States. If not,
this way of proceeding is dangerous, as it may exclude the architects of
some Member States from the benefit of free movement if their training is
not compatible with the requirements of the directive.

Lawyers

Free movement for lawyers raises particular problems: each Member
State has its own laws and legal traditions which are not easily accessible to
the foreign lawyer. For this reason, the mere recognition of national qualifications seemed inappropriate. The proposal made by the Commission in
1969 was therefore limited to the provision of services. As a first measure,
lawyers practising in one Member State were to be allowed to provide

services in another Member State. In 1975 a working document elaborated by the services of the Commission after consulting the profession – and furthermore taking into account the judgment of the Court of Justice in the *Reyners* and *Van Binsbergen* cases as well as the situation of the profession in the enlarged Community – was submitted to the Council. A formally amended proposal was sent to the Council at the end of July 1975. On this basis it is hoped that the Council will be able to agree on the directive in 1976.

It may be worth mentioning that a new approach has been chosen in order to allow lawyers to provide services in other Member States: the proposal does not envisage recognition of qualifications, but of the quality of lawyer as such. This way of proceeding makes things much easier all around. The directive will only have to regulate the use of the professional title, relationships with the local bar and tribunal, and so on, the main point being, probably, the question of professional rules applying to a lawyer providing cross-frontier services.

Other Professions

The dossier on pharmacists was deferred some time ago because of the considerable difficulties encountered in this field, and it is still uncertain just when work will be resumed. The services of the Commission are at present preparing new working documents concerning both coordination and recognition of qualifications in this field.

As to dentists, opticians, midwives, veterinary surgeons, chartered accountants and financial advisers, proposals on recognition of qualifications or on transitional measures are before the Council, awaiting discussion.

IV. Particular Problems

During the many years spent on the proposals made by the Commission in the field of recognition of qualifications, a great number of problems had to be dealt with at all stages of Community legislation. Amongst these problems, only a few can be dealt with here. They are taken from recent experience with the doctors' directives and have been selected because of the general interest they seem to have for other professions as well.

Particular Aspects of Coordination

It has already been stressed that coordination of national rules concerning training requirements should not be regarded as an end in itself but rather as one stage on the road towards recognition, the extent of coordination deemed necessary being subject to political appreciation. In connection with the directive adopted in respect of the activities of doctors, some further comments on this point seem appropriate.

The first point to be made is that, in the case of doctors, Member States have agreed on "full" coordination, in so far as Member States will have to adhere to certain rules concerning the training which will lead to a qualification in medicine, even if only a very small proportion of doctors will ever benefit from free movement in the Community. As laid down in Article 1 of the directive, (all) "persons wishing to take up and pursue medical profession" shall be required to hold a qualification in medicine referred to in the directive on recognition, a stipulation which guarantees that the person concerned has had thorough training as specified by the directive. This seems all the more noteworthy since in the case of the directive, (all) "persons wishing to take up and pursue a medical profession" shall be required to hold a qualification in provide – as was proposed by the Commission in 1969[23] – that qualifications in general nursing listed in the directive on recognition are to be conferred only on persons who have passed an examination subsequent to a training as specified in the directive. It seems unlikely, but it is not excluded, that Member States will adopt other qualifications in nursing than those listed in the directive. This would be quite permissible – but the holders of such qualifications would not be entitled to recognition in the Community.

As to architects, it has already been mentioned that the Council wants to include training requirements in the directive on recognition. The result might possibly be that Member States will proceed as if there had been a real coordination. But it is not legally impossible that a Member State will organise a training for architects of a lower standard: holders of such qualifications would not benefit from recognition. Finally, it ought to be borne in mind that free provision of services will be organised for lawyers without any coordination as to training. As lawyers providing services in another Member State will not be restricted as to the law on which they give advice – it may be the law of the home country or that of the host country – one wonders how it will ever be possible to provide coordination if one day the right of establishment of lawyers is to be facilitated by recognising their national qualifications.

The second point concerns the training requirements. These requirements are always taken to be minimum training requirements, Member States being free – without incidence on recognition – to ask for higher standards. The enlargement of the Community had a tremendous impact on the formulation of training requirements. The six Member States had agreed on having only so-called "quantitative" criteria inserted in the directive on coordination. When discussion opened in the enlarged Community, there was a strong feeling that provision should be made for "qualitative" criteria as well. This tendency, strongly supported by the British Government, prevailed, and the text of the coordination directive for doctors lists several qualitative criteria. These qualitative criteria are of course written in very general terms. The implementation of these criteria will largely be a matter of mutual trust among Member States. The Commission can ensure that Member States fulfil the requirement that general medical training should "comprise at least a six-year course or 5,500 hours of theoretical and practical instruction...", but there is hardly any way of checking if the training provides a student with "adequate knowledge of clinical disciplines and practices, providing him with a coherent picture of mental and physical diseases...".

Linguistic Knowledge

When discussions resumed on the doctors' directives following the enlargement of the Community, there was considerable concern amongst the new Member States on the linguistic knowledge which, it was felt, foreign practitioners ought to possess. In fact, this matter had been thoroughly discussed by the six Member States years before. The conclusion was reached then that it was inexpedient to seek for a special provision to be inserted in the directives. Since then things have gone the other way and it seems now of some interest to draw attention to this question.

One can easily see the implications of the matter. It is evident, on the one hand, that a doctor should be able to understand his patient and to communicate with him. On the other hand, it is equally clear that a requirement of this nature could easily turn out to be a serious barrier to free movement. It would be throwing a new obstacle into the way of free movement in the Community if Member States were allowed to require foreign doctors, before registration, to pass a language examination, possibly including a

solid knowledge of Shakespeare or Molière. It is understandable that
nobody wants to envisage the possibility of such a measure. Besides, as the
Earl of Halsbury mentioned in this connection in the House of Lords[24]
when the matter was discussed, the danger should not be exaggerated: the
general practitioner who speaks not a word of English would not have any
patients. In other words – and all doctors are aware of this fact – the first
thing they will attend to when wanting to practise in another country is to
learn the language of its inhabitants. This, by the way, is a problem which
exists even within one language area. A person from Hanover might well
have some difficulties in understanding people in the Bavarian mountains
– comparable difficulty might be encountered, says the Earl of Halsbury, if
a doctor trained in the Home Counties wants to practise in the industrial
North.

On the Community level, things have been settled by a compromise at
the very last meeting of Ministers. There is now a new paragraph providing that "Member States shall see to it that, where appropriate, the
persons concerned acquire, in their interest and in that of their patients,
the linguistic knowledge necessary to the exercise of their profession in the
host country". This clause enables Member States to suggest to foreign
doctors the advisability of studying the local language to the extent where
it can be called a "working knowledge", and, at the same time, prevents
them from introducing any linguistic barriers which would have most
unhappy results.

Recognition and National Authorities – The Advisory Committee

The functions attributed to national authorities in the case of foreign
professional persons seeking employment, or wishing to practise as self-
employed persons, are another matter of considerable interest. This
question has, of course, many aspects; only a few of them can be dealt with
in this paper.

As a matter of principle, the role attributed to national authorities as to
the registration of doctors as well as to the national regulations, remains
unchanged, provided they are not discriminatory. Under the recognition
directive, nationals of any Member State possessing the necessary qualifications for practising in their home country automatically have the right to
be entered in the register of any of the other Member States, without any
further examination as to their training. The procedure of registration
must be completed not later than three months after presentation of the

documents, and there are further provisions which aim at facilitating the exercise of the rights granted by the directive. Where, for instance, host Member States require of their own nationals proof of good character or good repute, or a certificate of physical or mental health, they are bound to accept the presentation of the corresponding document required in the Member State from which the foreign national originates. The foreign doctor will normally seek information on the health and social security laws of the host country. Under the directives, Member States are required to furnish all the information he needs, and "information centres" may be set up for this purpose.

What happens in the event that a Member State expresses doubts as to the authenticity of the foreign documents presented for registration? In case of possible forgery, the recognition directive provides for the host Member State to ask the other Member State for confirmation. The same applies if doubts exist as to whether or not the applicant has fulfilled the training requirements of the coordination directive.

But what if the competent authorities of the host Member State consider that the teaching establishment where the applicant received his training falls short of the standard required by the coordination directive?[25] Can the General Medical Council decline registration in such a case? Obviously, such a right would go too far, since it might easily ruin all efforts towards mobility in the Community. Another solution had therefore to be found.

As a matter of principle, it is up to the Commission to survey the implementation of directives by Member States. In the event of any doubts on this point arising, Member States may inform the Commission, and it is up to this institution to conduct the necessary inquiries. If the Commission considers that a Member State has not complied with the training requirements, it may refer the matter to the Court of Justice. This procedure is the usual one under the Treaty (Article 169). In order to make this point perfectly clear, however, a Council statement has been entered in the Minutes of the Council – and was even published in the Official Journal. It is explicitly stated there that in case of "serious doubts" as to whether a given national qualification is based on training complying with the minimum standards of the coordination directive, "it shall be incumbent on the said Member State to inform the Commission thereof".[26] The Commission will then undertake the necessary investigations. As a result, the Commission will either "confirm...that the training standards have been complied with"[27] – or open a procedure under Article 169 against the Member State concerned.

This very clear statement excludes the possibility of national authorities declining or deferring registration. In other words, holders of national qualifications listed in the recognition directive can be certain of their right to practise in other Member States.

The rights of the individual thus being preserved,[28] it must be added that the Commission, in its role as supervisor of the faithful implementation of the directives by Member States, is to be assisted by an Advisory Committee. This Committee – the existence of which is mainly due to a British request in the Council – will consist of experts from the practising professions, from the medical faculties of the universities and from the competent authorities of the Member States. In general terms, its task will be to help to ensure a comparably demanding standard of medical training in the Community. Almost certainly, in the case of "serious doubts" as to the value of certain qualifications – and even long before such doubts may be raised officially – this Committee will be informed. It will be in a position to obtain full information very quickly and see whether the doubts are well founded. The task of the Commission should be greatly facilitated by the work of this Committee.

Third Countries' Diplomas

A short time ago, it was reported in the press[29] that immigrant doctors who qualified outside the EEC, and who are fully registered as practising physicians in the United Kingdom, complained about being excluded from freedom of movement. A word of comment seems to be indicated on this.

As stated above, recognition applies only to qualifications listed in the recognition directive. These are qualifications awarded in one of the Member States. As to qualifications obtained in other countries, the directives do not change the present situation. Member States remain free to authorities holders of such qualifications to practise as doctors in respect of their own territory.[30] At the present time, however, holders of these qualifications – even if actually practising in a Member State – do not benefit from the right of free movement in the Community. The same applies equally to a doctor having post-graduate qualifications awarded in one of the Member States, since under the terms of the coordination directive a qualification in specialised medicine is only to be recognised if the holder is also in possession of a primary qualification awarded in a Member State.[31]

The fact that doctors having qualifications awarded by third countries do not have the same rights in the Community as their colleagues who had their training in one of the Member States, may be particularly resented by the immigrant doctors in the United Kingdom. But it should be stressed that other Member States also have a considerable number of immigrant doctors. In Germany, for instance, nearly 5,000 doctors out of 42,000 working in hospitals are foreigners;[32] many of them received their training in third countries. Furthermore, an increasing number of German students, rebuffed by the "numerus clausus" from German universities, try to get their qualifications in Austria, Switzerland, the United States or elsewhere. Back home, their third countries' qualifications are recognised without difficulty, provided their training was equivalent to German standard. But these German doctors remain excluded from free movement in the Community. The only step thus far made towards free movement for holders of qualifications which have been awarded in third countries concerns the nationals of Luxembourg, on the ground that there is no complete university training in this country. A Council recommendation therefore invites other Member States to allow nationals of Luxembourg having third countries' qualifications, previously recognised in Luxembourg, to practise as doctors within other Member States.[33]

The position adopted so far by the Council as to third countries' diplomas seems entirely consistent with the Treaty. Article 57 implicitly refers to national qualifications, as they alone can be subject to "mutual" recognition. At a later stage, however, it will not be legally impossible to amend the directives in order to facilitate to a certain extent free movement for holders of qualifications awarded outside the Community.[34] Before undertaking this, however, it appears appropriate, at any event, to examine the repercussions of free movement as actually guaranteed by the directives.

Conclusion

Freedom of movement in the Community, irrespective of the Member State of which the individual is a national and in which he obtained his professional qualifications, is certainly one of the most noble aims of the Treaty of Rome. As to the first obstacle – nationality – the Court of Justice has definitely cleared the field. As to qualifications, it appears – taking into account the many difficulties which exist between the Member States in the educational field – that this objective is really a very ambitious one.

It can be realised only step by step. In the course of this paper it has been stressed that there is a close link between "recognition" of qualifications and the – previous or simultaneous – "coordination" of training requirements leading to professional qualifications. This link, however, is not a rigid one. Coordination is not a legal condition for recognition, and the practice which the Community has hitherto observed in respect of the directives on doctors, nurses, architects and lawyers, shows the Council's readiness to agree on various patterns which are supposed to be adequate for the activities concerned. In all endeavours the Council has shown considerable flexibility as to the extent to which coordination is found necessary. It is here that the great chance of further progress lies in the field of recognition. Once Member States have two or three times essayed the big step towards recognition, and no catastrophe has come as a result, they will more easily be prepared to confide in mutual trust and thus to accept the principle of recognition without asking for item-by-item coordination. One can therefore be reasonably optimistic about the future.

Notes

¹ Article 3(c) of the EEC Treaty.

² Article 48 *seq.*

³ Article 52 *seq.*

⁴ Article 59 *seq.*

⁵ As stipulated for employed persons under Article 48, para. 2, of the Treaty.

⁶ In the words of the Court of Justice in Case 2/74 *Reyners* [1974] ECR 631.

⁷ See Regulation No. 38/64 of 25 March 1964, which entered into force on 1 May 1964 (O.J. No. 62 of 17 April 1964, p. 965), now replaced by Regulation No. 1612/68 of 15 October 1968, in force since 8 Nov. 1968 (O.J. No. L 257 of 19 October 1968, English version see Special Edition 1968(II), p. 475).

⁸ See footnote 6.

⁹ Case 33/74, *Van Binsbergen* [1974] ECR 1299.

¹⁰ The principle of non-discrimination, it ought to be recalled, is subject to a few exceptions: Following Articles 55, 48, para. 3 and 56, an exception is made for activities connected with the exercise of official authority, and Member States may continue to apply special rules to foreign nationals on grounds of public policy, public security and public health. Besides, the provisions on free movement for employed persons do not apply to employment in the public service (Article 48, para. 4).

¹¹ The existing arrangement between France and Belgium provides that up to ten (!) doctors of one country can be allowed to practise in the other country (*Moniteur belge* of 15 May 1974, p. 7084).

¹² Article 66 of the Treaty.

¹³ The Council – but perhaps not the authors of the Treaty – was quite aware of the problem arising, see Article 45 of Regulation No. 1612/68 (footnote 7).

¹⁴ See Maestripieri, "Freedom of establishment and freedom to supply services", *Common Market Law Review*, 1973, p. 150.

¹⁵ O.J. No. 56 of 4 April 1964, p. 850; for English version see Special Edition 1963-1964, p. 117.

¹⁶ The titles of the doctors' directives have been modified accordingly. Oddly enough, the directive on recognition still mentions "measures to facilitate the effective exercise of the right of establishment and freedom to provide services". But Article 24 makes it clear that these measures equally apply to employed persons.

¹⁷ The academic aspect of recognition is traditionally dealt with by other institutions, such as the Council of Europe. A short time ago, however, the Ministers of Education, meeting within the Council, agreed on the setting up of an Education

Committee designed to study (among other things) "improved possibilities for academic recognition of diplomas and periods of study" (O.J. No. C 98 of 20.8.74, p. 2). Needless to say, this goes beyond the possibilities of Article 57.

[18] For a comparative report see *The Times*, "Europa", May 1975.

[19] O.J. No. C 98 of 20 August 1974, p. 2.

[20] See Written Question No. 39/75 of Mr Rivierez (O.J. No. C 170 of 28 July 1975, p. 19).

[21] O.J. No. L 167 of 30 June 1975 and No. C 146 of 1 July 1975.

[22] See *Wägenbaur*, "Où en est la reconnaissance mutuelle des diplômes de médecin dans la C.E.E.?", *Revue trimestrielle de droit européen*, 1973, p. 426 *seq.*

[23] Proposals of 14 October 1969 (O.J. 1969, No. C 156, p. 19).

[24] Parliamentary Debates (Hansard), Vol. 355, No. 24, 9 December 1974, p. 515.

[25] This matter was discussed in the House of Lords, see Parliamentary Debates (Hansard), Vol. 355, No. 24 of 9 December 1974, p. 502, *seq.*

[26] Council statement A. 2 (O.J. No. C 146 of 1 July 1975, p. 1).

[27] This is the only alternative which is explicitly taken into consideration in the Council statement.

[28] The opposite interpretation could perhaps have found support in Article 2 of the recognition directive. Under this provision, recognition seems to be subject to a double condition: The qualification must be listed in the directive, *and* it must have been awarded "in accordance with Article 1" of the coordination directive, i.e. with the training requirements mentioned in this provision. One might have argued that, if the latter condition is not fulfilled, Member States remain free to refuse recognition. Such an interpretation would be misleading. The statement of the Council quoted above makes this perfectly clear.

[29] See *The Times* of 15 April 1975.

[30] Upon British demand, this has been made clear under para. 5 of Article 1 of the coordination directive. The criteria of the coordination directive are not applicable if Member States grant equivalence to holders of third countries' diplomas.

[31] This results from Article 4 of the recognition directive combined with Article 2, para. 2 of the coordination directive.

[32] See "Zur Reform des Gesundheitswesens", *Schriftenreihe des Marburger Bundes*, Bd. 6, 1974.

[33] O.J. No. L 167 of 30 June 1975, p. 20.

[34] Not to forget that, conceivably, agreements will be reached one day between the Community and third countries in respect of recognition of doctors' qualifications.

7

Citizen Access to Judicial Review of Administrative Action in a Transnational and Federal Context[*]

ERIC STEIN and G. JOSEPH VINING

The Individual Citizen in International Law

In an international legal order dominated by states, the individual citizen is generally viewed as lacking international legal personality. It is true with little exception that an individual cannot appear in an international forum – political or judicial – to press his rights. Despite the dramatically increased emphasis upon international protection of basic human rights, individuals have been given access to international dispute settlement machinery in only a few isolated instances within the United Nations system, and on a regional level pursuant to the European convention on human rights.[1]

The Paris Treaty establishing the European Coal and Steel Community (ECSC), and the Rome Treaties establishing the European Atomic Energy Community (EURATOM) and the European Economic Community (EEC the Common Market) are the only international agreements providing for a judicial tribunal of general compulsory jurisdiction open not only to Member States and Community institutions but individual citizens as well. The purpose of this essay is to explore the case law of the Court of Justice of the Communities and the considerations that may have motivated that Court in its effort to define limits on access by individuals seeking judicial review of acts of Community institutions, and to inquire whether experience with judicial review of administrative action in a federation may be relevant to the evolution of transnational European administrative law.

113

F.G. Jacobs, ed. European Law and the Individual © *1976, North-Holland Publishing Company*

Three Cases

A convenient way of introducing the subject is to present three little dramas in contemporary costume, drawn from three different milieux:

1. The Federal Comptroller of Currency, an agency supervising federal banks in the United States, issued a regulation allowing federal banks to expand their activities into the business of selling data processing services. A trade association of companies also engaged in selling data processing services and claiming loss of profit and customers sued the Comptroller to obtain review and annulment of the regulation. The data processing companies relied on a federal statute which prohibited banks from engaging in any activity other than the performance of bank services. In 1970 the Supreme Court of the United States upheld their standing to sue. *Association of Data Processing Service Organizations* v. *Camp,* 397 U.S. 150 (1970).

2. In the nineteen sixties, The Parliament of the German Federal Republic appropriated funds to the individual German States (*Länder*) for the purpose of subsidizing construction of wine vaults by German wine producers and thus increasing their competitive position in the Common Market by improving the quality of their wine. The Land in question allocated the subsidies to wine producers but refused the application of a company engaged in wine marketing. The company sued for review and annulment of the Land decisions granting the subsidies to producers, alleging illegal denial of an equal opportunity to compete. Its business consisted of entering into long-term contracts with wine producers for the annual purchase of quantities of wine at a minimum price, storing the wine, and ultimately marketing it. As a result of the subsidies, the producers were now able to market wine directly to consumers at a cheaper price than competing retailers who like the plaintiff company did not have access to the subsidy. The Federal Administrative Court upheld the plaintiff company's standing to institute judicial review: Judgment of August 30, 1968, BVerwGE vol. 30, p. 191.

3. In 1968, the Commission of the European Communities decided to grant substantial subsidies from Community funds to three Italian sugar refineries to enlarge their production. The award was conditioned upon enlargement by the Italian Government of the production quotas allotted to the three refineries within the Italian quota fixed by the Community.The plaintiffs, competing sugar refinery enterprises who did not get any subsidies, sued in the Court of Justice of the Communities for review and annulment of the Commission's decisions, alleging unlawful distortion of competition in violation of Treaty articles on subsidies, because their own production quotas were to be reduced to make possible the required enlargement of the quotas of the three subsidized competitors. The Court denied standing to sue on the ground that the plaintiffs failed to demonstrate a direct and individual concern. Cases 10 and 18/68, *Società Eridania Zuccherifici Nazionali et al.* v. *Commission of the European Communities,* 15 Recueil de la jurisprudence de la Cour de Justice des Communautés Européennes (Rec.) 459 (1969).

Thus in the United States private plaintiffs claiming consequential harm have been given standing to contest a general regulation. In Germany they have been permitted to contest decisions addressed to third parties. But in analogous situations in the European Economic Community (EEC) they have been denied standing to sue. Two of the three milieux are more or less mature federations in which citizens are directly subject to federal and state laws. The third is different – a hybrid, "a new legal order of international law".[2] It is a treaty-based international organization, but is distinctive among such organizations in its broad impact upon the rights and obligations of individual citizens.

To what extent does – or should – this distinction make a difference? Should or will the experience of the Community follow that of mature political federations? Or should we approach each *sui generis,* and see nothing remarkable in current differences in treatment of apparently similar problems?

The Federation and the Community: Some Dissimilarities

The comparative method, in law or in any other discipline, has its problems. Above all there is a danger of losing sight of controlling dissimilarities behind the smoke-screen of superficial likeness. It may help to avoid pitfalls if we review some of the relevant similarities and differences between the European Economic Community and a federal system as exemplified by the United States.

At the core of our inquiry is the position of the individual before governmental authority in an increasingly complex and technology-based society, which now exists on both sides of the Atlantic. On one hand government regulation steadily widens, and on the other individuals and groups demand ever greater recognition and participation in governmental processes. In the United States as in the Community, governmental authority is divided among separate hierarchies of institutions exercising normative powers. The United States has States with different constitutions, a federal government, fifty state judiciaries and a federal judiciary. But in the United States, the power of the federation dwarfs the States' power. In the Community the balance goes the other way. In the United States there is little question about the basic legitimacy of the governmental institutions – even though today the Watergate cloud is still hovering over them – while in the Communities the institutions are brittle and as yet have little grass roots participation. Moreover, Community lawmaking is in the hands of an executive. There is no popularly based legislature. In the American federation, federal agencies and federal courts execute federal legislation (with some important exceptions such as federal grant programs where implementation is left in considerable part to the States). But in the Community, Member States carry the bulk of the responsibility for implementing Community law: State officials issue import licences and collect customs duties; State parliaments transform major directives into national law; and State courts decide controversies involving Community law, albeit after preliminary ruling on Community law questions by the Court of Justice.[3] This broad decentralization and delicate symbiotic relationship between national and Community institutions at the political as well as the judicial levels, to which there is no real analogy in America, is a feature of crucial importance in evaluating the case law on standing before the Court of Justice. The Community is a body at the borderline between the federal and the international – and in international law the very notion of an individual having independent standing to sue before an international tribunal is little short of revolutionary.

The Standing Question: What the Court of Justice Said

With these differences in mind, let us turn to the similarities between the American federation and the Community bearing directly upon the standing question. In each the formal source of law determining the requirements of standing can be found in principle in a single normative provision: in Article 173 of the EEC Treaty[4] and in section 10 of the federal Administrative Procedure Act.[5] In addition, however, federal statutes often provide specifically for judicial review of specified types of administrative action. Similarly, in the Community certain regulations, such as Regulation 17 implementing the Treaty rules of competition, might have the effect of broadening individual access to judicial review.[6]

Article 173 sets no limitations whatsoever upon the standing of Member States to contest *any* normative act of the Commission or the Council, nor for that matter upon the standing of the Commission to contest acts of the Council and *vice versa*. It is the much discussed second paragraph of that Article that provides that

> [a]ny natural or legal person may...institute proceedings against a decision addressed to that person or against a decision which, although in the form of a regulation or a decision addressed to another person, is of direct and individual concern to the former.

The posture of the Court of Justice with regard to this provision was set in two groups of early cases in which the question of individual standing was raised for the first time: cases 16-17/62 and 19-22/62 in which associations of producers and associations of traders respectively sued for annulment of Council regulations,[7] and the *Plaumann* case 25/62,[8] in which a German importer of citrus fruit sought to contest a Commission decision addressed to the German Government refusing to authorize a reduction of the common external tariff on certain fruit imports from third states. The Court denied standing in both instances and adopted a strict reading of the requirement of "direct and individual concern". It did so despite an express recognition of the principle – in the *Plaumann* case – that provisions for access to legal remedy should never be narrowly construed.[9]

Judging by what the Court *said*, the factor that influenced it most was the difference between the language in the second paragraph of Article 173 and the the corresponding provision in the earlier Treaty Establishing the Coal and Steel Community.[10] That latter provision, which expressly grants standing to contest acts of general application on the ground of *détournement de pouvoir* (misuse of powers, abuse of discretion) affecting a plaintiff, had been given a rather liberal interpretation by the Court. The Court concluded from the differences between the two treaties that the authors of the EEC Treaty deliberately intended to restrict access of individuals to the Court, presumably because of the much broader power to issue general regulations granted to the EEC institutions and the much wider range of persons affected by the EEC Treaty. "It is not for the Court to pass upon the merits of such system", the Court stated, "since the latter clearly stems from the text under scrutiny".

The formula that the Court evolved in the early cases for the application of the second paragraph of Article 173 may be summarized as follows:

1. An act is a "regulation" – as opposed to a "decision in the form of a regulation"[11] – if, by its "legal nature", it applies to categories of persons treated theoretically. Private persons may not contest such a general regulation under any circumstances.[12]

2. "Decisions" may be contested, but persons other than those to whom a decision was addressed must show not only a *direct* concern but also an *individual* concern. They can claim an individual concern only if the decision affects them because of factors peculiar to them or by reason of circumstances "in which they are differentiated from all other persons and by virtue of these factors distinguishes them individually just as in the case of the persons addressed".[13]

Professor Waelbroeck has called the second part of this formula "not enlightening", which is a resounding understatement. The real question, he wrote, is to know just what the characteristics or fact situations are that "individualize" a person.[14] It is nevertheless this formula or its variant that the Court has repeated in every case and applied to deny standing to all the "natural or legal persons" who thus far have come before it as plaintiffs,[15] with the exception of three cases. Let us consider this triad in some detail since it may be easier to divine the Court's criteria from cases where standing was granted than from the much more numerous cases where it was denied.

The Triad Where Standing Was Allowed

In the *Toepfer* case,[16] the German Government import agency posted a zero levy on the import of corn for a specific date as a result of a Commission error. Seizing this opportunity, plaintiffs, large grain wholesale enterprises, applied for import licences on the zero-levy basis. When the error was discovered, German and Commission officials consulted and agreed on a course of action. The German Government invoked its safeguard power under a Council regulation which enabled the German agency to reject the requested licences. The Commission, pursuant to the same regulation, issued a decision directed to the German Government and "authorizing" its safeguard measure retroactively. It was this Commission decision that the plaintiffs sought to have annulled. The Court held that the plaintiffs had standing. They were concerned "directly" because the Commission decision was "directly applicable" to them[17] – *there was no need for any further action by the German Government*. The plaintiffs were also concerned "individually" because the number and identity of the parties affected by the Commission's act ("no less than 27 companies") were determinable at the time the decision was adopted.

In the *Bock* case,[18] as in the *Toepfer* case, the Commission responded to a request from the German Government and addressed a decision to that government authorizing it to reject already pending applications for import licences, including one by the plaintiff. In this case also the Court granted standing: The plaintiff was concerned directly (even though the formal rejection of the licences required an act of the German Government and *in theory* – it was argued – that government may have decided not to use the authorization to reject). The plaintiff was also concerned individually, because, as in *Toepfer*, his licence application was already pending at the time of the Commission decision and "the number and identity of importers thus affected was certain and determinable".[19]

Finally, in the *International Fruit* case,[20] the Commission, as part of a safeguard system designed to ensure stability of the apple market was given authority to consider the total quantity of apples for which import licences were requested and to decide what percentage, if any, of that quantity should be admitted. In that context, the Commission issued a "regulation" limiting the percentage and preventing acceptance of the applications for import licences filed during a specified past period with the Dutch Government. Plaintiffs whose applications were among those rejected were given standing to sue for annulment of the regulation which, the Court said, was in effect a bundle of individual decisions.[21] Plaintiffs were concerned directly because after the Commission had acted, the Member governments had no intervening power, no discretion whether or not to accept or reject that action. The plaintiffs were also concerned individually because the Commission based its regulation upon applications already filed. Hence the number of the parties concerned was determined at the time of the adoption of the regulation even though the Commission, acting upon the aggregate quantity of apples for which import licences were requested as reported by the Dutch Government, had no knowledge of the identity or even of the number of the parties affected.

The Court of Justice in Search of a Rationale

The manner in which the Court and the Advocates General have employed the prerequisite of "direct concern" manifests an intense interest in maintaining the delicate balance between Member State and Community power, and we shall turn to this shortly. But the three cases where standing was allowed, seen against the background of all the cases where standing was denied, demonstrate the difficulties the Court and the Advocates General have encountered in drawing a line between what is and what is not of direct concern. Is the presence or absence of administrative discretion on the part of the Member State under the challenged Community act the determining factor? And in which situations is such discretion present? In the *Toepfer* case where a Commission decision granted the requested authorization to the German Government the Court found a direct effect upon the plaintiff, although the Advocate General disagreed. In theory the German Government still had discretion whether or not to make use of the Commission's authorization but this did not seem to bother the Court.[22] Yet in the *Eridania* case denying standing, one of the three dramas at the beginning of this article, the most remote possibility that the Italian Government might not make use of an authorization, which in fact it had recommended and to which it was financially committed, was enough for the Court to deny direct effect.[23] In the *Alcan* case[24] where the Commission in a decision addressed to a Government refused an authorization, the Court found no direct effect on the plaintiff although the refusal eliminated any discretion on the part of the addressee government. (The Advocate General found a scintilla of discretion in the possibility that the Government might appeal the decision to the Court.[25]

The Court has struggled in a similar way with the second prerequisite, that of "individual concern". In the *Eridania* case, with which we began, the Court denied individual (as well as direct) effect – contrary to the advice from the Advocate General – to Italian sugar producers who were affected by a Commission decision granting subsidies to their competitors. But there were only twenty-five sugar producers affected. In another case, the *Zuckerfabrik Watenstedt*, not more than 30 raw sugar producers in the entire Community were *in fact* directly affected by a Council regulation and there was no real chance of new producers being added in view of the depressed conditions in the sugar market and the size of the necessary investment.[26] Such *"de facto* individualization" satisfied the Advocate General but not the Court. Again, in *Getreide-Import*, despite the *Toepfer* ruling, a German importer-plaintiff was held not to be "individually" concerned by the Commission's decision fixing a price on imports for a specific date although he was ultimately the only one to request an import licence on that date.[27] It would seem that in the Court's view, the plaintiffs can be considered "individually" affected only if they are members of a group of persons whose identity and number are fixed and, in addition, if the challenged act has a retroactive effect on their *legal* position, that is, if the act affects their "vested rights". But it is not the unfairness or the actual harm in retroactive lawmaking that moves the Court to grant standing. In two more recent cases where a retroactive effect clearly existed, the Court found no standing.[28]

We might note that in the *Glucoseries* case, the Court, after reciting the *Plaumann* formula, proceeded to inquire into the "general economic scope" and "purpose" of the Commission's act.[29] The preoccupation with the "purpose" of the challenged act may suggest one reason why the Court may have granted standing in *Toepfer* and *Bock*, two of the three Community cases where standing was allowed. In *Toepfer* there was some evidence suggesting a collusion between national and Commission officials to erase an administrative error through means not entirely compatible with good administration,[30] and in *Bock* an improper delay and perhaps arbitrary recourse to a protective measure. It is significant that in both cases the Court ultimately annulled the contested act in proceedings on the merits. In the *International Fruit* case, the third case of the triad, the Court may have been concerned, in granting standing, that the Commission should not be in the position of precluding judicial review of its act by labelling it "regulation" rather than "decision".[31] This somewhat speculative line of analysis would suggest that in reality the Court may be inclined to look beyond jurisdictional arguments and grant standing where it senses an element of irregular administration.

This possibility aside, it is fair to say in summary that with respect to "direct concern", the Court of Justice has sought to give content to the requirement by invoking a Community interest in preserving the discretion of Member governments; but the distinctions the Court has made on this basis are so illogical that one may question whether there is yet a workable or meaningful doctrine of "directness". As for the "individual concern" prerequisite, the Court seems to require that a plaintiff show something in the nature of an exclusive legal right analogous to a "vested right" – something similar in its impact, as we shall see, to the original common law standing test in American federal law.

Elements of Legal Policy

One may well wonder what considerations have induced the Court to reject even the modicum of flexibility suggested by its own Advocate General,[32] particularly if we recall – by way of a contrast – the Court's imaginative and teleological approaches to other institutional questions.[33]

1. We have already mentioned the political concern with respect to Member Governments. A real likelihood of the exercise of Member State discretion in implementation does appear to be relevant to the technical definition of a "direct" concern in the Community act being challenged. But Advocate General Gand went so far as to invoke "diplomatic courtesy" dictating that state discretion and state "sovereignty" not be impaired[34] – language reminiscent of the International Court of Justice which umpires international disputes among states.

While prudence is obviously in order for a freshly established judicial tribunal in a body politic where States play a crucial part, the method by which the Court has sought to limit its jurisdiction is – as we have suggested – open to question. Moreover, can the Court seriously assert respect for States' rights and sovereignty when a plaintiff, claiming present harm, is offering to show that the contested Community act is illegal and thus can not serve as a legal basis for further state action?

2. Another and perhaps more compelling consideration was articulated by Advocate General Lagrange: Since the Treaty is largely a *"traité cadre"* or framework law which normally must be implemented by general regulations, the possibility of even a partial annulment of such a regulation poses "an extreme danger" to the system, if – as is frequently the case – the regulation represents a laborious compromise reached in the Council pursuant to the unanimity rule or practice.[35] The solution, he suggests, lies in increasing the role of the European Parliamentary Assembly in the legislative process so that there is less danger of paralysis if the compromise is annulled. In the present circumstances, there may also be a recognition that it is difficult to brand a Council regulation unanimously adopted by representatives of the Member States as "illegal" even where it appears to be inconsistent with the Treaty: it would be to a degree a modification of the basic law albeit in disregard of the amending procedure. These considerations, however, would hardly apply to standing with respect to Council regulations of lesser stature, routine regulations of the Commission or to

Commission decisions addressed to other persons (particularly to private parties).

The Court may also have had in mind another argument advanced by Commission jurists with respect to Council regulations which the Commission is required to implement. Even where a plaintiff feels directly injured by a general regulation which he considers illegal, he should be denied standing – it is said – until the regulation is actually applied to him by a Commission decision addressed to him, at which time he would have standing to contest the decision.[36] Apart from making rational business planning impossible, the argument does not take into account a potentially serious or even irreparable harm that might result from the delay.

It has been suggested that the Court ought to develop more nuanced standing criteria depending upon whether the act is predominantly "legislative" or purely "administrative", such as a Commission decision addressed to a government[37] and responding to its request for a special exemption from a general rule.[38]

3. The political considerations are no doubt buttressed by the inherent aversion of administrators everywhere (including the United States) to judicial control. Attorneys appearing in defense of the Council and the Commission have been uncompromising and consistent in their opposition to plaintiff standing. The Court of Justice is not a federal court – and even the Supreme Court of the United States would hesitate to rule in a controversial matter against both the Congress and the Executive. In very few instances has the Court of Justice ventured substantially beyond the Commission's position in important systemic questions. The opposition of the Commission and Council makes it difficult to do so on the standing issue. While the Commission has invariably urged liberal, purpose-oriented interpretations in defining the scope of its own power or the power of the Communities generally, it has taken the narrowest and the most mechanistic position in the standing-to-sue cases where the question was of potentially curbing its own power.[39] However, at this stage of development the opposition of Community attorneys to a more liberal interpretation may be due as much to the customary bureaucratic aversion to any deviation from an established policy line, as to a strong attachment to principle.

4. The Court has said that it cannot modify the Treaty. In one case the plaintiff contended that if recourse to Article 173 were denied to him because of a narrow interpretation of the text, he would be deprived of all judicial safeguards both under Community law and under national law, which would be contrary to the basic principles governing all Member countries.[40] The Court responded that these considerations could not "be allowed to override the clearly restrictive wording of Article 173, which it is the Court's task to apply".[41] Yet at least in the case of an individual contesting a decision addressed to a third party, the question involved – the interpretation of the words "direct and individual concern" – is hardly a matter of Treaty modification.[42]

Of course in many, though not in all cases, the plaintiff would in fact have recourse to national courts, and – *via* the procedure of Article 177 – to the Court of Justice which then would have an opportunity to pass upon the validity of a decision or regulation in a "preliminary ruling", with a binding effect upon national courts. This procedure involves substantial cost and delay.[43] Nevertheless, from the very outset the Court has interpreted access to national courts for the purpose of enforcing individual rights derived from Community law in a most liberal way, far beyond what may have been the intent of the authors of the Treaty. The Court has clearly preferred to enhance its jurisdiction – and the protection of individuals – through this avenue which is particularly appropriate to the symbiotic Community system, rather than by opening up the individual's direct access pursuant to Article 173. In this, the Court has succeeded beyond any expectation, considering the many cases referred to it by national courts from the Member States. Because of the political problems which a Member State or a Community institution faces in initiating an action against an institution or a State before the Court, the Article 177 procedure has become the most frequently employed course for enforcing Community law. More recently, the Court has also given a more liberal interpretation to the Treaty provisions allowing private persons to sue the Community for damages caused by an act of a Community institution.[44] The question for the future will be whether these procedures are sufficient.

5. It is interesting to speculate whether the Court has been influenced in this field by the laws of the Member States.

The Court's records show that the Advocates General, if not the Court itself, have at least had in mind the relevant national laws and practices. But there has been no unanimity of opinion. M. Lagrange, the distinguished first Advocate General from the French Conseil d'Etat, was prepared to discount the fact that "the legal situation within the Community is undoubtedly less favorable [to the plaintiff] than that which has been reached for a greater or lesser length of time by some of the Member States, but it is similar to that known in other States".[45] His counterpart, the able Mr. Roemer, coming from private corporate law practice in Germany, appeared troubled – in 1968 at any rate – by the Court's formalistic approach as compared with rules applied by the German Federal Administrative Court, and particularly by the possible constitutional implications of leaving a citizen without any remedy.[46] The current German and Italian Advocates General appear to take somewhat different views on the relevance of national administrative law solutions to analogous Community cases.[47]

In any event, although the Court has not hesitated in other contexts to canvass national laws for "general principles" that may be common to them, we cannot find any evidence that the Court may be getting ready to soften its strict posture in this area to reflect some of the more liberal trends in national laws. The Court's present position is reminiscent of the earlier German standing requirement that plaintiff show infringement of "subjective public *right*" rather than the more flexible formula evolved by German doctrine holding "legally protected *interest*" sufficient. Obviously the liberal French jurisprudence has also had little impact.[48]

6. One factor which may explain the apparent absence of effective pragmatic pressures on the Court to grant broader access is the still relatively limited scope of the Community regulatory power, confined essentially to customs union, movement of factors of production and competition. Some of the economic and non-economic forces and interests such as environmental and consumer protection, which have had such impact on the liberalization of the American rule, operate thus far, if at all, at the national level, and are only beginning to be reached by Community power.

7. Finally, although the Court has been reticent on the subject, an important concern may be the possibility of multiplicity of suits should citizen access to the Court be defined in broad terms. We shall return to this problem after a discussion of the American experience.

Standing in United States Federal Courts: the Common Law Test and its Demise

The Community Court's difficulties in applying its current interpretation of Article 173 are similar to those experienced by American federal courts in the decades before 1970. American doctrine has not been troubled by a basic distinction between "decisions" and "regulations". Both have long been judicially reviewable "administrative action".[49] But, as we have seen, in specific circumstances "regulations" can be viewed in Community law as a "bundle of individual decisions",[50] and it is likely that the classification of Community action as a "regulation" or not for purposes of the first part of the second paragraph of Article 173 will follow and simply express the resolution of the real problems of standing, which have to do with the "individuality" and "directness" of the plaintiff's stake in the case. Here the parallels between American and Community developments are striking.

A concern that the judiciary not undermine the sense of responsibility within administrative agencies for the legality of their programs, or interfere with the process of interest-group accommodation carried on by agencies in the development of a program, has led to doctrines in American federal administrative law designed to allow postponement of judicial review where there are discretionary agency steps still to be taken before enforcement of an agency decision or regulation. These, the doctrines of "finality" and "ripeness", are now treated separately from the law of standing. Whether that part of the Community standing test that focuses on Member State discretion is meant to take into account similar concerns is difficult to know, in view of the way the "directness" prerequisite has been administered. It is quite clear, however, that access to judicial review under the American doctrines of "finality" and "ripeness" does not turn simply on whether or not there is discretion. A showing of discretionary implementation is only the beginning of an analysis of the relative costs and benefits of delaying judicial review. The argument that a plaintiff has too indirect and attenuated a concern with administrative action if it does not fix rights or obligations – an argument still made by government attorneys – has been labeled by the Supreme Court as having "the hollow ring of another era".[51]

With regard to "individuality", the basic rule of standing in the United States until the late nineteen sixties was the common law test, under which the plaintiff could invoke the jurisdiction of a court only if he could point to a *private legal right* that would be violated by a named government official if that official failed to show that his action was authorized – a test which still obtains in many of the States today and which resembles the formula now employed in the Court of Justice. It was only in 1970 that the United States Supreme Court expressly "discredited" this test and turned to the Administrative Procedure Act for a definition of standing.[52] However, the formula drawn from the Act to replace the so-called "private legal right" test did not burst upon us full blown. There is a history which merits a brief account, for it indicates that we may be dealing with underlying currents of thought and concept that are likely to have an impact on societies functioning in a comparable frame of reference.

The attack upon and demise of the "legal right" test had two main historical roots. One involved "economic" interests and the other "non-economic". On the economic side it has been a rule of the common law that no person has a "right" to be free of competition. When a person came into court and complained that he had suffered injury through the increased competition of someone else made possible by an allegedly illegal government act or subsidy, the classic response was that he had no standing to seek an injunction against the illegal act hurting him because he had shown the invasion of no legal right of his "own". For instance, in 1938 competing private utilities were held to have no standing to challenge the legality under the National Industrial Recovery Act of a program of public work grants to municipalities for construction of electric distribution systems – and in reading this case one immediately thinks of *Eridania*. The United States Supreme Court held that a person injured by government action could not challenge that action in court unless the injury resulted in the violation of a legal right,[53] which the Court later defined as "one of property, one arising out of contract, one protected against tortious invasion, or one founded on a statute which confers a privilege".[54]

There was never a self-evident logic to a position that because a business had no right to be free of competition it had no right to be free of illegally created competition, and as government was seen to intervene more and more into the market and affect and determine the relative advantages of the players in the market, business interests became more and more determined to gain access to the courts to review the legality of administrative actions affecting them in this most important way. One response by courts was to view the specific standing provisions often written into statutes creating the regulating agencies and often couched in vague terms – conferring standing for instance on "aggrieved" persons – as congressionally mandated exceptions to the courts' own self-imposed and restrictive requirement of a legal right.[55] Much more threatening to the conceptual integrity of the legal right test, however, was the conclusion that if a person or group of persons could show that they were in some sense the intended beneficiary of the establishment of an administrative regulatory scheme or any part of it, they could be viewed as having "quasi-property" rights in the common law sense, and standing followed when government officials administered the scheme in such a way as to deny the benefit. This was a transparent circumvention of the legal right test, for such persons as the private utilities operating around the territory of the Tennessee Valley Authority, and claiming to be the beneficiaries of that authority's limited geographical jurisdiction, had no private legal rights under the common law of property and none granted them by the statute. Nor was their standing arguably mandated specifically by Congress. Their quasi-property rights were recognized solely for the purpose of standing to challenge the administrative action.[56] This search for and discovery of "beneficiaries" of the regulatory scheme was extended into a number of fields beyond those of economic competition. The concept recalls the "legally protected interest" test in German administrative law which, as we have mentioned earlier, German doctrine constructed as a more flexible alternative to the rigid standing requirement that the plaintiff must show a "subjective public right".[57]

The second major thrust against the common law test concerned non-economic values. It is usually impossible to claim any private or exclusive right to the beauty, health, safety, or recreational opportunities so widely regulated by modern administrative bodies. The money loss resulting from a bureaucratically dictated change in relative economic advantage was at least discrete and theoretically measurable, like other private harms which the common law traditionally considered and sometimes prevented. A non-economic loss often did not resemble a loss of "property" in any way. Yet it might be of even greater importance to an individual; and as the growth of legislation and regulation established causal connections between non-economic losses and official action, lower federal courts began to give remedies to individuals against such action when it was illegal. Consumers of television were granted standing to challenge the licensing of particular television stations[58] and consumers of food were granted standing to challenge the legality of adding color to oleo margarine.[59] Frequently the courts claimed to be interpreting the general language contained in specific statutory standing provisions in various licensing acts, provisions which most observers would have originally thought were included for the benefit of persons and groups, such as manufacturers of food or chemicals or television licensees, economically associated with the regulatory scheme in question and subject to administrative sanctions. These cases in the lower courts go back to the 1940's and 50's, but appeared in great numbers during the 1960's and were ultimately cited with approval in the 1970 decisions of the Supreme Court which brought about the major change.

The New Test

Technically, the change was effected by holding that the Adiministrative Procedure Act, which had been enacted more than a quarter of a century earlier, was a source of standing independent of both the common law and the special standing provisions incorporated into the various acts setting up administrative agencies. The Act applies to all agencies unless they are specifically excepted, and provides that any person is entitled to judicial review of agency action if he "suffers legal wrong or is adversely affected or aggrieved within the meaning of a relevant statute". Even though the term "legal wrong" was used in the statutory language, the Court declared that the legal right test of the common law, under which, it will be remembered, the plaintiff stated a cause of action only if he showed a private legal right invaded by a government official acting under the color of law, was discredited. The Court used the word "discredited" and was unanimous in this regard. The Court then went on to construct a new formula for the standing of private parties in challenges to administrative action, namely that the party must be "injured in fact" and must show that "the interest he is seeking to protect" – to quote the language which the Court has since repeated in subsequent cases – is "arguably within the zone of interests protected or regulated by the statute in question", the "statute in question" being the statute setting up the administrative agency and providing substantive standards for judging the legality of its actions. A French lawyer reading the language of this formula might immediately think of his own "*intérêt à agir*", the rather liberal standing[60] test developed by the Conseil d'Etat.

Applying the new test, the United States Supreme Court granted standing to a trade association of independent data processing companies, and later to a travel agency, to challenge the legality of regulations issued by the Comptroller of the Currency which permitted federal banks to compete with them by expanding into the fields of data processing and travel services.[61] The Court made clear that it was not relying on any evidence that Congress had intended to make data processors or travel agents specific beneficiaries of bank regulation.[62] Two years later, the Court seemed to imply that it would hear the challenge of the Sierra Club, a conservationist group, to actions by federal officials of dubious legality which had permitted Disney Enterprises to begin the development of a wilderness area in a national forest in California, providing that the club showed that it spoke on behalf of members who were injured, whether in economic or non-economic fashion, in their use of the wilderness area.[63] Then, in 1973, the Court did grant standing to a group of law students who used a national park and who challenged a railroad rate regulation that might have the effect of polluting the park.[64] In none of these cases could a claim to a personal legal right be made out, nor were there specific provisions in the statutes governing the agencies in question for judicial review of the agency decision at the request of the plaintiffs.

One cannot doubt that the conceptual and pragmatic pressures that led to these results would have succeeded in finding some other mode of expression if the language of the Administrative Procedure Act had not been at hand ready for use.[65] Had the judiciary truly conceived itself as limited to the protection of private rights except in those instances where the legislature expressly instructed it to go beyond that role, a quite reasonable interpretation of the standing language of the Act was available. As we have noted, many of the special standing statutes providing for judicial review of certain agency actions in specified circumstances use the term of art "aggrieved" to designate those persons who may seek redress, and it was open to the Court to conclude that the language of the Administrative Procedure Act which suggested a ground of standing other than "legal wrong", or invasion of private and personal legal right, was meant to do no more than refer to those situations where specific statutory standing was given to individuals by such statutes. But the Court did not do so, and held instead that standing emanated from the Administrative Procedure Act itself. Though grounded in legislative language – as the formula for standing in the Court of Justice is grounded in Article 173 – the decision to hear challenges to the legality of administrative action in a larger number of situations was clearly a matter of *judicial* choice.

It is, however, far easier to see what American courts have put behind them than to see what lies ahead. Lower federal courts have found the new standing formula difficult to administer without opening their doors to all litigants who have demonstrated a personal concern for the values affected by the challenged government action sufficiently strong to support the costs of litigation.[66] Explicit approval of such a result would not be incompatible with existing jurisprudence,[67] and as we shall note below, might cause relatively few practical difficulties. But there are indications that the Supreme Court is not prepared to go so far. In constitutional judicial review of congressional action, litigants have sought to use developments in the review of administrative decisions to establish the standing of persons in their capacity as "citizens" to enforce the Constitution. In its most recent decisions, the Court has explicitly rejected the concept of the "public action"[68] and while, as we have noted, review of acts of Congress involves considerations different from those governing the review of administrative action and has proceeded on doctrinely separate routes, the Court used language in justifying its limitation on constitutional standing that may apply to both the administrative and the constitutional areas.[69] Ironically, the difficulties in charting the reach of the new American administrative law standing formula and in determining whether a constitutional challenge is more than a "public action" are now discussed in terms of whether the plaintiff's injury or interest is sufficiently "individual" and "direct",[70] the very terms mandated by Article 173 for equivalent discussions in the Community. But all we can say with assurance is that the questions of "directness" and "individuality" are not to be answered in the United States according to whether or not a private and established right is at stake in the case.

Concluding Observations: How Relevant is Federal Experience?

What has happened in the United States is a reflection of and indeed now a principal symbol of a significant change in the conception of the role of a judiciary in a modern administrative state. Courts are no longer to be viewed as restricted to the settlement of private disputes and protecting vested private rights against government intrusion. The very notion of a self-sustaining sphere of private rights into which government action "intrudes" is now difficult to grasp. And with the growth of government it has been increasingly widely perceived that leaving government activities outside that sphere to take care of themselves may well mean leaving individual government officials essentially unchecked. Neither bureaucratic processes nor the legislature itself is in fact capable of policing the activities of government agencies on a day to day basis. Not even the American Congress with its massive staff of experts can attend to details or tend to them in time. The burden of inertia is such that relegating a challenger to a legislative remedy is itself a decision on the merits.

In sum, we think the American courts and Bar have at last acknowledged that they and their processes play an integral part in the business of

government. Of course in a pluralistic democratic society it is the elected
legislature that in principle has power and responsibility to determine the
hierarchy of common values and resolve conflicts among them. But no
society pursuing a multitude of public values of different weight and importance through a multitude of largely independent implementing agencies
can do without courts and still hope to achieve a satisfactory realization of
its goals. The Supreme Court now speaks of "private attorneys general", a
phrase which appeared as early as 1943 in the American judicial vocabu-
lary.[71] Responding to their initiative, American courts are holding in
check and inquiring into the legality of challenged agency action on behalf
of interests of a broader and more general concern than the private interests in contract and property traditionally protected.

The Rome Treaty has made the Court of Justice an important part of its
mechanism for achieving its goals. In a body without an elected legislature, where law is made by national and transnational executives through
processes shielded from the glare of publicity, the judicial role is if anything
even more essential than in a mature federation. As a single tribunal
serving the entire expanse of the Community, the Court may understanda-
bly be concerned with judicial economy and avoidance of cranky proceedings and multiplicity of suits. Both these dangers have troubled American
courts. The burden of merely being required to respond to an argument on
the merits and the potential for harassment resulting from a broadened test
of standing are no doubt among the factors making the exploration of the
boundaries of the new American formula a rather cautious one, particularly in the non-economic area. But the State of Michigan and several
other American States are experimenting with environmental protection
legislation that permits extremely broad access to courts, and the experience to date is that no large scale multiplicity of suits is developing. Rather
the impact has been on the attitudes of the administrators and on proceedings before them.[72] If in fact a great number of suits, perhaps of an identical
nature, are brought with a shift from a "private right" basis for standing to
the new formula – and given the cost of litigation that is dubious – then
the problem can be handled through consolidation and class action procedures.[73] Whether a suit is cranky or not seems to us a matter for the merits.
If it is frivolous it can be disposed of far more rapidly by getting to the
merits than by litigating the question of standing.

It has clearly been a wise judicial policy for the Court of Justice to encourage private plaintiffs to bring their complaints before their own national
tribunal, despite the additional risks, cost and delay which this may entail.

But as the scope of the Community regulatory powers broadens to include other fields and affect other values, economic and non-economic – health and safety, environment, consumer protection, energy conservation – the Court may well feel called upon to broaden direct access by private complainants. If it does, we suggest that it will act not only to protect private interests but also to advance the common interest in effective enforcement of Community legality and broader participation of citizens in Community administration.

Notes

* This paper is reprinted from the American Journal of International Law with the permission of the American Society of International Law.

¹   International civil servants may press their service-connected grievances before administrative tribunals established by the U.N. and the specialized agencies. M.B. Akehurst, The Law Governing Employment in International Organizations (1967); Byung Chu Koh, The United Nations Administrative Tribunal (1966). If the State concerned consents, an individual may complain against it to a committee of experts under the U.N. sponsored Convention on the Elimination of All Forms of Racial Discrimination. Schwelb, The International Convention on the Elimination of All Forms of Racial Discrimination, 15 Int'l and Comp. L.Q. 996 (1966). Pursuant to procedures evolved in U.N. General Assembly Committees and in certain other U.N. bodies, individuals may file petitions and even may be heard in person. Individuals may complain directly to the European Commission of Human Rights if the State against which the complaint was lodged recognizes such jurisdiction, but only the States contracting parties and the Commission have access to the European Court of Human Rights. European Convention for the Protection of Human Rights and Fundamental Freedoms, Arts. 25 and 48, 213 U.N.T.S. 221 (1955).

²   The Court of Justice of the Communities in Case 26/62, *N.V. Algemene Transport en Expeditie Onderneming van Gend en Loos* v. *Nederlandse Tariefcommissie,* 9 Recueil de la jurisprudence de la Cour de Justice des Communautés Européennes (Rec.) 1 (1963), [1963] European Court Reports (ECR) 1 at 12, [1963] Common Market Law Reports (C.M.L.R.) 105, Commerce Clearing House, Chicago, Common Market Reporter (CCH Comm. Mkt. Rep.) §8008.

³   Article 177 of the EEC Treaty.

⁴   The corresponding articles in the other Community treaties are Article 33 of the ECSC Treaty and Article 146 of the Euratom Treaty.

⁵   5 U.S.C. §702 (Supp. V, 1965-1969). This discussion is limited to judicial review of acts of federal administrative agencies which have both rule-making and decision-making authority. We do not address the special problem of judicial review of Congressional acts for constitutionality.

⁶   Daig in H. von der Groeben, H. von Boeckh, J. Thiesing, 2 Kommentar zum EWG-Vertrag 209 at 234 (2nd ed. 1974); Peters in 3 C.M.L. Rev. 233 at 241 (1965).

⁷   Cases 16/62 and 17/62, *Confédération Nationale des Producteurs de Fruits et Légumes et al.* v. *Council,* 8 Rec. 901 (1962), [1962] ECR 471, [1963] C.M.L.R. 160, CCH Comm. Mkt. Rep. §8005 at 7186; Cases 19/62-22/62, *Fédération Nationale de la*

Boucherie en Gros, etc. v. *Council,* 8 Rec. 943 (1962), [1962] ᴇᴄʀ 491, [1963] C.M.L.R. 160, ᴄᴄʜ Comm. Mkt. Rep. §8006.

⁸ Case 25/62, *Plaumann and Co.* v. *Commission,* 9 Rec. 197 (1963), [1963] ᴇᴄʀ 95, [1964] C.M.L.R. 29, ᴄᴄʜ Comm. Mkt. Rep. §8013 at 7274.

⁹ In the above cases the attorneys for the defendant Council and Commission urged an even more restrictive interpretation that would have denied any association capacity to sue as such under any circumstances despite the specific Treaty language to the contrary ("any...legal person") and that would not recognize a government as a "person" within the meaning of the second paragraph of Article 173. The Court rejected these assertions and on this issue followed the conclusions of its Advocates General.

¹⁰ Article 33 of the ᴇᴄꜱᴄ Treaty reads: "...Undertakings or the associations referred to in Article 48 may, under the same conditions, institute proceedings against decisions or recommendations concerning them which are individual in character or against general decisions or recommendations which they consider to involve a misuse of powers (*détournement de pouvoir*) affecting them (*à leur égard – ihnen gegenüber*)": Compare the above language "decisions...concerning them" with the requirement of "direct and individual concern" in the corresponding ᴇᴇᴄ Article 173(2) *supra.* There is considerable literature comparing the ᴇᴄꜱᴄ and the ᴇᴇᴄ Treaties on this issue and commenting on the case law. See e.g. G. Bebr, Judicial Control of the European Communities 68-77 (1962); A. Tizzano, La Corte di Giustizia delle Communità Europee 396-415 (1967) and also in R. Quadri, R. Monaco, A. Trabucchi, 3 Trattato Istitutivo della Communità Economica Europea, Commentario 1277-1285 (1965); Daig in H. von der Groeben, H. von Boeckh, J. Thiesing, 2 Kommentar zum ᴇᴡɢ-Vertrag 222-236 (2nd ed. 1974); C. H. Ule, Empfiehlt es sich, die Bestimmungen des europäischen Gemeinschaftsrechts über den Rechtsschutz zu ändern und zu ergänzen?, Gutachten für den 46. Deutschen Juristentag 13-32 (1966); Bebr, "Recours en annulation et en carence" in W. J. Ganshof van der Meersch (ed.), Les Novelles, Droit des Communautés européennes 309-319 (1969) with bibliography at 309; Rasquin et Chevallier, "L'article 173, alinéa 2 du Traité C.E.E.", 2 Rev. trim. dr. eur. 31(1966); Barav, "Direct and Individual Concern: An Almost Insurmountable Barrier to the Admissibility of Individual Appeal to the ᴇᴇᴄ Court", 11 C.M.L. Rev. 191 (1974).

¹¹ According to Art. 189, a "regulation" is "directly applicable" by national courts and other authorities throughout the Community territory.

¹² Cases 16/62 and 17/62, *Confédération Nationale, supra* note 7. The Court added in *Confédération Nationale* that it would look beyond the official designation of the act as a "regulation": "Consequently, in order to determine in doubtful cases whether one is concerned with a decision or a regulation, it is necessary to ascertain whether the measure in question is of individual concern to specific individuals. In these circumstances, if a measure entitled by its author a regulation contains provisions which are capable of being not only of direct but also of individ-

ual concern to certain natural or legal persons, it must be admitted, without prejudice to the question whether that measure considered in its entirety can be correctly called a regulation, that in any case those provisions do not have the character of a regulation and may therefore be impugned by those persons under the terms of the second paragraph of Article 173." [1962] ECR at 478-479 (at 186 CCH Comm. Mkt. Rep.). In support of a more liberal interpretation, A. Tizzano, *supra* note 10 at 404-411 (1967). But see Bebr, "Recours en annulation et en carence", *supra* note 10 at 318. On above cases, see note by Cartou in [1963] Sirey Jurisprudence 126.

¹³ Case 25/62, *Plaumann, supra* note 8 [1963] ECR at 107 (at 7274 CCH Comm. Mkt. Rep.). Since the plaintiff in this case was not concerned "individually", the Court found it unnecessary to deal with the question of "direct" concern.

¹⁴ Waelbroeck, Les compétences de la Cour de Justice (II) [1971] Revue Critique de Jurisprudence Belge 513 at 530.

¹⁵ The cases in which this paragraph was applied or discussed are: Cases 16 and 17/62, *Confédération Nationale des Producteurs de Fruits et Légumes et al.* v. *Council,* 8 Rec. 901 (1962), [1962] ECR 471, [1963] C.M.L.R. 160, CCH Comm. Mkt. Rep. §8005; Cases 19-22/62, *Fédération Nationale de la Boucherie en Gros et du Commerce en Gros des Viandes et al.* v. *Council,* 8 Rec. 943 (1962), [1962] ECR 491, [1963] C.M.L.R. 160, CCH Comm. Mkt. Rep. §8006; Cases 31 and 33/62, *Milchwerke Heinz Wöhrmann & Sohn KG et Alfons Lütticke GmbH* v. *Commission,* 8 Rec. 965 (1962), [1962] ECR 501, [1963] C.M.L.R. 152, CCH Comm. Mkt. Rep. §8007; Case 25/62, *Plaumann and Co.* v. *Commission,* 9 Rec. 197 (1963), [1963] ECR 95, [1964] C.M.L.R. 29, CCH Comm. Mkt. Rep. §8013; Case 1/64, *Glucoseries Réunies* v. *Commission,* 10 Rec. 811 (1964), [1964] ECR 413, [1964] C.M.L.R. 596, CCH Comm. Mkt. Rep. §8024; Case 38/64, *Getreide-Import Gesellschaft* v. *Commission,* 11 Rec. 263 (1965), [1965] ECR 204, [1965] C.M.L.R. 276, CCH Comm. Mkt. Rep. §8033; Case 40/64, *Marcello Sgarlata et al.* v. *Commission,* 11 Rec. 279 (1965), [1965] ECR 215, [1966] C.M.L.R. 314, CCH Comm. Mkt. Rep. §8034; Cases 106 and 107/63, *Alfred Toepfer et Getreide-Import Gesellschaft* v. *Commission,* 11 Rec. 525 (1965), [1965] ECR 405, [1966] C.M.L.R. 111, CCH Comm. Mkt. Rep. §8031; Case 30/67, *Industria Molitoria Imolese et al.* v. *Council,* 14 Rec. 171 (1968), [1968] ECR 115, CCH Comm. Mkt. Rep. §8060; Case 6/68, *Zuckerfabrik Watenstedt GmbH* v. *Council,* 14 Rec. 595 (1968), [1968] ECR 409, [1969] C.M.L.R. 26, CCH Comm. Mkt. Rep. §8063; Cases 10 and 18/68, *Società "Eridania" Zuccherifici Nazionali et al.* v. *Commission,* 15 Rec. 459 (1969), CCH Comm. Mkt. Rep. §8099; Cases 63 and 64/69, *La Compagnie française commerciale et financière, SA* v. *Commission,* 16 Rec. 205 (1970), [1970] C.M.L.C. 369, CCH Comm. Mkt. Rep. §8090, §8091; Case 65/69, *La Compagnie d'approvisionnement, de transport et de crédit, SA* v. *Commission,* 16 Rec. 229 (1970), [1970] C.M.L.R. 369, CCH Comm. Mkt. Rep. §8092; Case 69/69, *SA Alcan Aluminium Raeren et al.* v. *Commission,* 16 Rec. 385 (1970), [1970] C.M.L.R. 337, CCH Comm. Mkt. Rep. §8110; Case 15/70, *Amedeo Chevalley* v. *Commission,* 16 Rec. 975 (1970), CCH Comm. Mkt. Rep. §8115; Cases 41-

44/70, *NV International Fruit Co et al.* v. *Commission,* 17 Rec. 411 (1971), cch Comm. Mkt. Rep. §8142; Case 15/71, *Firma C. Mackprang, Jr.* v. *Commission,* 17 Rec. 797 (1971), [1972] C.M.L.R. 52, cch Comm. Mkt. Rep. §8155; Case 62/70, *Werner A. Bock* v. *Commission,* 17 Rec. 897 (1972), [1972] C.M.L.R. 160, cch Comm. Mkt. Rep. §8150; Case 42/71, *Nordgetreide GmbH & Co. KG* v. *Commission,* 18 Rec. 105 (1972), [1973] C.M.L.R. 368, cch Comm. Mkt. Rep. §8174; Cases 9 and 11/71, *Compagnie d'approvisionnement, de transport et de crédit SA et Grands Moulins de Paris SA* v. *Commission,* 18 Rec. 391 (1972), [1973] C.M.L.R. 529, cch Comm. Mkt. Rep. §8177; Case 96/71, *R & V. Haegeman* v. *Commission,* 18 Rec. 1005 (1972) [1973] C.M.L.R. 365, cch Comm. Mkt. Rep. §8181; Case 134/73, *Holtz & Willemsen GmbH* v. *Council,* [1974] ecr 1, [1975] C.M.L.R. 91, cch Comm. Mkt. Rep. §8255; Case 175/73, *Union Syndicate et al.* v. *Council,* [1974] ecr 917, [1975] C.M.L.R. 131; Case 18/74, *Syndicat Général du Personnel des Organismes Européens* v. *Commission,* [1974] ecr 933, [1975] C.M.L.R. 144; Cases 44, 46 and 49/74, *Marie-Louise Acton et al.* v. *Commission,* [1975] ecr 383; Case 72/74, *Union Syndicate et al.* v. *Council,* [1975] ecr 401.

[16]   Cases 106/63 and 107/63, *Alfred Toepfer* v. *Commission, supra* note 15.

[17]   The Court equated "direct concern" with the important Community concept of "direct applicability" and this raises some interesting problems which are beyond the scope of this article. The former is a procedural prerequisite for action before the Community Court; the latter goes to the merit of an individual's claim against a Member State enforceable in a national court. For comments see Fromont in [1966] Rec. Dalloz-Sirey, Jurisprudence 58; Peters in 3 C.M.L. Rev. 233 (1965).

[18]   Case 62/70, *Werner A. Bock* v. *Commission, supra* note 15. For a comment, see Verougstraete, 8 Cahiers de droit eur. 666 (1972).

[19]   The Commission "was in a position to know that the decisions would affect only the interests and legal status of these importers. Under these circumstances the importers are set apart from all other persons in a manner similar to the addressee" (cch Comm. Mkt. Rep. at 7720).

[20]   Cases 41/70-44/70, *N.V. International Fruit Company et al.* v. *Commission, supra* note 15. For a comment, see V.C. in 99 Journal de droit international 687, 693 (1972).

[21]   Subsequently, the Court dismissed the case on the merits.

[22]   The Court said that the Commission decisions modifying or abolishing safeguard measures are "directly applicable" because Article 22 of the regulation under which the Commission acted provided that the Commission's decision shall take effect immediately and therefore "[i]t would be illogical to say that a decision to retain protective measures had a different effect...". Cases 106 and 107/63, *Alfred Toepfer* v. *Commission, supra* note 15, [1965] ecr at 411, cch Comm. Mkt. Rep. at 7460.

[23] Cases 10 and 18/68, *Eridania, supra* note 15; see also Adv. Gen. Roemer in Case 1/64, *Glucoseries Réunies* v. *Commission, supra* note 15, and in Case 26/62, *Plaumann and Co.* v. *Commission, supra* note 15, and also in Cases 106/63 and 107/63, *Alfred Toepfer* v. *Commission, supra* note 15.

[24] Case 69/69, *SA Alcan Aluminium Rearen et al.* v. *Commission, supra* note 15; see also Case 25/62, *Plaumann and Co.* v. *Commission, supra* note 15; cf. Adv. Gen. Gand in Case 38/64, *Getreide Import* v. *Commission, supra* note 15.

[25] Advocate General Gand relied here on the views of his colleague Roemer in Plaumann. In the *Alcan* case Advocate General Gand pressed the argument that if the Commission's decision had granted the requested authorization to the government the decision would not have direct effect on the plaintiff; consequently, the actual decision in this case refusing the authorization must be equally without direct effect on him – apparently in the interest of symmetry. Case 69/69, Alcan, *supra* note 15, CCH Comm. Mkt. Rep. at 7256. Daig distinguishes the decisions in which the Commission addresses an order, prohibition or authorization to a Member State. Daig in Kommentar, *supra* note 10 at 232-233.

[26] Case 6/68, *Zuckerfabrik Watenstedt* v. *Council, supra* note 15; see also Case 1/64, *Glucoseries Réunies* v. *Commission, supra* note 15, where both the Advocate General and the Court found no individual effect.

[27] Case 38/64, *Getreide-Import Gesellschaft* v. *Commission, supra* note 15. For comments on this case see Mailänder, "Privater Rechtsschutz im Recht der Europäischen Wirtschaftsgemeinschaft", [1965] Betrieb 1312; Ule, *supra* note 10 at 17-19. The Court attempted to distinguish the case from Toepfer on the ground that, unlike the Toepfer situation, the Commission did not know of the plaintiff's application at the time of its decision. Bebr feels this factual difference might explain the two different holdings "at least partially". Bebr, "Recours en annulation et en carence", *supra* note 10 at 315. See also Case 30/67, *Industria Molitoria Imolese* v. *Council, supra* note 15.

[28] In Case 69/69, *Alcan* v. *Commission, supra* note 15, the Court found no direct concern and remained silent on the issue of individual concern although Advocate General Gand held individual concern to be present. In Case 64/69, *La Compagnie française* v. *Commission, supra* note 15, the Court found no individual concern even though, according to the plaintiff, the contested provision of the Commission regulation applied to a group of specified enterprises (including the plaintiff) since these enterprises were positively known and identifiable even before the contested provision was issued. The Court stated: "The fact that a transitional rule concerns only certain situations created prior to a date which it sets and which are therefore often determined even before the rule goes into effect does not prevent such a rule from being an integral part" of and sharing the general character of a regulation. Thus retroactivity alone is not enough "unless there is a misuse of discretionary power". CCH Comm. Mkt. at 8323.

[29] Case 1/64, *Glucoseries Réunies* v. *Commission, supra* note 15.

[30] Kovar in 93 Journal de droit international 707 at 711-712 (1966).

[31] In his opinion in the International Fruit case, Advocate General Roemer stated: "[I]t is extremely doubtful that we are actually dealing with a regulation in the sense of the definitions that were so often given in previous decisions of the Court" (CCH Comm. Mkt. Rep. at 7635). But see Case 64/69 *La Compagnie française, supra* note 15. In that case, denying that a provision in a regulation was of individual concern to the plaintiff, the Court said: "Unless there is a misuse of discretionary power, such a provision shares in the general legal nature" of the regulation (CCH Comm. Mkt. Rep. at 8323).

[32] E.g. Advocate General Roemer in Case 6/68, *Zuckerfabrik Watenstedt* v. *Commission, supra* note 15. It is, however, difficult to reconcile Mr. Roemer's own position in this and in the Glucoseries case 1/64, *supra* note 15, unless one concludes that the lapse of four years and the intervening experience with the system led him to change his mind.

[33] See Stein, Review of Europäisches Gemeinschaftsrecht by Hans Peter Ipsen in 22 Am. J. Comp. L. 156 (1974).

[34] Case 69/69, Alcan, *supra* note 15, CCH Comm. Mkt. Rep. at 7256.

[35] M. Lagrange very likely had in mind the type of Council regulation comparable in substance if not in form to an act of Parliament which, according to the French conception of separation of powers, could not be made subject to judicial review.

[36] In that case, the Court could also consider the legality of the Council regulation; if it found that the regulation infringed the Treaty, it would annul the decision, holding the underlying regulation inapplicable pursuant to Article 184.

[37] It is, in any case, doubtful that the Court would want to adhere to its present narrow interpretation of "individual concern" should a private party contest a decision addressed not to a Member State but to another private party, as is likely to occur particularly in the field of competition. An example would be a Commission decision addressed to parties to a restrictive agreement which exempts the agreement from the Treaty prohibition and third parties (competitors) feel aggrieved by the decision. P.J.G. Kapteyn and P. VerLoren van Themaat, Introduction to the Law of the European Communities After the Accession of New Member States, at 169 (1973).

[38] A. W. Green, Political Integration by Jurisprudence – The Work of the Court of Justice of the European Communities in European Political Integration 111 (1969).

[39] Some of the Commission's extreme positions were criticized by the Advocates General. We were able to find only one case in which the Commission's counsel, having first taken a rather untenable position against standing on one of the two requirements, reversed himself in the course of the proceeding. Case 38/64, *Getreide Import Ges.* v. *Commission, supra* note 15, Opinion, [1965] ECR at 211, CCH Comm. Mkt. Rep. at 7489.

[40]   Kovar criticizes such potential "denial of justice", *supra* note 30 at 710.

[41]   The Advocate General buttressed this view by adding that "[t]his argument can only avail if the applicants first prove that the Treaty gives private individuals concerned a guarantee of direct and complete legal protection, for it clearly cannot fall within the powers of the Court of Justice to amend the Treaty on this point". Case 40/64, *Sgarlata et al.* v. *Commission, supra* note 15, Opinion, [1965] ECR at 235.

[42]   In defining the reach of Article 173(2) the Court must have had in mind the long-range consequences in national legal systems if it ignored the principle underlying national constitutions that in a system of power relationships based on law, an affected citizen must presumptively have some remedy against illegal official action. The German Federal Constitutional Court has ruled that at this stage of integration it retains power to review a Community act for compatibility with the Federal Constitution if it is claimed that the act violates a basic right protected by the Constitution. Dec. of May 29, 1974, 37 BVerfGE 271 (1974).

[43]   Since, according to Article 177, only the court of last instance is *required* to refer the Community law questions to the Court of Justice, it may take years before the case reaches the highest national court. Ule (*supra* note 10 at 19-20, 22) considers this route "a difficult and prolonged detour". He suggests (de lege ferenda) a modification of Article 173(2) that would omit the requirement of direct and individual concern and allow standing to contest a decision addressed to another if the plaintiff's "legally protected interests" are affected. Thus the Treaty would conform to German administrative law which allows standing in case of impairment of a right as well as legally protected interest. Ule cites J. H. Kaiser, Mailänder, and possibly Badura as supporting this suggestion. He cites Zweigert, Lagrange, Mathijsen, Catalano and Ehle as urging replacement of the requirement of "direct and individual" or (Daig) of "individual" so as to broaden access to the Court. Zweigert, "Empfiehlt es sich, Bestimmungen über den Rechtsschutz zu ändern?" Hauptreferat, Zehn Jahre Rechtssprechung des Gerichtshofs der Europäischen Gemeinschaften 580-597 (1965); Rapport fait au nom de la Commission juridique sur la protection juridique des personnes privées dans les Communautés européennes, Rap. M.A. Deringer, Parl. Eur. Doc. 39, 3 May 1967.

[44]   *Cf.* Case 25/62, *Plaumann and Co.* v. *Commission, supra* note 15, with Case 4/69, *Alfons Lütticke GmbH* v. *Commission,* 17 Rec. 325 (1971), CCH Comm. Mkt. Rep. §8136; *see also* Case 5/71, *Aktien-Zuckerfabrik Schöppenstedt* v. *Council,* 17 Rec. 975 (1971), CCH Comm. Mkt. Rep. §8153, Professor van Gerven's article in this book, pp. 1-17, and cases there cited; Gilsdorf, "Die Haftung der Gemeinschaft aus normativem Handeln auf dem Hintergrund der Rechtssprechung des Europäischen Gerichtshofs", 10 Europarecht 73 (1975).

[45]   Cases 19/62-22/62, *Fédération Nationale* v. *Council, supra* note 15, [1962] ECR at 486; CCH Comm. Mkt. Rep. at 7192.

[46]   Case 6/68, *Zuckerfabrik Watenstedt* v. *Council, supra* note 15, [1968] ECR at 418, CCH Comm. Mkt. Rep. at 7973. Cases 10 and 18/68, *Società "Eridania* v. *Commission,*

supra note 15, CCH Comm. Mkt. Rep. at 8431-34.

[47] Case 175/73, *Union Syndicale et al.* v. *Council, supra* note 15, [1974] ECR at 930, [1975] C.M.L.R. 131 at 136 (Opinion by Mr. Reischl); Case 18/74, *Syndicat Général du Personnel des Organismes Européens* v. *Commission, supra* note 15, [1974] ECR at 948, [1975] C.M.L.R. 144 at 151 (Opinion by Mr. Trabucchi).

[48] The German courts and the doctrine have mitigated the rigor of the language of the statute requiring that plaintiff be injured "in his rights". §42(2) Verwaltungsgerichtsordnung of Jan. 21, 1960. See also *infra,* text at note 57.

[49] See, e.g., *CBS* v. *United States,* 316 U.S. 407 (1942); Administrative Procedure Act, 5 U.S.C. §551 (13), 7 U.S.C. §§702, 704, 706 (Supp. V, 1965-1969).

[50] *Supra* text at note 21.

[51] *Marine Terminal* v. *Rederiaktiebolaget Transatlantic,* 400 U.S. 62, 71 (1970); see Vining, "Direct Judicial Review and the Doctrine of Ripeness in Administrative Law", 69 Mich. L. Rev. 1443 (1971).

[52] *Supra* note 5.

[53] *Alabama Power Co.* v. *Ickes,* 302 U.S. 464, 479 (1938).

[54] *Tennessee Electric Power Co.* v. *TVA,* 306 U.S. 118, 137-138 (1939).

[55] *Associated Industries* v. *Ickes,* 134 F. 2d 694 (2d Cir. 1943), vacated as moot, 320 U.S. 707 (1943).

[56] *See e.g. Hardin* v. *Kentucky Utilities,* 390 U.S. 1 (1968).

[57] See *supra* text at note 48. See also Ule *supra* note 10 at 21-22. Fromont believes, referring to the Toepfer case, that the Court of Justice in fact adopted the "subjective public right" test without saying so in so many words. Fromont, "L'influence du droit français et du droit allemand sur les conditions de recevabilité du recours en annulation devant la Cour de Justice des Communautés européennes", 2 Rev. trim. dr. eur. 47, at 63 (1966). See also Fromont, "Der Rechtsschutz gegen Massnahmen der Verwaltung im Europa der Sechs", 4 Europarecht 202 (1969).

[58] *Office of Communication of United Church of Christ* v. *F.C.C.,* 359 F.2d 994 (D.C. Cir. 1966).

[59] *Reade* v. *Ewing,* 205 F.2d 630 (2d Cir. 1953).

[60] Commissaire du gouvernement Mosset stated in his well-known conclusions that standing to institute judicial review of administrative action will be given if the contested decision "injures the plaintiff materially or morally" and if the consequences of the decision affect plaintiff in his capacity as a member of a "defined or limited category". C.E. 26 oct. 1956, Association Générale des administrateurs civils, R.D.P.,1956, 1309, cited in Fromont, "L'influence du droit, etc." *supra* note 57 at 56.

[61] The principal case was *Association of Data Processing Service Organisations Inc.* v. *Camp,* 397 U.S. 150 (1970), described *supra* under "Three Cases". See also *Barlow* v. *Collins,* 397 U.S. 159 (1970); *Arnold Tours, Inc.* v. *Camp,* 408 F.2d 1147, 1151 (1st Cir. 1969), vacated 397 U.S. 315 (1970), reaffirmed 428 F.2d 359 (1st Cir. 1970),

reversed 400 U.S. 45 (1970).

[62]   *Arnold Tours, Inc.* v. *Camp, supra* note 61.

[63]   *Sierra Club* v. *Morton,* 405 U.S. 727 (1972).

[64]   *United States* v. *S.C.R.A.P.,* 412 U.S. 669 (1973).

[65]   The Court commented at the time and has emphasized since that rules of standing are developed by the Court "for its own governance". *Data Processing Service Organizations* v. *Camp, supra* note 61, 397 U.S. at 154; *Warth* v. *Seldin,* 95 S. Ct. 2197, 2205, 2215 (1975). The Court had never required a statutory basis for its legal right test. In essence the Court shifted the judicial presumptions within which legislatures must work. Legislative materials are now searched for a specific intent to deny standing rather than a specific intent to grant it.

[66]   *See, e.g., Coalition for the Environment* v. *Volpe,* 504 F.2d 156 (8th Cir. 1974); *Diggs* v. *Schultz,* 470 F.2d 461 (D.C. Cir. 1972), *cert. den.* 411 U.S. 931 (1973); *Ballerina Pen Co* v. *Kunzig,* 433 F.2d 1204 (D.C. Cir. 1970).

[67]   See e.g., Jaffe, "The Citizen as Litigant in Public Actions: The Non-Hohfeldian or Ideological Plaintiff", 116 U. Pa. L. Rev. 1033 (1968); Sax, Defending the Environment (1970).

[68]   See. e.g., *Warth* v. *Seldin, supra* note 65; *United States* v. *Richardson,* 418 U.S. 166 (1974).

[69]   In addition, in one case following the announcement of the new formula three members of the Court turned again to a special standing statute using the term "aggrieved" to justify hearing the challenge of a white resident of a housing project to the legality of the housing agency's alleged exclusion of black applicants. The Justices did, however, concur in the majority decision to grant standing, which was based on general principles rather than any specific permission by the legislature. *Trafficante* v. *Metropolitan Life Ins. Co.,* 409 U.S. 205 (1972).

[70]   *See, e.g., Linda R.S.* v. *Richard D.,* 410 U.S. 614 (1973); *Sierra Club* v. *Morton, supra* note 63.

[71]   *Associated Industries* v. *Ickes, supra* note 55. See also *F.C.C.* v. *Sanders Bros. Radio Station,* 309 U.S. 470 (1940); *Association of Data Processing Service Organizations* v. *Camp, supra* note 61.

[72]   Sax and Dimento, "Environmental Citizen Suits: Three Years' Experience Under the Michigan Environmental Protection Act", 4 Ecology L. Q. 1 (1974).

[73]   See *Abbott Laboratories* v. *Gardner,* 387 U.S. 136, 155 (1967). Although the Court of Justice has made full use of the consolidation procedures, most recently it has defined the standing to sue of associations so as to cause numerous separate actions to be filed by individual association members instead of a single action by the association itself. Case 18/74, *Syndicat Général du Personnel des Organismes Européennes* v. *Commission, supra* note 15. See Cases 44, 46 and 49/74, *Marie-Louise Acton et al.* v. *Commission,* and Case 72/74, *Union Syndicale et al.* v. *Council, supra* note 15. The Court held, with the support of the Advocate General, that although an association has a general capacity to appear in court as a "legal person" – and may also partici-

pate as an intervenor – it cannot sue for annulment in its own name unless it can show that it was aggrieved in its own functional rights (e.g. violation of its contract with the public agency) or upon an express "mandate" from the aggrieved members.

8

The Protection of Fundamental Rights in the Community

M. HILF

The subject of this paper[1] calls for three preliminary remarks.[2] First, it deals with fundamental rights in the Community and not with the protection of these rights in the Member States. Secondly, the expression "fundamental rights" is difficult to define. Fundamental rights were originally defensive in nature; but the case-law of the German Constitutional Court for example shows how such rights have often been transformed into offensive rights which enable citizens to demand State action in their favour. Thus the right of free choice of one's own profession, once construed as a defence against undue State limitations, has more recently been interpreted as enabling the individual to demand access to State universities.[3] Without entering into the various problems of classification one may understand by "fundamental rights" all those legal rights and situations which must not be violated by any action of the public authorities, whether by the legislature, the executive or the judiciary; one may also include those rights which are mainly limited to setting out programmes for the legislature, like certain social and economic rights. Thirdly, if one speaks of the "protection" of these rights one has to think in terms of substance as well as in terms of procedure. As the procedural aspects are dealt with in another paper[4] this contribution will concentrate more on questions of substance.

Why has the present subject become so important in the last few years, or even, one could say, in the last few months? There are two major reasons: first, we have been confronted recently with relevant decisions of

F.G. Jacobs, ed. European Law and the Individual © *1976*, *North-Holland Publishing Company*

national courts; secondly, preparatory work is under way on the elaboration of a constitution for a European Union.

The question whether joining the Community and transferring powers
to it would mean a loss of protection of fundamental rights was at the time
the subject of lengthy debate in the German Parliament. While still
divided on this issue in 1951, in 1957 the two major parties in deciding to
join the Community were evidently of the opinion that fundamental rights
would be protected as effectively by the Community as under the constitution of the Federal Republic of Germany and elsewhere.

Since then a large number of well known authors have dealt with this
problem. But the intensity of the discussions diminished after the German
Bundesverfassungsgericht (Federal Constitutional Court), in 1967, started to
acknowledge the autonomous legal order of the Community and to restrict
its power of control strictly to acts of the German public authorities[5]
However, on 29 May 1974 this Court – after three years of reflection –
held to be generally admissible requests to it for rulings from lower Courts
which consider that a provision of Community law seems to be in conflict
with fundamental rights guaranteed by the German Constitution.[6] It is
this recent decision which has provoked a whole variety of reactions. The
many judgments and comments range from "it can stand comparison with
the best decisions of the United States Supreme Court"[7] to "decision
which is entirely wrong in all aspects, both procedural and substantive,
whether according to legal or political criteria".[8] I will not hesitate to add
my own personal judgment.

As to the second reason mentioned, the problem of the protection of
fundamental rights is relevant in the process of framing a new constitution
such as that of the proposed *European Union*: to safeguard the basic liberties,
rights and interests of the individual in such a Union is clearly essential. At
the request of the Paris Summit Conference of December 1974[9] the
European Parliament, the Court of Justice and the Commission have
drawn up their reports on an overall concept of European Union. The
Court of Justice in its report of 11 July 1975 favours a general formula
indicating the obligation to protect the fundamental rights of the citizen.
Thus for example Article 164 of the EEC Treaty could read: "The Court of
Justice shall ensure that in the interpretation and application of this
Treaty the law and especially the fundamental rights of the citizens are
observed."

The Commission in its report of 25 June 1975 prefers a list of specific
rights to be incorporated in the basic act on which the Union will rest.

Such a list would assist in the exercise of economic and social rights, where implementing measures of a legal nature are necessary.[10]

Finally the European Parliament in a resolution of 10 July 1975 favours the elaboration of a "Charter of the rights of the peoples of the European Community" as part of a wider programme for immediate action designed to transform the present Community into a truly unitary organization.[11]

The present subject has an historical dimension which may be traced back at least to the 1776 Bill of Rights of Virginia or to the French and German revolutions of 1789 and 1848. It has an international background and it also finds it roots in the various legal systems of the nine Member States.

None of these three aspects can be neglected if one tries to analyse the Community legal order (I), the difficulties being faced at present by the Community (II) and the possible courses of action to be taken in the future (III).

I.

The absence of a catalogue of fundamental rights in the Community seems to be the outstanding feature of the Community Treaties. And this seems to some on the Continent sufficient reason to pass a negative verdict on the Community legal order. In fact, apart from the recognition of certain freedoms, such as freedom of movement for workers, freedom of establishment of nationals of one Member State in the territory of another, freedom of voluntary association of undertakings under the Coal and Steel Treaty (Article 48) and the freedom to provide services within the Community, and the recognition of the principle of equal pay for equal work, there is only one other explicit provision, but at the same time it is the most important, stating the general principle of prohibition of discrimination on grounds of nationality (e.g. Article 7 of the EEC Treaty).

Other rights such as property, professional or social rights did not seem to exist if one reads the early decisions of the Court of Justice such as the *Storck* case of 1959,[12] the *Nold* case[13] of the same year, the *Chairman of Ruhrkohlenverkaufsgesellschaft* case of 1960[14] and the *Sgarlata* case of 1965.[15] When confronted with arguments taken from corresponding national constitutional thinking the Court regularly rejected them stating that its sole duty was to control the application of Community law; it felt it had no jurisdiction to apply provisions of any domestic law, even if these provisions concerned fundamental rights guaranteed in a State's constitutional law. These decisions appear to us today like the sins of youth.

Later, however, the Court started to acknowledge the existence of general principles of law and recognized that fundamental rights are included among these principles which have their source in the constitutional traditions common to the Member States. Leaving aside some cases involving staff matters there are three relevant cases.

The *Stauder* case of 1969[16] dealt with an alleged violation of the rights to human dignity and to the free development of one's personality: a pensioner in Germany had to give his name to obtain cheap butter subsidised by the Community. In the second case, the *Internationale Handelsgesellschaft* case of 1970,[17] the Court had to consider an alleged violation of the freedom to exercise a profession. In this case a German company had lost a £ 3,000 deposit for not using export licences for ground maize. And most recently another *Nold* case, decided in 1974.[18] The applicant Nold, having set up his own company to handle the mass of litigation in which he was involved, felt himself threatened in the free exercise of his business activities, even to the point of endangering his very existence: The European Commission had authorised the German Ruhrkohle AG to restrict the number of direct wholesalers by requiring the contracting of a minimum of 6,000 metric tons of coal a year. And Nold was unable to reach this minimum quota.

The Court, though not following Nold in his submission, took the opportunity to sum up its relevant case-law:

Fundamental rights form an integral part of the general principles of law; and one has to note that the Court did not limit itself to general principles of Community law as it was still expressed in the Stauder case.

In safeguarding these rights, the Court is bound to draw inspiration from constitutional traditions common to the Member States, and it cannot therefore uphold measures which are incompatible with fundamental rights recognized and protected by the Constitutions of those States.

International treaties – including the European Convention on Human Rights – for the protection of human rights on which the Member States have collaborated or of which they are signatories, can supply guidelines which should be followed within the framework of Community law. One may assume that the Court would not reject any developing source or international standard for finding its guidelines. It is here that for example, the European Social Charter has its place and even the UN Covenants though they have not been ratified by all Member States.

The constitutional laws of all the Member States protect the right of ownership and similarly the right freely to choose and practise one's trade or profession; the German text – German being the language of the case – speaks of the freedom of work, trade and other professional activities.

As to the restrictions to these rights the Court held: These rights are far from constituting unfettered prerogatives, but must be viewed in the light of the social function of the property and activities protected thereunder. For this reason, rights of this nature are protected by law subject always to limitations laid down in accordance with the public interest. Within the Community legal order it likewise seems legitimate that these rights should, if necessary, be subject to certain limits justified by the overall objectives pursued by the Community on condition that the substance of these rights is left untouched.

The judgment of the Court in this case was generally very well received. Apparantly the Court did not bind the Community to the traditions common to *"all"* constitutions of the Member States, but to those rights protected by *"the"* constitutions of those States. This change in wording seems at times to have been overlooked.

Indeed, this formula indicates that the Court does not intend to bind the Community to a common denominator of all constitutions or to a common minimum standard. Such a mathematical principle, based on a general reduction of all higher standards, is unsound in law. Neither in comparative law nor in the interpretation of multilingual treaties has this principle been maintained. The reference to "the" constitutions of Member States indicates that the Court will observe a *maximum standard*, that is to say, it will invalidate any rule of Community law which is in conflict with any of the rights guaranteed by any of the Member States constitutions.[19]

This construction is inevitable in a Community of States in which one of the basic tenets is that of common loyalty and solidarity. This tenet which is well developed in federal States, not only binds the Community in relation to the Member States but also vice versa. And it binds the Member States amongst themselves. The essence of it is that no one should use its respective powers without taking into account the repercussions this may have on the legal order of the partner. In consequence, this tenet binds the Community not to legislate if possible in any way which could be contrary to essential rules of the constitutions of Member States.[20]

But the *Nold* judgment has provoked other more critical comments, so that it might seem that the Court of Justice has fallen between all possible stools: On the one hand it has been argued that the acknowledgment of such a vast variety of rights, such as to ownership, profession, work and other activities, has exceeded even the limits of judicial legislation and has bound the Community to a more or less liberal concept of economy, whereas the authors of the Treaties intended this to be decided by the political institutions.

On the other hand, it has been argued that the limitations, such as "social function", "public interest", "overall objectives pursued by the Community", are much too imprecise and in effect water down the good intentions of the Court.[21] Personally I think that none of these criticisms is justified, but the Court will have to prove this in the years to come.

Should one hope that there will be a large number of cases brought before the Court involving violation of fundamental rights by the Community? Of course not. One should be satisfied that there have been only the few instances before the Court cited above. This is partly due to the still limited powers of the Community which affect the individual with the same intensity as he may experience from his national authorities. It is also partly due to the combined efforts of legal experts from all Member States and from the institutions which have eliminated doubtful provisions in any drafts of Community legislation. But partly it may well be due to the limited access for the individual to safeguard his rights before the Court of Justice. Under Articles 173 and 175 of the EEC Treaty for example there is generally no possibility for the individual to attack Community regulations or directives.[22]

On the other hand, only a developing case law of the Court of Justice can bring any certainty as to which rights will be protected by the Court and as to which restrictions the Court will be prepared to accept.

II.

Having dealt with the position as it is at present in the Community, I will turn now to the second part of my considerations. Does this system of the protection of fundamental rights seems satisfactory? The courts in most of the Member States have not yet adopted a clear position though accepting generally the principles of unity and of priority of Community law over national law. As to the protection of fundamental rights the German and the Italian constitutional courts have expressed themselves.

The Italian *Corte Costituzionale* in its decision of 18 December 1973[23] refused any national control over secondary rules of Community law. But, and this is to be stressed, it reserved the possibility to question the basic Act of ratification should the Community interfere unlawfully with the rights of its citizens. For the moment it considers such a situation as more than unlikely.

The decision of the German *Bundesverfassungsgericht*[24] is in effect along the same line, though different in its method. The Court expressed clearly its dissatisfaction with the Community system of the protection of human rights though it turned out to be only a 5:3 decision. In 1971 the German legislature had given the judges of the Constitutional Court the possibility of giving a dissenting opinion – thus following Anglo-American traditions. The dissenting opinion of the minority in this case is an excellent analysis of the legal order of the Community, clear both in its language and in its reasoning.

The majority said: Article 24 of the German Grundgesetz (Basic Law) does allow a transfer of sovereign powers to an interstate organization. But there are limits. Article 24 does not open the way to altering or affecting the inalienable and essential part of the constitutional structure of the Basic Law, including, beyond any doubt, the system of protection of fundamental rights. The new organization should at least have an equivalent system. And in the opinion of the five judges this is not yet the case for the European Community.

The case-law of the European Court of Justice may have its merits, but as long as the Community does not have a codified catalogue of fundamental rights which has been approved by a parliament, is generally applicable and is equivalent to that contained in the Basic Law, the Constitutional Court will retain its powers to control Community law (or more precisely to control acts of the German public authorities such as lower courts applying Community law) in respect of the fundamental rights guaranteed in the Basic Law. The Constitutional Court does not claim to be able to invalidate Community law which would in any event remain effective in eight other Member States. But it maintained its power to declare such a conflicting rule of Community law as inapplicable within the territory of the Federal Republic of Germany.

This decision though generally in favour of the protection of fundamental rights is in my opinion dangerous and seems to be in violation of the Community Treaties.

The decision is dangerous because it may destroy the uniform application of Community law throughout the Member States; discriminations would be created if some rules were not applied in Germany; it will, by admitting new internal procedures even after the European Court of Justice has pronounced an opinion, extend the period of uncertainty as regards the effective application of Community law in Germany, and it will constitute a precedent for other Member States invoking other constitutional principles to ignore their obligations under the Community Treaties.

On the merits the German Court reached the same result as the European Court of Justice. In effect the latter decided in this same *Internationale Handelsgesellschaft* case on the deposits for import/export licences some 4 years earlier that no violation of any fundamental right could be found.[25] Could one speak nevertheless of a *violation* of the Community Treaties, which could give rise to a procedure under Article 169 of the EEC Treaty? Or should the present conflict be considered as a pure dispute of principle and on respective powers of jurisdiction?

The answer must be that there is a violation. First, Article 5(2) of the EEC Treaty obliges the Member States to "abstain from any measure which could jeopardize the attainment of the objectives of the Treaty". And, just as in international law, it does not make any difference whether these measures are initiated by a national legislature, the administration or an independent Court. Courts are independent of the other constitutional institutions, but not of the State as such.

Secondly, one may speak of a violation of Article 177 of the EEC Treaty. If the European Court of Justice by means of a preliminary ruling has interpreted Community law or has pronounced on the validity of Community law these results may not, under any circumstances, be denied by a national authority. I must admit that German Courts, and national Courts generally may question whether a particular aspect of Community law is in conflict with national law (indeed the European Court never decides on this matter); but in none of the national procedures could the result possibly be the inapplicability of Community law, as the judgment of the Court of Justice has definite and binding effects in this report.

Though one has to posit a violation of Articles 5 and 177 in connection with Article 189 of the EEC Treaty, the Commission has not so far opened an infringement procedure under Article 169. Answering two parliamentary questions[26] the Commission indicated the risks inherent in the position of the Constitutional Court, but did not think it urgent to send even a reasoned opinion under Article 169. Instead the Commission sent a letter to the German Government stating its serious preoccupation.[27] In an answer, the German Government expressed its conviction that none of the risks indicated would ever materialise.

It is difficult to interpret the Commission's intentions, especially as the door is still open. But plainly it could be extremely hazardous to open legal proceedings on such a sensitive question as that of the protection of fundamental rights. And above all: What would be the effects of a judgment by the Court of Justice stating that there had been a breach of the Treaty?

The Federal Republic would have to change its constitution in order to withdraw the jurisdiction claimed by the Constitutional Court. But could one really imagine that there would be the required two-thirds majority in both houses of Parliament? Certainly not, as the Constitutional Court still has a high reputation and particular merits in the effective protection of human rights. But let us assume that Parliament changed the constitution – could not the Constitutional Court then itself outlaw this amendment stating that it was unconstitutional? Article 79(3) of the Basic Law states that amendments to the constitution affecting the basic principles of guaranteed fundamental rights shall be inadmissible. And as the Constitutional Court has power to control the legislature to ensure that Article 79(3) is respected, they could find themselves going round in circles.

In such a situation it might be wise to wait and see whether any real conflict arises out of the jurisdiction claimed by the Constitutional Court. One may be sure that there will be a common endeavour to avoid any major conflict: the Community legislature will respect national constitutional traditions, the European Court of Justice will keep itself informed about developments in the case-law of the highest national courts. And these courts – and especially the German Constitutional Court – will attempt, when interpreting their constitutional principles, to conform as much as possible with the law of integration. The former President of the Commission, Hallstein, has recently proposed a more formalized procedure which would allow the European Court, before deciding any question on fundamental rights, to ask the relevant courts of the Member States for their opinion and case-law.[28] This, in effect, would go a long way towards avoiding any major incidents.

I do not think that the German Constitutional Court will change its attitude, at least not in the foreseeable future. And instead of waiting for a possible overruling by the plenary grouping all the 16 judges of the Court, one should recognize that a serious problem exists and one should ask oneself what can be done within the Community framework to remedy the situation.

III.

I do not want to comment upon suggestions calling for an Ombudsman for the Community, nor for the setting up of special machinery for data protection, which is currently under study.

If one takes up the more or less political suggestions of the German Constitutional Court one has to decide whether a more democratic structure and whether a written catalogue of fundamental rights would help.

Leaving aside the question whether the principle of democracy is essential for the protection of fundamental rights (certainly, democracy alone is no guarantee of freedom!)[29] the demand for a written catalogue of fundamental rights for the Community seems at first glance to be entirely justified – at least in the eyes of Continental lawyers. But at present this concept is even being discussed for a new constitutional settlement for England.[30]

However at least three major problems exist:

The first problem is one of *selection*, as it is not possible to add all the existing rights which may be found in national and international instruments. Freedom from extradition, the rights of conscientious objectors, the right of heritage and the freedom to choose one's life partner are hardly within the sphere of a European Union. But if defence should be within the powers of such a Union or if it is to have a diplomatic service whose members would be forbidden to choose their partner from the country where they are designated, even these rights may have to be protected.

If one thinks further of the protection of the family, of one's belief and religion or for example of the prohibition of forced labour we find that there may already be cases under the existing system. Migrant workers must be in a position to be accompanied by their families, which should be able to enjoy the same social advantages as indigenous members of the population.

Thus in the *Casagrande* case[31] the Court of Justice held in 1974 that a Bavarian law was in conflict with Community law in that it provided for educational grants of nearly 13 per month only to those school children who were German nationals. And the freedom of religion was in question when a candidate with Jewish beliefs refused to take part in an entrance examination for service with the Community institutions, because the date of the examination fell on a Jewish holiday. And as I am a civil servant myself I do not want to comment on forced labour.

The activities of the Community are developing. Under the present system there are already hardly any of the traditional rights which might not be affected. For example whether you can force farmers to refrain from planting or replanting certain argricultural products is a typical question which has to be decided within the common agricultural policy as well as in any system of interventionist economic policy.

To summarize: a selection of certain rights will only be a real problem if one tries to restrict a catalogue to certain economic and social rights. Such a restriction might mean that the Court of Justice would again have to take recourse to general principles of law common to the constitutions of all Member States.

The second problem, that of *restriction* of these rights, is clearly the most serious one. An article which states: "private ownership is protected" is of no use, as there are and must be certain restrictions, if not in the interest of the rights of other citizens, at least in the public interest. A catalogue would only be of value if it indicated the relevant limitations and restrictions. It is obvious that by making these restrictions one may pre-judge the entire economic policy of a legal order, either in a more liberal direction or by opening up interventionist possibilities.

Numerous decisions of the German Constitutional Court show the difficulties which the Court has had in avoiding any interference in the genuine political powers of the legislature. It is the latter who should have exclusive power to decide on overall economic policy.

If one imagines today the Council of Ministers sitting together in order to elaborate such a catalogue one may wonder whether anything more would emerge than a very restricted standard on the basis of perhaps even less than the common denominator of the relevant national traditions. One may argue whether in the present political climate even the very limited European Convention on Human Rights would have any chance of achieving a consensus amongst Member States.

This leads to the third problem:
The elaboration of a catalogue for the Community is to be recommended only within the framework of the constitution for a European Union. An *isolated catalogue*, not accompanied by a reform of the institutional set-up and the judicial procedures, would be of little value. Perhaps it is a lesson which we may take from history. People, Parliaments and Governments have often framed catalogues of rights, but only those which were forged in times of political oppression and put into force within a new constitution turned out to be of any considerable value.

On the other hand, any plans for a European Union would be incomplete and of no value if they did not point out in clear terms the fundamental rights of the citizens and especially their economic and social rights which might involve specific programmes for the legislature. There must be effective judicial remedies for the individual and there must be effective limits to the possible restrictions of fundamental rights. Otherwise this Union would again fail to realize the aim already set out in the preamble of the European Convention and of the EEC Treaty, that is to "lay the foundations of an ever closer Union amongst the people of Europe".

Such a constitution must include a number of essential rights for citizens who take advantage of living in any other Member States and who should not suffer discrimination under the national legal order. The Commission, following the demand of the last Paris Conference (1974) of the heads of states,[32] is at work on provisions for the protection of specific rights to be exercised within the legal order of the Member States. One need only think of the right to vote in local government elections or even the right to hold public office.

Such a codified system of protection would certainly give more legal security as to the possible standard of fundamental rights of the citizen than the slowly developing case-law of the Court of Justice. But one could argue that such a standard, agreed on the basis of political compromise, would be inferior to anything which could develop out of the case-by-case decisions of the Court of Justice.

Are there any alternatives for the moment?

With the accession of France to the European Convention on Human Rights all Member States of the Community are bound by the Convention, though France and Italy are still reluctant to accept individual applications which might be brought against them. The Court of Justice is willing, as the *Nold* case shows, to take the Convention into account as evidence of the existence of general principles of law. If it should ever be necessary it is likely that the Court of Justice will go further and apply the Conventions directly, in view of its decision in the *International Fruit Company* case.[33] However, in this Convention the Court of Justice will not find those rights which are most relevant to the Communities' activities such as the freedom to exercise a profession and the right of private ownership. Nevertheless the Court of Justice will find a great deal of valuable comparative work in the decisions of the European Court of Human Rights and in the work of the Human Rights Commission. The Convention is full of express restrictions such as "prescribed by law and are necessary in a democratic society", "interest of national security", "public safety" and "economic well-being of the country" and others. Thus the Court of Justice would be well advised to use the results of the relevant studies.

Does one have to fear any divergent interpretation of the Convention? It seems most unlikely that any major problem will arise, and if it did – one could live with it: It would be too complicated and not in the interest of speeding up the procedures, to oblige the Luxembourg Court to obtain preliminary rulings from the Strasbourg Court.

Another approach would be to envisage accession by the Community to the European Convention on Human Rights. But here again one is confronted with more questions than answers: does the Community have the power to accede? Is not the European Convention partly beyond the scope of the Community? Again the Convention is only open to the signature of States and an additional protocol would therefore be necessary for the accession of the Community.

Within the Strasbourg system the Committee of Ministers of the Council of Europe, a political organ, may be called upon to take the decision on whether the Convention has been violated, if the case is not referred to the Court of Human Rights. A decision by a political organ may be unacceptable with regard to the activities of the Community institutions. Furthermore, if the Community as such joined the Convention its rules would become directly applicable in all Member States, which at present is not the case as the effects of transformation differ from one country to another. If the law of the Convention came into force like any other Community law, the Luxembourg Court would have jurisdiction and then possibly the Strasbourg Court. Again one has to ask how conflicts could be avoided.

Whatever solution is found, in the near future one will have to live with the case-law of the Court of Justice and unfortunately with that of the German Constitutional Court as well. And one will have to live with draft programmes and aspirations. The stronger these aspirations are, the nearer the day when European citizens will be effectively protected against any violation of their fundamental rights by any public authority.

[1] This paper was completed in August 1975.

[2] This paper reflects the personal opinion of the author. For more details of. H.P. Ipsen, "BVerfG versus EuGH re 'Grundreckte'", 10 Europarecht 1975, I *seq.*, 3.; P. Pescatore, "La protection juridictionnelle des droits fondamentaux". Rapport communautaire to the VII International Congress on European Law, Bruxelles October 2-4, 1975 (to be published); C.D. Ehlermann, "Primaute du droit Communautaire mise en danger par la Cour Constitutionnelle Federale Allemande", (1975) Revue du Marche Commun, no. 181, p. 10-19 and M. Hilf, "Sekundäres Gemeinschaftsrecht und deutsche Grundrechte, Stellungnahme aus der Sicht des Gemeinschaftsrechts", 35 ZaöRV 1975, 51-66.

[3] Cf. BVerfGE 33, 303 concerning the limits on a numerus clausus system.

[4] Cf. below p. 113 the article by Professors Stein and Vining.

[5] Cf. the decisions of 18 October 1967, BVerfGE 22, 293 and of 9 June 1971, BVerfGE 31, 145.

[6] Internationale Handelsgesellschaft, BVerfGE 37, 271 and [1974] 2 C.M.L.R. 540.

[7] N. March Hunnings in a letter to The Times, 30 December 1974.

[8] H.P. Ipsen, *loc. cit.*, note 1, p. 3.

[9] Cf. Communiqué of the Paris meeting of the Heads of Government Bull. EC 12-1974, p. 9.

[10] Bull. EC Suppl. 5/75, no. 83.

[11] Provisional procès-verbal of the session of 10 July 1975, PE 41.303.

[12] Case 1/58, 5 Recueil 1958-1959, 43.

[13] Case 18/57, 5 Recueil 1958-1959, 89.

[14] Case 36/59 *et seq.*, 6 Recueil 1960, 857.

[15] Case 40/64, [1965] ECR 279.

[16] Case 29/69, 15 Recueil 1969, 419.

[17] Case 11/70, 16 Recueil 1970, 1125.

[18] Case 4/73, [1974] ECR 491, 507.

[19] Cf. P. Pescatore, "Les exigences de la démocratie et la légitimité de la Communauté Européenne", 5 Cahiers de droit européen 1974, 499, 513.

[20] Cf. for further details M. Hilf, *loc. cit.*, note 1, p. 58 *et seq.*

[21] Cf. e.g. G. Meier, 27 N.J.W. 1974, 1704 and H.H. Rupp, "Zur bundesverfassungsgerichtlichen Kontrolle des Gemeinschaftsrechts am Masstab der Grundrechte", 27 N.J.W. 1974, 2153.

[22] Cf. the article by Professors Stein and Vining, below p. 113.

[23] *Frontini* case [1974] 2 C.M.L.R. 372.

[24] *Loc. cit.*, note 6.

[25] *Loc. cit.*, note 7.

[26] Question No. 414/74, O.J. 1975, C 54/1 and No. 23/75, O.J. 1975, C 161/11.

[27] Cf. Bull. EC 12-1974, no. 2501.

[28] W. Hallstein, "Europapolitik durch Rechtsprechung", Festschrift für Franz Böhm, Tübingen 1975, 205, 211 *et seq.*

[29] Cf. in detail the arguments in the dissenting opinion, *loc. cit.*, note 6.

[30] Cf. L. Scarman, *English Law – The New Dimension* (The Hamlyn Lectures, 26th Series), 1974, p. 81.

[31] Case 9/74 [1974] ECR 773; cf. also the *Alaimo* case 68/74 [1975] ECR 109.

[32] Cf. Bull. EC 12-1974, 8, no. 11.

[33] Case 21-24/72, 18 Recueil 1972, 1219 concerning the Community being bound by the GATT; cf. further P. Pescatore, *loc. cit.*, note 1.

9

Remedies in the United Kingdom: Some Practical Problems of Direct Applicability

LAWRENCE COLLINS

Introduction

The experience of the impact of Community law on the law of the United Kingdom is necessarily limited by its short period of membership of the European Communities. There has, however, been sufficient time for some trends to have developed and, in particular, for the attitude of the judiciary to have become reasonably clear.

It may perhaps be helpful to look at the developments not in the abstract but in the context of a recent reported decision of an English court involving Community law. In *EMI Records Ltd.* v. *CBS United Kingdom Ltd.*[1] the plaintiffs were a well-known English record company and the defendants were an English subsidiary of the well-known American record company CBS Inc. The plaintiffs, EMI, owned the rights in the trade mark "Columbia" in the United Kingdom and in all the other countries of the EEC. The parent company of the defendants, CBS, owned the mark "Columbia" in the United States. The defendants had been importing records bearing the mark "Columbia" from the United States into Britain, although in many cases the mark was obliterated from the product. EMI sought an interlocutory injunction to restrain infringement of its trade mark "Columbia" in the United Kingdom by the sale of records made by CBS. The defendant company resisted the motion on the ground (among others) that it was necessary to refer a question to the European Court in view of the fact that (according to the defendants) Community law gave the defendants a

F.G. *Jacobs*, ed. *European Law and the Individual* © *1976*, *North-Holland Publishing Company* defence to the action. The defendants argued that Article 36 of the EEC Treaty and the decisions of the European Court (particularly the decisions in the *Deutsche Grammophon* case,[2] *Van Zuylen Frères* v. *Hag AG*[3] and the *Centrafarm* cases[4]) were a complete defence to the action. On the basis of these decisions the defendants argued that where goods were lawfully produced and marketed, even in non-Member States, by an economic unit which traded within the Community, which once owned a particular mark in the United Kingdom, and which later brought the goods into the United Kingdom, the principles of the Common Market and the import-ance of free circulation of goods prevented the present owner of the trade mark in the United Kingdom from exercising those rights in the goods.

This is not the place for a discussion of the substantive rules relating to the existence and exercise of trade mark rights as a result of the interpreta-tion of Articles 36 and 85 of the EEC Treaty by the European Court. The importance of the case for present purposes is the way in which it shows how easily European Community law fits into English law and procedure and also for the light it throws on the attitude of the judiciary to Commu-nity law. The following questions arose explicitly or implicitly in this litiga-tion: first, could the defendants rely on Article 36 of the EEC Treaty in the English court? Second, did the Judge have a discretion to refer a question to the European Court under Article 177, and if so, should he exercise it in favour of the defendants? Third, if he did refer a question to the European Court under Article 177, should that prevent him from granting an inter-locutory injuction in the English proceedings?

Direct Applicability – The Legislative Technique

There has not, of course, been a domestic legal revolution as a result of the accession of the United Kingdom to the European Communities. In the first place, the framework of the European Communities Act 1972 is entirely non-revolutionary. A discussion on sovereignty would be outside the scope of this paper, but the 1972 Act is expressive of, and consistent with, the sovereignty of Parliament in the old-fashioned sense, in the sense that in legal theory there is nothing Parliament cannot do, including repealing the 1972 Act itself. Although the House of Lords Select Commit-tee on the European Communities has expressed the view that this is an unsettled question,[5] it is likely that the courts would give effect to subse-quent inconsistent legislation.[6] In a different context, that of the European

Convention on Human Rights, Lord Denning M.R. has reaffirmed, in *R.* v. *Secretary of State, ex parte Bhajan Singh,*[7] the orthodox view that the courts have no power to declare a statute void for non-compliance with international obligations.

Secondly, the practical impact of Community law on everyday practice of law is not yet pronounced. Although there are obvious exceptions (e.g. *Van Duyn* v. *Home Office*[8] dealing with immigration and perhaps also *Bulmer* v. *Bollinger*[9] on unfair trade practices) most of the cases which have arisen in the United Kingdom courts have been concerned with the EEC competition rules. All of the direct applications to the European Court have been in connection with the merger provisions of the European Coal and Steel Community Treaty, the most recent being the application for interim measures in *Johnson & Firth Brown Limited* v. *E.C. Commission.*[10]

The basic principle of direct applicability developed by the European Court is that individuals may invoke certain provisions of the Treaties as conferring direct rights, upon which the individuals concerned may rely in proceedings in national courts.[11] According to the European Court, the effect of the last sentence of Article 36 of the EEC Treaty is to prevent the exercise of trade mark rights from constituting a means of arbitrary discrimination or a disguised restriction on trade between Member States. Although the Court has never articulated the reasons, it appears from the *Deutsche Grammophon* and *Hag*[12] cases that the last sentence of Article 36 is by Community law a directly applicable provision.

That, therefore, is the position in Community law. The position in English law is reasonably clear. It is trite law that a treaty cannot of itself affect private rights in England.[13] The technique used to achieve the incorporation of directly applicable Community law is that of Section 2 of the European Communities Act 1972. Sub-section 1 provides that, broadly, all rights created under the Treaties are to be recognised and available in law and enforced accordingly in the United Kingdom. It is in this way that directly applicable Community law becomes effective in the United Kingdom. By virtue of Section 3 of the Act, whether a Treaty provision has direct applicability is a question of Community law, which is to be treated as a question of law in the English Court, and not as a question of fact, like foreign law, and is to be determined in accordance with the principles laid down by, and any relevant decision of, the European Court.

Although Section 2(2) is directed primarily to the subordinate legislation designed to give effect to Community law which is not directly applicable, nevertheless Section 2(2)(b) does give similar powers in relation to

directly applicable law. It provides that the Minister may, for the purpose
of dealing with matters arising out of or related to directly applicable
obligations or rights, by regulations make provision. In so doing the
relevant Minister may have regard to the objects of the Communities and
to any "such obligation or rights as aforesaid", i.e. directly applicable
rules.

In practice, there have been very few ministerial regulations which have
dealt with directly applicable law. In theory one might expect to find a
large number of English ministerial regulations dealing with directly applicable law, and in particular with Community regulations. But a glance at
the table of Rules and Orders in the Encyclopaedia of European Community Law, edited by Professor Simmonds, will show that very few of such
rules and orders can be regarded as implementing Community regulations. Most of them deal with directives where, until the recent decision of
the European Court in *Van Duyn* v. *Home Office*,[14] the British authorities
had to work on the basis that in general directives were not directly applicable. It is not difficult to guess at the reasons why very few orders have
been made in relation to regulations.

One reason, no doubt, is the line of decisions of the European Court that
Member States are prohibited from altering the scope of Community
regulations when applying their provisions in domestic law.[15] In one
case,[16] a German court referred a question on the interpretation of Council
and Commission Regulations to the European Court under Article 177.
The question was whether national authorities had power to categorise
doubtful products by interpreting them as being within one of two groups
under the agricultural regulations in question. The German government
argued that where a reference to products in a regulation is not sufficient to
achieve an exact classification, additional rules for interpretation and
definition of products had to be issued by Member States. The Court held
that Member States were not entitled, by means of national provisions, to
explain and differentiate from one another the categories of products
subject to the relevant levy. That was because the regulation in question
was directly applicable and in the absence of specific provision to the
contrary, Member States were prohibited from adopting measures for the
implementation of the regulation intended to modify their scope or add to
their provision.

A second reason why the United Kingdom authorities have made little
use of subordinate legislation in relation to directly applicable law, may be
the principle laid down by the European Court in *Variola* v. *Italian Minister*

of Finance[17] that Member States were under an obligation not to introduce any measure whereby the Community nature of a legal rule was concealed from those subject to it. In particular, the Court held, the jurisdiction of the Court under Article 177 should be unaffected by any provision of national legislation which purported to convert a rule of Community law into national law. That was a case where the Italian law abolishing a statistics duty and an administrative services duty (declared to be incompatible with Community law by the European Court in 1969 and 1970) had only abolished the relevant duties from 1971.

Directives which are directly applicable may raise more difficult questions, e.g. the Council directive of 1964 on the co-ordination of measures concerning the movement and residence of foreign nationals which are justified on grounds of public policy, security or health – it was put into effect by rules under the Immigration Act 1971. It was this directive which was in issue in the *Van Duyn* case.[18] While it was clear that directives did not have direct effect, no problem would arise in relation to the role of national implementing subordinate legislation. Problems of interpretation might arise, but no doubt the orthodox English approach would have been adopted. If the subordinate legislation were ambiguous, then recourse could be had to the terms of the directive: *Salomon* v. *Commissioners of Customs and Excise*.[19] But once directives have direct effect, more difficult problems arise. The first question would be whether the directive in question indeed had direct effect. That question would be decided as a matter of Community law, and in a doubtful case recourse could be had to the European Court under Article 177. If the directive had direct effect, a further question would arise, as to the relationship between the rights (if any) given under that directive and the right given under the English subordinate legislation. How would the subordinate legislation be interpreted? Many rules and orders[20] provide that the Interpretation Act 1889 shall apply for their interpretation as it applies for the interpretation of an Act of Parliament. Is such a provision perhaps *ultra vires*, since it purports to apply English rules of interpretation instead of Community rules? It is suggested that subordinate legislation which is inconsistent with directly applicable law will be *ultra vires* so long as Section 2 of the 1972 Act remains in force. That is because the Minister's powers are limited to making provision for the purpose of implementing Community obligations and dealing with matters arising out of directly applicable law, and in so doing the Minister is to have regard (by virtue of the express terms of Sections 2(2)) to the objects of the Communities and to directly applicable law. If he went beyond them, and enacted subordinate legislation which was inconsistent with Community law, such legislation would be *ultra vires.* In so far as directly applicable law and subordinate legislation cover the same ground and are not in conflict, there will in a sense be two co-ordinate systems, on either of which the individual may rely – perhaps not entirely unlike a statute which is merely declaratory of the common law.

The Attitude of the Judiciary

It may be helpful to return to the case of *EMI Records Ltd.*, v. *CBS United Kingdom Ltd.*[21] in order to consider the judicial atmosphere in which Graham J. was called upon to make his decision. The judges of the Chancery Division have exhibited a cautious attitude to Community law in general and to the necessity to make applications under Article 177 to the European Court in particular. It is only necessary to mention the decisions of Graham J. himself in *Löwenbräu München* v. *Grunhalle Lager International,*[22] of Whitford J. in *Bulmer* v. *Bollinger*[23] and Pennycuick V-C in *Van Duyn* v. *Home Office.*[24] What one makes of the attitude of the Court of Appeal is not so certain. The Court of Appeal has a role in the English legal system which is central, both in a literal and metaphorical sense. It is the Court of Appeal, and not the House of Lords, which is the principal judicial law-making body in England. In relation to Community law one senses, perhaps, a paradox. On the one hand, there is the enthusiasm for Community law and its methods which is expressed in several judgments of Lord Denning M.R. On the other hand, there is the evident reluctance to refer cases to the European Court which underlies the decision in *Bulmer* v. *Bollinger.*

There can be no doubt about the enthusiasm shown by Lord Denning for the principles of interpretation of Community law. In *Bulmer* v. *Bollinger* he said:[25]

> In future, in transactions which cross the frontiers, we must no longer speak or think of English law as something on its own. We must speak and think of Community law, of community rights and obligations, and we must give effect to them.

A similar attitude may be found in his judgments in *Application des Gaz* v. *Falks Veritas*[26] and *Schorsch Meier* v. *Hennin.*[27]

On interpretation, Lord Denning has contrasted the principles of Community law of interpretation with those of English law. In *Bulmer* v. *Bollinger,* after indicating that English judges "interpret a statute applying only to the circumstances covered by the very words" and referring to the rejection by the House of Lords in *Magor and St. Mellons Rural District Council* v. *Newport Corporation*[28] of the suggestion by Denning L.J. (as he then was) that it was the duty of judges to fill in the gaps in legislation, he went on:[29]

> How different is this Treaty! It lays down general principles. It expresses its aims and purposes. All in sentences of moderate length and commendable style. But it lacks precision. It uses words and phrases without defining what they mean. An English lawyer would look for an interpretation clause, but he would look in vain. There is none. All the way through the Treaty there are gaps and lacunae. These have to be filled in by the judges, or by regulations or directives. It is the European way.

But one detects in *Bulmer* v. *Bollinger* a strong inclination on the part of Lord Denning to the view that, wherever possible, English judges, and not the Community Court, should interpret Community law. In *Schorsch Meier* v. *Hennin* he said, in relation to Article 106, "in interpreting this article we need not examine the words in meticulous detail. We have to look at the purpose or intent. There is no need to refer the interpretation to the European court at Luxembourg. We can do it ourselves."[30]

What is the explanation of this apparent paradox? Perhaps Lord Denning's reference to the rejection in the *Magor and St. Mellons* case of his old ideas on the interpretation of English statutes was a little tongue in cheek. It will be recalled in *Seaford Court Estates* v. *Asher*[31] he said the Judge "must set to work on the constructive task of finding the intention of Parliament, and he must do this not only from the language of the Statute, but also from a consideration of the social conditions which gave rise to it, and of the mischief which it was passed to remedy and then he must supplement the written word so as to give "force and life" to the intention of the legislature". Although this approach was heavily criticised in the House of Lords in the *Magor and St. Mellons* case, in *Ministry of Housing and Local Government* v. *Sharp*[32] Lord Denning, dissenting, said "but we do not now in this court stick to the letter of a statute. We go by its true intent. We fill in the gaps. We follow what I said in *Seaford Court Estates* v. *Asher.*"

There is clearly a close parallel between the approach to the interpretation of English statutes which Lord Denning has for so long advocated and the approach which he finds to interpretation under Community law. The latter approach therefore clearly has a great attraction for him. The reason why he prefers English courts to apply these principles, and not the European Court, is, of course, a matter of speculation but it is possible to suggest an answer. When the *Atlantic Star*[33] (in which the House of Lords re-interpreted the expression "vexatious and oppressive" for the purposes of staying actions) was before the Court of Appeal, Lord Denning, stating the traditional law that it was extremely difficult to divest the English Court of jurisdiction, said:

> This right to come here is not confined to Englishmen. It extends to any friendly foreigner. He can seek the aid of our courts if he desires to do so. You may call this 'forum shopping' if you please, but if the forum is England, it is a good place to shop in, both for the quality of the goods and the speed of service.[34]

The position, therefore, appears to be this: the principles of interpretation of Community law are to be embraced wholeheartedly, but it is for the English court to apply them wherever possible.

In *EMI Records Ltd.* v. *CBS United Kingdom Ltd.* Graham J. did decide to refer to the European Court the question of the right to import goods lawfully produced and marketed in a non-Member State which trades within the Community, as against a present owner of the trade mark in the United Kingdom. But it was perhaps as a result of the influence of the decisions of the Court of Appeal referred to above (or perhaps as a result of the considerable criticism of the trade mark decisions of the European Court found in the academic literature[35] and among practising lawyers) that Graham J. took the step of indicating that, although the case was not a simple one, and therefore required a reference to the European Court, he was able to give his own view of the answer, in these words:[36]

> I should, however, at this point perhaps say that on the arguments before me, if I had to decide the matter now, I would accept the plaintiff's contentions and decide in their favour.

The Role of the Courts and Judicial Remedies

One of the striking features of the formulations by the European Court of the nature of directly applicable law is the emphasis which it places on the role of the national courts. In general, if a state has an international obligation, it is for the state to decide which of its internal organs it will use to comply with that obligation. But in a consistent line of cases the European Court has emphasised that directly applicable rights must be protected by national *courts*. One need refer only to the formulations in the *Molkerei Zentrale* cases[37] and in *Salgoil* v. *Italian Ministry of Foreign Trade*.[38] This is not, of course, unique. In the famous *Danzig Railway* case[39] the Permanent Court of International Justice held:

> But it cannot be disputed that the very object of an international agreement, according to the intention of the contracting Parties, may be the adoption by the Parties of some definite rules creating individual rights and obligations and enforceable by the national courts. . . . The intention of the Parties, which is to be ascertained from the contents of the Agreement, taking into consideration the manner in which the Agreement has been applied, is decisive.

It is moreover commonplace that in certain branches of international law the existence of judicial remedies is just as important as the standard and content of the substantive rules which they apply – much of the law of state responsibility relating to denial of justice rests on such a foundation, as do several of the provisions of the European Convention on Human Rights.

This, however, casts a heavy responsibility on the national judge. It is the judge who has to protect individual rights. The European Communities Act 1972 provides in Section 2(1) that directly applicable law shall be recognised as available in law, and be enforced, allowed and followed accordingly – but a formulation in such a general manner is not very helpful to a national judge. If the national judge is to provide remedies beyond those which already exist, such a formulation goes, it is suggested, against the whole grain of judicial law-making in this country. Judges fill in gaps, they build upon rules – it is very difficult for them to introduce new rules which are of the specific type essentially related to law making by legislatures. A modern example of judicial law making which goes beyond the bounds of what would normally be regarded as appropriate for judges is the line of cases culminating in *Yorkshire Electricity Board* v. *Naylor*[40] concerning the figure which may be awarded in actions for personal injury in relation to damages for loss of expectation of life.

It is not in fact likely that this will be a problem in the United Kingdom, since the judicial remedies available in this country are sufficiently flexible to allow judges to enforce directly applicable Community law. It may be helpful to consider how an English court would have dealt with the problem which arose before the Dutch courts in *Walrave and Koch* v. *Cyclists Association.*[41] That was the case in which Dutch plaintiffs sought to challenge the rules of the International Cyclists Association, which provided that a pace-maker should be of the same nationality as the stayer. The plaintiffs argued that the provision was incompatible with Articles 7, 48 and 59 of the EEC Treaty since it prevented the pace-maker of one Member State from offering his services to a stayer of another Member State. The precise procedure adopted in the Dutch courts in that case is not clear from the report. On a reference under Article 177, the European Court held that although discrimination based on nationality was prohibited by the Treaty, it did not affect matters which were questions of purely sporting interest and had nothing to do with economic activity. The European Court left the national court to decide the very difficult question whether the activities of pace-makers were essentially economic or sporting.

If such a case arose in England, what would the appropriate remedies be? It is suggested that the declaration and the injunction are sufficiently flexible remedies to cover not only this type of case but most others. It will be recalled that in *Nagle* v. *Feilden*[42] Mrs. Nagle had been a racehorse trainer for twenty-four years, when she applied for a licence from the Jockey Club for a Trainer's Licence. According to the rules of the Stewards of the Jockey Club, they had power at their discretion to grant and withdraw licences to officials, trainers and jockeys. Mrs. Nagle was refused a licence, without reasons, and she alleged that the sole reason for the refusal of a licence was that she was a woman. One of the main pieces of evidence on which she relied was that the Stewards had granted licences to men employed by her and in particular to her "head lad". Mrs. Nagle sued for a declaration that the practice of the Stewards was void against public policy; an injunction restraining them from following that practice; and an injunction ordering them to grant her a licence.

The Judge at first instance struck out the action because Mrs. Nagle did not have an existing contractual relationship with the Stewards of the Jockey Club. Lord Denning allowed the appeal in terms which may have very considerable implications in relation to the direct effect of the EEC rules relating to freedom of movement and establishment. According to Lord Denning

> The common law of England has for centuries recognised that a man has a right to work at his trade or profession without being unjustly excluded from it. He is

not to be shut out from it at the whim of those having the governance of it. If they make a rule which enables them to reject his application arbitrarily or capriciously, not reasonably, that rule is bad.[43]

Salmon L.J. added[44]

one of the principal functions of our courts is, whenever possible, to protect the individual from injustice and oppression. It is important, perhaps today more than ever that we should not abdicate that function. The principle that the courts will protect a man's right to work is well recognised... The courts use their powers in the interests of the individual and of the public to safeguard the individual's right to earn his living as he wills and the public's right to the benefit of his labours.

Clearly the Court of Appeal thought that the declaration was an appropriate remedy in that type of case. The case is reported only at the interlocutory stage, where the defendants sought to strike out the action and failed and the only question for the court was whether Mrs. Nagle had an arguable case. The litigation was subsequently settled, when Mrs. Nagle was eventually given her licence.

The use of the declaration, however, has its limits. First, the plaintiff must have an adequate interest to support his claim. The problem of *locus standi* is not an easy one, and the many cases on this aspect will be found in the standard works on administrative law.[45] The authorities were recently considered by Megarry J. in *Thorne R.D.C.* v. *Bunting.*[46] In that case it was not the *locus standi* of the individual which was in question but that of a Council seeking a declaration that the defendant had no right to commons registration. After citing such well-known decisions as *Dyson* v. *Attorney General*[47] and *Anisminic* v. *Foreign Compensation Commission*[48] he went on:

I accept that the remedy by way of declaration is wide and flexible, and that in recent years the tendency of the courts towards width and flexibility have, if anything, been accentuated; the remedy is indeed a valuable servant. But there must be some limit.[49]

In practice the decisions are not very helpful if one seeks to formulate any general rule, but the tendency is unmistakably liberal. When Mr. Blackburn sought a declaration that by signing the EEC Treaty Her Majesty's Government would unlawfully surrender the sovereignty of the Crown in Parliament, his action was struck out on the ground that it disclosed no cause of action because the treaty-making power of the Crown could not be challenged in the courts: *Blackburn* v. *Attorney General.*[50] So far as the standing of Mr. Blackburn was concerned, Lord Denning said:

> A point was raised whether Mr. Blackburn has any standing to come before the court. That is not a matter which we need rule on today. He says that he feels very strongly and that it is a matter in which many persons in this country are concerned. I would not myself rule him out on the ground that he has no standing. But I do rule him out on the ground that these courts will not impugn the treaty-making powers of Her Majesty, and on the ground that in so far as Parliament enacts legislation, we will deal with that legislation as and when it arises.[51]

In deciding what is a sufficient legal interest, the English court would of course be deciding a quite different question from that which the European Court decides when it considers the question of what amounts to "direct and individual concern" under Article 173. The subject matters covered are quite different. The English court would be concerned with the right of an individual to invoke directly applicable law in a national court. The European Court would be considering the question whether an individual was directly and individually concerned by some provision of Community law (most probably a regulation) which he was seeking to challenge.

A second limitation on the right to a declaration under English law is that there must not be some other alternative statutory remedy which is both exclusive and available.

This often arises in practice in relation to disputed points of tax law. It is well-established that a taxpayer cannot avoid the machinery of an assessment and appeal to the Special Commissioners etc. by merely applying for a declaration in the Chancery Division.[52] But it may be that the scope of this exception is not very large. In *London Borough of Ealing* v. *Race Relations Board*[53] in 1971 the Ealing Borough Council issued a summons claiming a declaration against the Race Relations Board that the Council was entitled to decline to place an alien on the housing list on the ground that he was not, at the material time, a British subject. The Race Relations Board argued that the court had no jurisdiction to grant the declaration because the procedure laid down by the Race Relations Act 1968 (an action by the Race Relations Board in the County Court) was a complete and exclusive code. The House of Lords held that clear words were necessary to oust the jurisdiction of the court and the proceedings contemplated by the Race Relations Act were purely proceedings brought by the Race Relations Board and therefore the relevant prohibition relating to courts other than the County Courts did not apply because the Council was in a different position.

The other important weapon is the injunction. In practice the most crucial stage of any litigation where an injunction is sought is the interlocutory stage, where an interim injunction is sought pending trial. The use of the interim injunction is likely to become more common, perhaps more dangerous, as a result of the decision of the House of Lords in *American Cyanamid Co.* v. *Ethicon.*[54] The general practice before that case (although it cannot be said to have been completely consistent) was that the plaintiff had to show a strong prima facie case before he could obtain an interim injunction against the defendant. Once he had established a strong prima facie case, the next question was whether on the balance of convenience it was right that the status quo should be maintained.[55] In the *American Cyanamid* case the House of Lords has held, unanimously, that there is no such rule that the plaintiff must establish a prima facie case. All that is necessary is that the claim should not be frivolous or vexatious and there must be a serious question to be tried. Provided that the court is satisfied that there is a serious question to be tried the only question is the balance of convenience and the relative strength of each party's case is only a minor factor in that balance. In two cases since *American Cyanamid* the majority of the Court of Appeal have followed the approach laid down by that case, but Lord Denning (in one of the cases dissenting) has expressed the strongest distaste for the decision and has attempted to limit its application.[56]

In *EMI Records Ltd.* v. *CBS United Kingdom Ltd.* Graham J. was concerned with two questions relating to interlocutory injunctions. The first was the test which he should apply in deciding whether or not to grant one. As to this he said:[57]

> This point can, I think, be dealt with quite shortly and indeed since the recent decision in *American Cyanamid Co.* v. *Ethicon Ltd.*, it is clear that once the plaintiff is able to establish that his claim is not frivolous or vexatious and that there is a serious question to be tried, the Court should go straight to the question of balance of convenience.

The second question was the relationship between interlocutory injunctions and Article 177. As to this, he decided that there was nothing about the nature of interlocutory proceedings which meant it might not be necessary for a national judge to refer a question to the European Court at such a stage.[58] Nevertheless, he decided that it would be possible to grant an interlocutory injunction pending the reference to the European Court. He said:[59]

> It seems to me, therefore, essential in the meantime to do anything which can be done to make it less likely that such an unfortunate position will occur [namely, different decisions by courts of different countries leading to chaotic results], and this can best be done by a reference as quickly as possible. That, however, does not mean to say I ought not to grant an injunction pending the trial to preserve the status quo....

Thus the declaration and the injunction are remedies which are still in the process of being widened by the English courts and which will no doubt provide very valuable tools in the hands of resourceful plaintiffs. It is possible, also, that another recent judicial development will allow the courts to give full effect to directly applicable law and to avoid the delicate constitutional questions involved in a possible clash between Community law and the law of the United Kingdom. That development is the quite novel development which has its source in the decision of the House of Lords in *Waddington* v. *Miah.*[60]

Before that decision it was well-established that, for the purpose of interpretation of statutes, there is a presumption that Parliament does not intend to legislate in a sense contrary to the international obligations of the United Kingdom. If, therefore, there is ambiguity in a piece of legislation which is designed to give effect to a Treaty obligation the Treaty may be looked at to resolve the ambiguity: *Salomon* v. *Customs & Excise Commissioners.*[61] That case and other recent cases show that even if it does not appear on the face of a statute that it is intended to give effect to treaty obligations, nevertheless, the courts will not require strict proof of the fact that a piece of domestic legislation was enacted to give effect to a Treaty or Convention.[62] What is involved in the recent developments is something far more fundamental. In *Waddington* v. *Miah* the question was whether the penal provisions of the Immigration Act 1971 were retrospective. Lord Reid, in whose speech all of the other four Law Lords concurred, decided as a matter of interpretation that the Act did not have retrospective effect. He relied mainly on the common law presumption against retrospective legislation but he also referred to the United Nations Declaration of Human Rights and the European Convention on Human Rights and said:[63]

It is hardly credible that any government department would promote or that Parliament would pass retrospective criminal legislation.

In two subsequent decisions the Court of Appeal has also relied on the European Convention for the purpose of interpreting the Immigration Act 1971. In *R.* v. *Secretary of State, ex parte Bhajan Singh*[64] Lord Denning, referring to the earlier decision in *Birdi* v. *Secretary of State for Home Affairs,*[65] said:[66]

> What is the position of the Convention in our English law? I would not depart in the least from what I said in the recent case of *Birdi* v. *Secretary of State for Home Affairs.* The Court can and should take the Convention into account. They should take it into account whenever interpreting a statute which affects the rights and liberties of the individual. It is to be assumed that the Crown, in taking its part in legislation, would do nothing which was in conflict with Treaties. So the court should now construe the Immigration Act 1971 so as to be in conformity with the Convention and not against it.

He also added that he went too far in the case of *Birdi* v. *Secretary of State* in suggesting that an Act of Parliament which did not conform to the Convention might be invalid, and went on:[67]

> That was a very tentative statement, but it went too far. There are many cases in which it has been said, as plainly as can be, a Treaty does not become part of English law except and in so far as it is made so by Parliament. If an Act of Parliament contain any provisions contrary to the Convention, the Act of Parliament must prevail. But I hope that no Act will ever be contrary to the Convention. So the point should not arise.

This development means that any legislation, whether or not it is specifically intended to give effect to the international obligations of the United Kingdom, should be construed in the light of the existing international obligations of the United Kingdom. It would appear therefore that any ambiguity or difficulty of interpretation of a statute may now be resolved by considering the international obligations of the United Kingdom, however remote those obligations may be from the actual piece of legislation involved. It must follow, therefore, that pre-existing Community obligations, such as directives, may be resorted to in the interpretation of English statutes even though statutes are not designed to give effect to the relevant directives. It may be objected that they are not on the same plane as the European Convention on Human Rights. But the principle does not appear to be limited to a fundamental treaty such as the Convention. The principle stated appears to have general application and may yet have the most profound effect on the interpretation and application of Statutes in the law of the United Kingdom.

Conclusions

This paper began with the suggestion that the experience of the impact of Community law on the law of the United Kingdom was limited and yet certain trends had developed. For practising lawyers remedies are no less important than substantive rules. The experience to date has suggested that there is room for imaginative development of procedural law on the basis of well-tried and well-tested principles of English procedural law.

Notes

¹ [1975] 1 C.M.L.R. 285.

² Case 78/70 [1971] C.M.L.R. 631; 17 Rec. 487.

³ Case 192/73 [1974] ECR 731.

⁴ Case 15/74, *Centrafarm BV* v. *Sterling Drug Inc.* [1974] ECR 1147; Case 16/74, *Centrafarm BV* v. *Winthrop BV* [1974] ECR 1183.

⁵ 10th Report, 1974-1975, para. 12.

⁶ See, e.g. *Blackburn* v. *Att.-Gen.* [1971] 1 W.L.R. 1037, 1040-1041.

⁷ [1975] 2 All E.R. 1081 at 1083.

⁸ [1974] 1 W.L.R. 1107 (Pennycuick V-C) and Case 41/74 [1975] 1 C.M.L.R. 1; [1975] 2 W.L.R. 760.

⁹ [1974] Ch. 401 (C.A.).

¹⁰ Case 3/75 R.I. [1975] ECR 1.

¹¹ For recent examples see Case 33/74, *Van Binsbergen* [1975] ECR 1299 and Case 36/74, *Walrave and Koch* v. *Association Union Cycliste International* [1974] ECR 1405.

¹² See notes 2 and 3 *supra*.

¹³ *Att.-Gen. of Canada* v. *Att.-Gen. for Ontario* [1937] A.C. 326, 347-348 and for recent examples *The Atlantic Star* [1974] A.C. 436 at 455 and 467 and *R.* v. *Secretary of State, ex parte Bhajan Singh, supra* n. 7.

¹⁴ *Supra* n. 8.

¹⁵ Case 40/69, *Hauptzollamt Hamburg-Oberelbe* v. *Bollmann* [1970] C.M.L.R. 141; 16 Red. 69; Cases 72 and 74/69, *Hauptzollamt Bremen-Freihafen* v. *Bremer Handelsgesellschaft mbH* [1970] C.M.L.R. 466; 16 Rec. 427.

¹⁶ First case cited at n. 15, *supra*.

¹⁷ Case 34/73 [1973] ECR 981.

¹⁸ *Supra* n. 8.

¹⁹ [1967] 2 Q.B. 116 and more recent cases discussed in Collins, Treaties and/or Statutes [1974] C.L.J. 181.

²⁰ E.g. Motor Vehicles (Compulsory Insurance) (No. 2) Regulations 1973, S.I. 1973 No. 2143.

²¹ *Supra* n. 1.

²² [1974] 1 C.M.L.R. 1.

²³ Only the decision of the Court of Appeal is reported: [1974] Ch. 401.

²⁴ *Supra* n. 8.

²⁵ [1974] Ch. 40 at 419.

²⁶ [1974] Ch. 381 at 393.

27 [1974] 3 W.L.R. 823.

28 [1974] A.C. 189.

29 [1974] Ch. at 425. See also *Application des Gaz* v. *Falks Veritas* [1974] Ch. at 393-394 and *Schorsch Meier* v. *Hennin* [1974] 3 W.L.R. at 830.

30 [1974] 3 W.L.R. at 830.

31 [1949] 2 K.B. 481 at 499.

32 [1970] 2 Q.B. 223 at 267.

33 [1974] A.C. 436.

34 [1973] Q.B. 367 at 382. Criticised by Lord Reid [1974] A.C. at 453.

35 See Mann, Industrial Property and the EEC Treaty (1975) 24 I.C.L.Q. 31 and other material referred to by Graham J.: [1975] 1 C.M.L.R. at 292.

36 [1975] 1 C.M.L.R. at 296.

37 Case 28/67 [1968] C.M.L.R. 187 at 216; 14 Rec. 211.

38 Case 13/68 [1968] ECR 453 at 462-463.

39 P.C.I.J. Series B, No. 15 at p. 17.

40 [1968] A.C. 529.

41 *Supra* n. 12.

42 [1966] 2 Q.B. 633.

43 *Ibid.,* at 644-645.

44 *Ibid.,* at 654-655.

45 See de Smith, Judicial Review of Administrative Action, 3rd ed. 1973, pp. 452-456.

46 [1972] Ch. 470.

47 [1911] 1 K.B. 410.

48 [1969] 2 A.C. 147.

49 [1972] Ch. at 477.

50 [1971] 1 W.L.R. 1037.

51 *Ibid.,* at 1041.

52 See, e.g. *Re Vandervell's Trusts* [1971] A.C. 912 at 934, 938 and 944.

53 [1972] A.C. 342. See Hucker, The House of Lords and the Race Relations Act: A Comment on *Ealing* v. *Race Relations Board* (1975) 24 I.C.L.Q. 284.

54 [1975] 2 W.L.R. 316; [1975] 1 All E.R. 504.

55 See, e.g. *Stratford* v. *Lindley* [1965] A.C. 269; *Hubbard* v. *Vosper* [1972] 2 Q.B. 84 and *Evans Marshall & Co. Ltd.* v. *Bertola S.A.* [1973] 1 W.L.R. 349; [1973] 1 All E.R. 992.

56 See *Fellowes* v. *Fisher* [1975] 3 W.L.R. 184; [1975] 2 All E.R. 829 and *Hubbard* v. *Pitt* [1975] 3 W.L.R. 201; [1975] 3 All E.R. 1.

57 [1975] 1 C.M.L.R. at 287.

58 Cf. Collins, Article 177 of the EEC Treaty and English Interlocutory Proceedings (1974) 23 I.C.L.Q. 840 and Collins, European Community Law in the United Kingdom (1975) 101-104.

59 [1975] 1 C.M.L.R. at 297.

⁶⁰ [1974] 1 W.L.R. 683 sub. nom *R.* v. *Miah* [1974] 2 All E.R. 377.

⁶¹ [1967] 2 Q.B. 116.

⁶² See Collins, European Community Law in the United Kingdom (1975), pp. 66-70.

⁶³ [1974] 1 W.L.R. at 694; [1974] 2 All E.R. at 379.

⁶⁴ [1975] 2 All E.R. 1081.

⁶⁵ *The Times,* 12th February 1975.

⁶⁶ [1975] 2 All E.R. at 1083.

⁶⁷ *Ibid.*

10

The European Social Charter

O. KAHN-FREUND

This workshop is concerned with the law of the European Communities, and the emphasis is on the social and labour aspects of Community Law. However, I propose to talk about a European source of international obligations in the fields of labour law and social policy which, at first sight, seems to have nothing to do with the European Communities at all. I am going to speak about the European Social Charter.

In the first place I shall say something about its legal nature and its structure, I shall then compare the provisions of the Charter with the corresponding provisions of the European Treaties, and especially the EEC Treaty, and refer to the links between them. Lastly I shall compare the Charter with the work of the International Labour Organisation, particularly with regard to application and interpretation.

I. Structure and Legal Status of the Charter[1]

(a) The European Social Charter is part of the growing body of European law laid down and formulated under the auspices of the Council of Europe. Its Preamble refers to the aim of the Council to achieve greater unity between its members for the purpose of safeguarding and realising the ideals and principles which are their common heritage and of facilitating their economic and social progress, in particular by the maintenance and further realisation of human rights and fundamental freedoms. In this

F.G. Jacobs, ed. European Law and the Individual © 1976, North-Holland Publishing Company

context the Preamble to the Charter mentions the European Convention for the Protection of Human Rights and Fundamental Freedoms of 1950 and the Additional Protocol of 1952. In fact the European Social Charter which was signed in 1961 and which came into force in 1965 is, in a sense, a big footnote to the European Convention on Human Rights and Fundamental Freedoms. It is an emphatic pronouncement of certain principles governing social policy and labour relations, and at the same time a formulation of certain international obligations concerning specific standards to be applied to labour and social legislation and administration, and to judicial practice in these fields.

(b) Only Members of the Council of Europe can be Parties to the Charter (Article 35(1)). Of these eighteen Members ten have, up to now, ratified the Charter, or (which, as we shall see, is possible) a part of it. All the nine Members of the European Communities are also Members of the Council of Europe and all have signed the Charter, but only six of the nine have so far ratified it or part of it, and thus become bound by all or some of its provisions. The three Benelux countries are not, or not yet, Parties to the Charter, whilst on the other hand it applies to Sweden and Norway, Cyprus and Austria. This means that the territorial scope of the European Treaties and that of the Charter are like intersecting circles with a very large area of common coverage. But however much the two sources of law may have in common in geographical scope, in their legal nature and effect they are, as we shall see, very different indeed.

(c) The Charter is unique in that it combines a proclamation of general principles[2] (in Part I) with the formulation (in Part II) of more or less, often less than more, precise obligations designed to give effect to the general rights and principles previously proclaimed. By ratifying the Charter, a State accepts as the aim of its policy "to be pursued by all appropriate means, both national and international in character", "the attainment of conditions" in which these rights and principles may be effectively realised.

The principles are not only general but, partly at least, also very vague. But this is a characteristic which they share with all catalogues of fundamental rights, international and national, and we know that the indeterminacy of, say, the *Déclaration des Droits de l'Homme et du Citoyen* of 1789, of the first Ten Amendments of the United States Constitution, of the *Grundrechte* of the Bonn Basic Law, or of the Universal Declaration of

Human Rights, does not prevent any of these texts from being either the source of positive rules of law or of "general principles" guiding the courts in the interpretation of legislation. In fact, the American, and more recently the German experience seems to show that the value of such catalogues as sources of principles and of rights depends on their vagueness: their lack of specificity ensures that they can live up to their function of supplying a blank cheque to be filled in by the judge or administrator. One of the nineteen "General Principles" of the Charter is to the effect that "everyone shall have the opportunity to earn his living in an occupation freely entered upon". Others say that "all workers have the right to just conditions of work", "to safe and healthy working conditions", "to a fair remuneration sufficient for a decent standard of living for themselves and their families". Still others proclaim for workers and employers the "right to freedom of association" and the "right to bargain collectively". "Special protection against physical and moral hazards" is assured to children and young persons, and special protection in their work is also assured to women in case of maternity, but to other employed women only "as appropriate". Appropriate facilities for vocational guidance and training must be vouchsafed to everyone. Moreover, there is contained in this list of general rights and principles a charter of minimum guarantees of social policy which, in my opinion, is strictly parallel, and indeed on elementary principles of justice, a necessary corollary, to the guarantee of property rights found in so many constitutions. Everyone has the right "to benefit from any measures enabling him to enjoy the highest possible standard of health attainable", the right "to benefit from social welfare services", and, if he is "without adequate resources", "the right to social and medical assistance", but only "workers and their dependants" have the "right to social security" – the sharp distinction between social security and social assistance services is codified in the Charter. Disabled persons, however, whatever the origin and nature of their disability, are entitled to vocational training, rehabiliation and resettlement. Nor should we underestimate the potentialities inherent in the vague promise of "appropriate social, legal and economic protection" held out to "the family as a fundamental unit of society" "to ensure its full development" or to that of "appropriate social and economic" (but not legal) protection of "mothers and children" "irrespective of marital status and family relations" – one cannot help being aware of the precarious compromise between opposed systems of social ethics underlying these formulas. Lastly, the right to free migration – or at least elements of such a right – figures in this catalogue of social rights and freedoms, but it is in the nature of things that in both its aspects – equality of access to gainful occupation between the nationals of all Contracting Parties, and equal rights to protection and assistance for migrant workers and their families in the territories of all Contracting Parties – the Charter is far behind the corresponding common labour market provisions of European Community law.

(d) This catalogue of fundamental social rights has, it seems to me, potentially at least, a threefold legal significance:

(i) In the first place, the "acceptance" by a Contracting Party of these principles is translated into a positive international legal obligation by Article 20(1)(a) of the Charter, in virtue of which each Contracting Party undertakes to consider Part I as a declaration of the aims it will pursue by all appropriate means (*par tous les moyens utiles*). This is incumbent – and incumbent as regards *all* the principles enunciated in Part I – on every State Member of the Council of Europe which has ratified the Charter, or – and this is decisive – any part of it. Perhaps we can here see the true *raison d'être* of Part I of the Charter. As we shall see, any Member of the Council of Europe can, within certain limits, choose between provisions of Part II of the Charter it wishes and others it does not wish to accept as binding on itself – choose, that is, between strictly legal obligations it wants to impose upon itself by ratification and others it does not want to undergo. But there is no such choice of "general principles". The ratification of any part of Part II makes it incumbent on a State to implement the whole of Part I.[3]

This, however, sounds a little more grandiose than it is. The obligation imposed by Part I is what in the language of French Civil Law is known as an *"obligation de moyens"*, not an *"obligation de résultat"*, that is an obligation to use all means reasonably available towards the attainment of a result, but not a guarantee that it will be attained, whilst, as we shall see, the obligations imposed by Part II are mainly *"obligations de résultat"*, though there are some *"obligations de moyens"* among them. And even this obligation to make every possible effort to implement the Part I principles is, as it were, an *obligatio naturalis:* there is no provision comparable to the control mechanism applicable to Part II.

(ii) What is far more, at least potentially, important, therefore, is the "reflex effect" of Part I as a source of "general principles of law", *principes généraux* as used for the interpretation of positive legal norms and as direct sources of rights to an increasing extent in courts of various countries. In this sense the contrast between the provisions of Part I and of Part II is that between *"principe général"* and *"règle de droit"*,[4] or, to use Professor Esser's terms, between *Grundsatz* and *Norm*.[5] In this light, Part I appears as a series not of legal rules, but of matrices for legal rules. We know that the Universal Declaration of Human Rights and the European Convention for the Protection of Human Rights have served this purpose on a number of occasions – there is no reason at all why this should not also be the principal practical function of Part I of the Charter. The general jurisprudential significance of the Charter lies partly in the paradigmatic parallelism of "general principles" and legal rules shown by the contrast between Parts I and II, that same contrast which, for example, Professor Ronald Dworkin has discussed in the United States.[6]

(iii) Lastly, it is by virtue of this nature of its provisions as "general principles" and as principles of "fundamental rights" that Part I of the Charter constitutes what is perhaps the principal link between the Charter and the law of the European Communities, a matter to which I shall revert in a moment. It is for experts in international law to decide whether it would be open to the International Court of Justice to use Part I of the Charter for the elucidation of those "principles of law recognised by civilised nations" which any State ratifying the Charter undertakes to fulfil entirely or in for the Court.

(e) By contrast, Part II contains a catalogue of international obligations which any State ratifying the Charter undertakes to fulfil entirely or in part. The 19 articles of Part II correspond precisely to the nineteen principles of Part I. They translate them into positive legal obligations.

One can broadly divide these into six groups, of which the first three deal with the position of the individual in domestic labour law, i.e. with his access to work (Articles 1, 9, 10), his conditions of employment (Articles 2, 3, 4), and the protection of children, young persons and women (Articles 7, 8). A further – fourth – group seeks to establish minimum principles for the organisation of collective labour relations: freedom of organisation, the promotion of collective bargaining, the freedom to take collective action (Articles 5 and 6). These four groups of provisions, then, incorporate standards of what we commonly call labour law. In a broader sense one may also consider as an object of labour law the substance of a fifth group of international obligations (Articles 18 and 19): this seeks to guarantee for the nationals of all Contracting Parties a liberal admission to gainful occupation[7] (not only to employment) in the territories of the other Contracting

Parties, and, in a large variety of ways, to secure to migrant workers and their families minimum rights of protection and assistance, but – needless to say – this, like the corresponding principle in Part I, falls far short of the provisions of Articles 48ff. of the Treaty of Rome and of the Regulations passed to implement this part of the Treaty.

To this extent, then, the "Social Charter" may be called a "Workers' Charter",[8] but the remainder of the obligations under the Charter, seven out of the 19 Articles of its Second Part – that is, the sixth group of provisions – is totally different. This is a series of undertakings to maintain a number of general standards of social policy (Articles 11-17), such as protection of health, social security, social and medical assistance, welfare services, training, rehabilitation and resettlement of the disabled, protection of the family, protection of mothers and children.

All these are minimum standards. The Charter must, as I have said, be seen in the context of the European Convention on Human Rights and Fundamental Freedoms, and even if the Charter did not expressly say so in its Article 32, it would follow *ex natura rerum* that its provisions do not prejudice those of domestic law or of another Treaty under which the protected persons enjoy more favourable treatment.

In addition to these six groups of specific undertakings there is one which is incumbent on any Contracting Party whatever provisions it has otherwise selected for ratification. This (Article 20(5)) is to maintain a system of labour inspection "appropriate to national conditions". In view of the existing vast differences in administrative structures this qualification was inevitable – think only of the varying distribution of functions between central and local authorities, – and only a principle remains whose observance would, in a critical case, not be easy to enforce in practice. What matters here, as so often in international documents, is the enunciation of a required policy rather than the practical possibility of its implementation through international action.

(*f*) Like the General Principles in Part I, the positive legal obligations in Part II are formulated in terms of guarantees of subjective rights, rights of individuals, and, in one case, that of the provisions on collective bargaining in Article 6, of collective entities.[9] Nevertheless, it is clear that at least some of them have the intended effect of imposing on the Contracting Parties certain rules of social, economic, and administrative organisation. This is true of the provision on labour inspection in Article 20(5), it is equally true of the provisions on employment services, vocational guidance and vocational training (Articles 1, 9, 10, 15), and most certainly of the rules on social policy in general, on health and welfare services, social security, and social assistance (Articles 11-17). Consequently, it is one of the obligations of the relevant organs of the Council of Europe charged with the duty of supervising the application of the Charter, to make themselves acquainted with the administrative arrangements of the States Parties to the Charter. More than that: the rules on what I have called "access to work", the first of the six groups I have sought do distinguish, affect the basis of the economy. The promise (Article 1(1) to achieve and to maintain "as high and stable level of employment as possible, with a view to the attainment of full employment" touches the core of economic policy, and the accompanying promise to "protect effectively the right of the worker to earn his living in an occupation freely entered upon" goes to the root of the organisation of the labour market, and *inter alia*, embodies the prohibition of compulsory labour – experience has shown that even in the most advanced countries its observance is by no means a matter of course, especially not in the maritime services.[10]

(g) In another respect to which I have already alluded in connection with Part I the undertakings given by a ratifying State are of two different kinds: some of the provisions of the Charter make it incumbent on a State to take certain action and to do so immediately, e.g. "to issue safety and health regulations" with regard to working conditions (Article 3(1)), to "recognise the right of men and women workers to equal pay for work of equal value" (Article 4(3)), to provide that the minimum age of employment shall be 15 years (Article 7(1)) or that before and after childbirth women enjoy a leave of at least 12 weeks (Article 8(1)). To show that it has implemented such provisions (and they are the majority of the rules in Part II of the Charter), a State must be able to point to a state of affairs which has been achieved, a rule enacted, an institution created, a right conferred – in short a result produced. This is what French legal doctrine with a pungent and almost untranslatable word calls an *"obligation de résultat"*. Its opposite is the obligation to embark on a course of action with a view to achieving a result, and to do so by employing all the means reasonably available, e.g. to aim at a high and stable level of employment (Article 1(1)), progressively to reduce working hours (Article 2(1),[11] to "endeavour to raise progressively the system of social security to a higher level" (Article 12(3)), to "simplify existing formalities" (of admission to gainful occupation) and to "liberalise" regulations governing employment of foreign

workers (Article 18(2, 3)). These are what the French[12] call *"obligations de moyens"*, and this distinction between the duty to guarantee a result and the duty to take steps towards achieving it dominates the nature of the evidence a government has to produce to satisfy the organs of the Council that it has lived up to its duties. It corresponds precisely to the distinction in English law between, say, the obligations of a seller of goods, and those of an employee or an independent contractor, such as a professional man. For the work of the supervisory organs it is fundamental.

(h) On a previous occasion I have published some comments on that aspect of the Charter which concerns collective labour relations.[13] Here I should like to add a few comments on the provisions about conditions of individual employment, and more especially on some of the most problematical provisions of the Charter, viz. those on the right to what the Charter calls a "fair remuneration" (*rémunération équitable*) (Article 4). The application of this rule of "fair remuneration" has confronted the supervising organs of the Council of Europe with some of their most difficult tasks. The Charter says that:

> with a view to ensuring the effective exercise of the right to a fair remuneration, the Contracting Parties undertake to recognise the right of workers to a remuneration such as will give them and their families a decent standard of living.

How does one define a "decent standard of living" (*un niveau de vie décent*)? The concept is quite indeterminate, and it is not in the least clear whether for example, the standard of "decency" is to be taken from the general conditions of a particular country or from an (assumed) general standard prevailing throughout the area of application of the Charter. Is that which everyone would admire as a very "decent" standard of living in Sicily necessarily an even tolerably decent standard in Sweden? The whole Pandora box of "regional" problems is opened by this innocent looking (and very badly drafted) provision of the Charter. But this is only one aspect of the right to a "fair remuneration". Apart from some concrete and precise obligations referring to overtime pay, periods of notice, and restrictions on deductions from wages, the rule of "fair remuneration" also incorporates the "right of men and women workers to equal pay for work of equal value" – clearly the most far reaching and revolutionary provision of the whole Charter. One must observe that the fundamental social transformation which this implies is viewed by the Charter not as a process but an event: if you take the wording of the Charter *au pied de la lettre* each country which ratifies this provision (Article 4, No. 3) violates the Charter if men and women do not actually receive equal pay for work of equal value. It is an *"obligation de résultat"*, not an *"obligation de moyens"*, and in this respect different from the corresponding I.L.O. Convention No. 100 of 1953.[14] The United Kingdom has now ratified Convention No. 100, but it has exempted Article 4(3) from its ratification of the Charter. What else could it have done, considering that Parliament provided for five years of implementation for the similar principle laid down in the Equal Pay Act of 1970 which will not be operative until the end of 1975? One must remember that this obligation imposed by the Charter and by the I.L.O. Convention No. 100 of 1953 goes much further than the rule of "equal pay for equal work" in Article 119 of the Treaty of Rome, even if interpreted in the light of the recent Council Directive 65/117 of 10 February 1975, and who does not know of the difficulties the Commission has had in seeing even that implemented by the Member States of the EEC?[15] The Charter and the I.L.O. Convention do, but the Treaty of Rome does not, in effect presuppose the evolution of a general system of job evaluation. But whilst the wording of the I.L.O. Convention appears to recognise that this can only be an evolution, the Charter requires it as a *fait accompli*. The inevitable result is that a State Member of the Council of Europe which has ratified Article 4(3) of the Charter and which is developing a scheme of job evaluation with the loyal intent eventually to give effect to the principle of the Article is technically in breach, as long as this necessarily complex and expensive evolution is not complete. It illustrates the need for a cautious formulation of international standards of social policy.

(i) Let me turn to some of the problems of ratification. It would have been unrealistic to make the operation of this vast machinery of rules and principles dependent on its acceptance by Member States as a whole. After all, the substance of the Charter represents a whole corpus of I.L.O. Conventions and Recommendations, and each Member of the I.L.O. decides separately for each of these international transactions whether it wants or does not want to accept it.

This explains the principle of selective ratification to which I have already had to refer. It is a little complex because it combines three rules: viz. that each State may choose the obligations it wants to accept (principle of selection), that it must accept a minimum number of obligations (principle of the quantitative minimum), and that it must select a minimum number from a particular group of obligations (principle of the qualitative minimum). The matter is of very great practical importance. Of the ten nations which up to now have ratified the Charter, only one (Italy) has accepted the whole of it – all others have made use of the power to select. I have already said that e.g. the United Kingdom has refused to commit itself to the rule of equal pay for work of equal value, let me add that Austria (which like Germany denies the right to strike of a certain group of public employees known as *Beamte*) has not ratified the provision on the right to take collective action. Needless to say the supervision of the implementation of the Charter is not made easier by the principle of selection, yet I am convinced that it would have been totally unrealistic not to adopt it.

The principle of the quantitative minimum is double barrelled. Part II of the Charter consists, as we know, of nineteen Articles. A State must accept at least ten of these. Many (not all) of the Articles consist of two or more numbered Paragraphs. There are altogether 72 of these, of which the ratification must extend to at least 45 (Article 20(1)(c)).[16]

The principle of the qualitative minimum[17] means that the authors of the Charter ascribed special importance to seven of the nineteen Articles. It is interesting to see that these are taken from four of the six groups I have tried to distinguish, but do not include provisions on conditions of employment or protection of women or young persons. The right to work (Article 1) is one of these fundamental clauses, and so are the two clauses (Articles 5 and 6) which make up the contribution of the Charter to collective labour relations. Three of these fundamental provisions are taken from the group about social policy: the right to social security (Article 12), to social and medical assistance (Article 13), and the right of the family to social, legal and economic protection through family allowances, tax benefits, housing etc. (Article 16). Lastly, the protection and assistance of migrant workers and their families (Article 19) is regarded as fundamental. Each State must ratify at least five out of these seven Articles. It can therefore eschew (if it wishes to do so) the guarantees of freedom of organisation, collective bargaining and collective action. But all the ten States have in fact accepted them though – I have mentioned the case of Austria – not necessarily in their entirety. (Article 20(1)(b)).[18]

(j) A State implements the provisions of the Charter through legislation and through administrative or judicial practice. But this is not always necessarily the case. As is well known, it is now established practice that a

State Member of the I.L.O. can implement the provisions of a ratified Convention through collective bargaining practice which, if sufficiently comprehensive, obviates legislation.[19] This rule has, with regard to a number of its provisions, been codified in the Charter (Article 33), unquestionably under the influence of the I.L.O. representatives who participated in its drafting. In States in which certain matters are normally left to collective agreements "or are normally carried out otherwise than by law", no legislation is needed to implement the provisions dealing with these matters, provided they are in fact applied through such agreements or other means. The provisions which may be implemented in this manner include those on working hours, holidays, weekly rest periods and vocational training. The same or a similar system applies (Article 4) to all provisions on remuneration, including the equal pay rule, and the rules on overtime pay, deductions and notice. These can be implemented through collective agreements, statutory wage fixing machinery "or by other means appropriate to national conditions".

Moreover – and this is a kindred, but different point – there are a number of provisions of the Charter whose application to all workers would have been a pedantic and unrealistic requirement. It is therefore provided (Article 33) that the rules on hours, holidays, weekly rest periods and vocational training are considered as effectively implemented if they are in fact applied "to the great majority of the workers concerned", no matter whether this is done through legislation, collective bargaining or other means. The same applies (see the Appendix) to the rule against night work by persons under 18, and to the rule against deductions from wages (whilst the remaining provisions on remuneration must be applied to all workers).

(k) Obviously those responsible for the drafting of the Charter had to open to the Parties certain avenues of escape. There are in fact two, one of which refers to war and public emergency (Article 30) whilst the other, Article 31, which is inspired by the Universal Declaration of Human Rights, is of far greater importance in practice. This permits restrictions or limitations of the rights and principles of Part I or of their exercise under Part II, provided they are

> prescribed by law and are necessary in a democratic society for the protection of the rights and freedoms of others or for the protection of public interest,[20] national security, public health, or morals (*"pour protéger l'ordre public, la sécurité nationale, la santé publique ou les bonnes moeurs"*)

Clearly, a convicted prisoner has no "right to earn his living in an occupation freely entered upon" (Article 1(2)), but some situations are less simple. It is now only a matter of history, but under the Industrial Relations Act, 1971, I could not help reflecting on the extent to which the Cooling Off and Strike Ballot provisions were, in relation to the right to strike, covered by this – a knotty problem. I mention it here to illustrate the kind of problem linked with the application of this rule of the Charter. Restrictions of stoppages in the health services, in the police, and I think also in public services such as transport and power supply, seem to me to be covered by this clause. The Charter confirms in its Appendix that the exercise of the right to strike may be regulated by law, provided that any restrictions on the right going beyond those in the Charter itself can be justified under the terms of Article 31 to which I have referred.

II. The Charter and European Community Law

Let me now briefly compare the effect and the scope of the Charter with those of the social policy and labour law provisions in the European Community Treaties, and also say a word about the way the Charter may in practice impinge upon their application. The two bodies of rules are totally different in purpose and in effect: but this is just the reason why they may supplement each other.

(a) The outstanding difference is in their effect. The Charter gives rise to international obligations incurred by the States Parties to it in their relation to the Council of Europe. But unlike the Treaties and law made under the Treaties,[21] the Charter has no "supra-national" effect: it does not create municipal law within the States Parties to it, at least it does not do so *proprio vigore*. Like those of most of the I.L.O. Conventions,[22] most of its provisions are framed in such a way as to show that they are not intended or designed to be self-executing, i.e. "directly" to be law enforceable by the courts of the Member States. Moreover, even if they purported to be self-executing, any such direct effect could not emanate from the powers of the Council of Europe in virtue of its own Statute (here lies the big difference from the Community Treaties), but in a given State only from its own Constitution. The Constitution of any country may provide that Treaties have the force of law (in so far as their provisions are, by their own purpose and wording, self-executing), and, more than that, it may

ascribe to such Treaty provisions the force of a "higher law", [23] giving them that "priority" which may invalidate such subsequent legislation as is incompatible with them. But by the mere act of ratifying the Charter, even in so far as it can be regarded as "self-executing" (e.g. Article 5 (first sentence), Article 6(4), Article 7(1), Article 8(2), Article 19(6)), a State does not incorporate its provisions in its own legal system, except to the extent to which that legal system contains constitutional principles giving it the force of law. There is thus nothing to correspond to the direct effect of the European Treaties or e.g. of Regulations, and as we now know[24] certain Directives made under Article 189 of the Treaty of Rome. I say nothing here of course of the "reflex effect" which the Charter, and especially its First Part may have as a set of "general principles" – I have already referred to this. This is, as I have mentioned, not the direct effect of a legal rule as such, but the use of the legal rule as evidence for the existence of a general principle which it crystallises, and thus quite different from the incorporation of the European Treaties and of law made under them in the municipal laws of the Member States. The absence of any "direct" effect of this kind is *ex abundante cautela* expressed in the Appendix to Part III of the Charter which says:

> It is understood that the Charter contains legal obligations of an international character, the application of which is submitted solely to the supervision provided for in Part IV hereof,

and not, therefore, to that of the courts of any Member State. This Appendix forms an integral part of the Charter (Article 38). Nevertheless a number of writers in the Federal Republic[25] take the view that Article 6 para. 4 (which guarantees the freedom to strike) overrides the German principles denying that freedom e.g. to *Beamte* and indeed to all except trade unions and for all except certain defined purposes. That these principles are incompatible with the Charter has been repeatedly laid down by the Committee of Experts and is scarcely open to doubt. But this of course does not mean that, as a matter of German law, they have thereby been abrogated. Here is the fundamental difference between international and supra-national law.

To take two further concrete examples: the provision of Article 119 of the Treaty of Rome may, however ironic this may sound, have introduced into the laws of the Member States the rule that men and women receive equal pay for equal work. I do not think any argument to the contrary can be derived from the recent Council Directive 75/117. The matter is doubt-ful and now *sub judice*. Article 4 para. 3 of the Charter, however, which provides for equal pay for work of equal value has clearly had no effect on the municipal laws of the States Parties to the Charter. Or compare the provisions on the Common Labour Market in Articles 48ff. of the Treaty of Rome and of the Regulations and Directives made to implement them with the corresponding Articles 18 and 19 of Part II of the Charter. That the former, even some of the Directives, have a "direct" effect is clear – have we not seen it quite recently in the *Van Duyn* Case?[26] But no such effect attaches to the provisions of the Charter. This may mean that the rights of a national of a Community Member State, e.g. of an Italian, may, in the territory of another Community Member State which is also a Party to the Charter, e.g. in the United Kingdom, differ greatly from those of a national of a State Party to the Charter which is not a Community Member, e.g. a Cypriot. If both lawfully reside and regularly work in the United Kingdom, the United Kingdom is under an international obliga-tion to treat both on a footing of equality with United Kingdom citizens (see Appendix to the Charter). But the Treaty of Rome gives to the Italian a personal right which, in the event of discrimination, he can enforce through the appropriate remedies, whilst the Cypriot would have no right to complain, and all that could happen in his case would be that the Committee of Ministers of the Council of Europe would recommend to the United Kingdom Government to remedy the situation. Whether the express restriction of the scope of the Charter to nationals of Contracting Parties (which even excludes nationals of Members of the Council of Europe who have not ratified the Charter) yields to any most favoured nations clauses in other Treaties is a difficult problem of international law which cannot here be discussed.

(b) In so far, then, as the Treaties deal with social policy or empower the Community organs to make new law in that field, their effect is far stronger than that of the Charter. But the scope within which the Treaties seek to regulate labour law and social policy or enable the Community organs to do so is much more limited. Of course, the Community organs have deployed and are deploying a far-reaching and beneficial activity in these areas. But the Treaties do not and cannot profess to regulate large areas of labour law or of social policy as the I.L.O. and the Council of Europe do. The law-making powers of the Community organs are very important, but they are strictly confined to those matters which are germane to the

Community purposes as defined in Article 2 of the Treaty of Rome. They cannot regulate labour relations the way they can regulate, say, competition and monopoly, or the movement of goods and of capital, or agricultural prices. Exceptions apart,[27] Community law has nothing to say about collective relations between management and labour – peaceful or hostile – or about conditions of employment, such as wages.[28] It has a great deal to say about the organisation of the common labour market (Article 48ff.), including the social security of migrant workers, about measures to promote mobility, such as the European Social Fund (EEC Treaty, Article 123ff., and see the corresponding provisions under the Coal and Steel Treaty, Article 56). These are all matters directly or indirectly affecting the labour market as such – but there are others, such as equal pay for equal work (Article 119 EEC) to which I have referred more than once, and the at least potentially important power of the Commission (formerly the High Authority) over wages under the Coal and Steel Treaty (Article 68 which has no equivalent under the Treaty of Rome). Nor should we forget that the provisions on the harmonisation of company law (Article 54(3)(g)) of the Treaty of Rome are interpreted as a basis for directives on the participation of unions or employees in the corporate organs of commercial companies,[29] or that Article 235 of the Treaty of Rome is considered as a source of a far-reaching residual law-making power and perhaps as a possible basis of labour legislation even beyond the prospect of a European Company Statute embodying a blueprint for workers' co-determination.[30] Yet, though we cannot predict future developments nor gauge the extent to which Article 235 will eventually be allowed to override legislative limitations inherent in the main body of the Treaties, we can say that they are not and cannot be a basis for a comprehensive unification of labour law or social legislation in Europe. In saying this I am not ignoring the potentialities ascribed in Community practice to the "harmonisation" Article 100 of the Treaty of Rome, the principal instrument, it seems, for the implementation of the Community's Social Action Programme of 1974, and the basis for the recent Council Directives 75/117 and 75/129 on the application of the principle of equal pay for men and women, and on consultation about, and notification of, collective redundancies. These may, as Article 100 requires, "directly affect the establishment and functioning of the common market" (see also Article 3h), but of how many attempts to legislate on labour relations or conditions can this be said?[31]

In short: the great actual and even greater potential importance of the European Communities for the development of a European labour law and a European body of social legislation does not stem from the legal powers of the Communities to make new law. It does stem from the fact of European symbiosis and from the vastly increased incentive by voluntary action to arrive at a harmonisation of labour law and social legislation in Europe. In this I see a great difference between the activities of the Council of Europe and of their results (of which for our purpose the Charter is much the most important) and those of the Communities and their organs. The Community organs can make law in selected areas of labour law and social policy, areas more restricted than those accessible to the Council of Europe, but where they do make law, they do so with far greater effect than the work of the Council of Europe can achieve. The norm-making power of the Council of Europe is wider, but the supra-national sanctions available to the Communities, are stronger than those attaching to the international obligations based on the European Social Charter.

(c) The decisive element in the effect of the Communities on labour law and social policy in Europe is, I have suggested, not the law of the Communities or the law that can be made by their organs, but the fact of economic and political symbiosis, and this is clearly the view taken by the Treaty of Rome itself. It would of course be ridiculous to conclude from the limitation of the law-making powers of Council and Commission in these fields that they are condemned to a passive attitude. A picture painted in such contours and colours would be a caricature of what is happening and what, under the terms of the Treaty, is supposed to be happening. The Commission is extremely active, but Articles 117 and 118 of the Treaty – the decisive bases of these activities – do not envisage the Commission as an organ of legislation, but as an instrument promoting voluntary co-ordination. The scope of these provisions is very wide indeed. It is the duty of the Commission to "promote close cooperation between member states in the social field", and the illustrative list in Article 118, designed as an aid towards the definition of the "social field", includes practically the entire range of topics we commonly associate with labour law and social legislation, from "employment" via "labour law and working conditions" and "vocational training" to "social security", "prevention of occupational accidents and diseases" and "occupational hygiene" and lastly to the right of association and to collective bargaining. In all these matters it is by no means the task of the Commission to legislate – far from it – but to keep contact, to make studies, to deliver opinions, to arrange consultations: in short to persuade, not to compel, to assist

Member States in acting autonomously, not to take action so as to impose on them arrangements which, to them, would be heteronomous. Nothing illustrates the type of real significance which the Communities have in our field better than the immensely valuable Annual Reports on the Social Situation in the Community States which, in virtue of Article 122, the Commission has published since the Treaty came into force.

In a comparatively narrow area the legal impact of Community law on the labour and social legislation of the Member Countries is thus very intensive, much more so than that of the European Social Charter, but in a very wide area it is practically non-existent, whilst the political effect of the coordinating activities of the Commission may be very far-reaching. This policy-formulating power makes up in the extensity of its scope what it lacks in the legal intensity of its effect. The principal characteristic of the Chapter of the Treaty of Rome which bears the heading "Social Provisions"[32] is that its reach is enormous, and its legal effect is practically nil. All the greater its political importance.

The place of the European Social Charter between the area of Community law and the area of Community co-ordinating functions is thus determined. It has nothing like the legal impact of Community law in its narrow sphere, and more legal impact than the work of the Commission in its co-ordinating capacity. It can thus be said that in this way it supplements the legal rules as well as the extra-legal functions developed within the Communities.

(d) It is however possible that the Charter may have a further relation to Community law which is at the same time more subtle and more concrete. We have seen that, in its Part I, it contains a set of "General Principles", and, even apart from Part I, such "General Principles" may be found in at least some of the specific obligations codified in Part II. In any event there can be no doubt that, like the European Convention on Human Rights and Fundamental Freedoms, the European Social Charter is a source, or perhaps better, a crystallisation of "fundamental rights".

We all know that the European Court of Justice has now a *jurisprudence constante* to the effect that "fundamental rights form an integral part of the general principles of law, the observance of which it ensures". This is a quotation from what seems to be the most recent relevant case – *Nold* v. *Commission*[33] – where the Court continues:

In safeguarding these rights, the Court is bound to draw inspiration from the

constitutional traditions common to the Member States, and it cannot therefore uphold measures which are incompatible with fundamental rights recognised and protected by the Constitutions of those States. Similarly international
treaties for the protection of human rights on which the Member States have
collaborated or of which they are signatories can supply guidelines which should
be followed within the framework of Community Law.

Inevitably the European Convention on Human Rights and its Additional
Protocol are mentioned in this connection, and the Universal Declaration
of Human Rights belongs, and the United Nations Covenants of 1966 on
Civil and Political Rights and on Economic, Social and Cultural Rights
will, when in force, belong, to the same context. But so, unquestionably,
does the European Social Charter.[34]

Thus the Charter may gain importance in Community law – not of
course as a source of legal rules to be applied by the European Court, but as
an "indication" of those "human rights" to which the Court gives effect.

To take the two most important examples: one cannot doubt that the
right to choose an occupation (i.e. the prohibition of compulsory labour)
codified in Article 2(1) and the right of association codified in Article 5 of
Part II of the Charter are among those rights: they are also two of the "principles" proclaimed in Part I. But what about a situation in which, whilst
appearing in Part II, a fundamental right is not enunciated among the
"principles" in the First Part? This is the case of the right to strike. Part I
merely says that "all workers and employers have the right to bargain
collectively", but Article 6, para. 4 in Part II makes it incumbent on
Contracting Parties "with a view to ensuring the effective exercise of the
right to bargain collectively", to "recognise" (subject to certain limitations) "the right of workers and employers to collective action in cases of
conflicts of interest, including the right to strike". If called upon to do so,
the European Court may perhaps see in this reference to the freedom to
strike its elevation to one of the "fundamental rights" to which it gives
effect.

III. The Application of the Charter Compared with that of I.L.O. Conventions

   (a) From what I have said it is clear that the substance of the obligations
incurred by Member States of the Council of Europe largely coincides
with that of obligations incurred under I.L.O. Conventions. Although, as
Dr. Valticos points out,[35] the latter are more detailed and more precise,

there is the closest possible affinity between the two *corpora* of Rules – so much so that it is general practice to allow the Parties to the Charter in their biennial Reports about its implementation to refer to the corresponding Reports made to the I.L.O. on ratified Conventions to the International Labour Office. To almost all of the provisions of Part II of the Charter (there are exceptions[36]) there correspond one or more I.L.O. Conventions or Recommendations.[37] Not only did the work of the I.L.O. inspire the Charter, but, as said before, the I.L.O. participated in its actual drafting. More than that, according to Article 26 of the Charter a representative of the International Labour Office participates in a consultative capacity in the deliberations of the Committee of Experts which, as I have already mentioned and shall further point out, has the task of supervising the implementation of the Charter by the States which are Parties to it. This participation of the I.L.O. representative in the work of the Committee is a matter of very great importance: it constantly enables the Committee in interpreting the Charter to make use of the rich experience accumulated at Geneva in the application of I.L.O. Convention.

It is however also clear that in one respect at least the Charter is quite different from the corpus of I.L.O. Conventions: the latter is a steadily growing body of Rules, whilst the Charter is fixed once and for all. Not only does the I.L.O. add to the existing body of Conventions every year – the Annual Conference also can and frequently does amend existing Conventions or replace them by others in the light of past experience.[38] The work of the I.L.O. is a flexible corpus, whilst the Charter is rigid.

To a certain extent the principle of selective ratification makes up for this, especially because the Charter enables a Party subsequently to add to its ratification provisions of the Charter not previously ratified (Article 20(3)) or withdraw its ratification of one or more of its provisions, as long as the number of ratified provisions remains within the prescribed minima (Article 37(2)).[39] This may be said to introduce an element of flexibility as far as the individual State Party to the Charter is concerned. Yet any amendment of the Charter as a whole requires acceptance by all Contracting Parties, i.e. all those Members of the Council of Europe which have ratified the Charter (Article 36) – whilst the adoption of a Convention requires only a two thirds majority of the votes cast at the I.L.O. Conference (I.L.O. Constitution Article 19(2)).

(b) The principal differences between the Charter and the Conventions of the I.L.O. emerge when we consider the methods of safeguarding their

implementation. These differences are rooted in those between the Constitutions of the I.L.O. and of the Council of Europe. The I.L.O.'s concern is, as the Preamble to its Constitution says, the improvement of the conditions of labour, and its organisation is geared to that purpose. The Council of Europe is a multi-purpose organisation and social policy is only one, though one of the essential, aspects of its activities.[40] Hence the tri-partite structure which is one of the principal characteristics of the I.L.O., i.e. the representation of Governments, of employers, and of workers in the Governing Body (Article 7 of the I.L.O. Constitution) and in the Conference (Article 3), has no parallel in the Council of Europe. Within the I.L.O., the General Conference, i.e. the nearest equivalent to a "Parliamentary" body, is the ultimate legislative organ, but the Consultative Assembly of the Council of Europe[41] has, as its name implies, no decision-making power. This vests in the supreme organ of the Council of Europe, viz. the Committee of Ministers. This is a group representing the Foreign Offices of the Member States[42] and is thus very different from the tri-partite Conference and from the tri-partite Governing Body of the I.L.O., a point of some relevance in practice. Moreover, it is a body which can at best make "Recommendations"[43] to the Member States, there is no ultimate decision-making body. It is true that in the origin of the Charter a "tri-partite" element was of decisive importance. Its draft was produced by the Government Social Committee – a sub-committee of the Committee of Ministers which in fact consists of the representatives of the Ministries of Labour. But, at the request of the Council of Europe, the I.L.O. organised in 1958 at Strasbourg a tri-partite conference which amended the draft in numerous respects, and – with a number of amendments proposed by the Consultative Assembly – most of these were incorporated in the final text.[44] Yet, if one contemplates the operation rather than the origin of the Charter, one can see no more than a marginal function of the tripartite element, and thus a vital contrast to the I.L.O. This will emerge from a consideration of the control mechanisms of the two organisations.

(c) The object of these mechanisms is the same in the I.L.O. and in the Council of Europe. It is to scrutinise the measures which a State has taken to implement its international obligations under an I.L.O. Convention[45] or under the Charter. The procedure provided for in the Charter (Part IV, Articles 21-29) is, as far as possible, modelled on the pattern prescribed by the I.L.O. Constitution or – more importantly – developed by the administrative practice of the International Labour Office. As far as possible –

this is the gist of the matter. As a result of the differences in the structures of the two organisations (themselves easily explicable in view of their different purposes) it was possible only within certain limits.

As under the I.L.O. Constitution Article 22, so under the Charter Article 21, a State which has become a Party to a Convention or to the Charter must send regular biennial Reports concerning the application of its provisions to the organisation – the text of the I.L.O. Constitution requires annual reports, but for many years *dira necessitas* has made a dead letter of this requirement.[46] The provisions I have quoted say that the I.L.O. Governing Body or the Committee of Ministers of the Council of Europe are to determine the form of these Reports, but in fact the Committee of Ministers has delegated this duty to the Committees of Experts which I am about to discuss. Before doing so, I should add that, according to the I.L.O. Constitution[47] the Members of the I.L.O. also undertake to make certain reports on non-ratified Conventions and on Recommendations, and that a similar obligation is imposed by the Charter Article 22 on Parties to it with respect to those provisions of its Part II which they have not accepted. But this depends on a further decision of the Committee of Ministers as to the provisions with respect to which such Reports shall be requested. No such decision has as yet been made, with the result that Article 22 of the Charter is not or not yet a provision which operates in practice. I must also add that both under the I.L.O. Constitution[48] and under the Charter (Article 23) copies of the Reports must be communicated to the representative organisations on both sides, i.e. those entitled to participate in the I.L.O. Conference or in the Council of Europe to be represented at the Sub-Committee of the Governmental Social Committee to be discussed. This attempt to introduce into the report procedure under the Charter a modest tripartite element has so far not been crowned with much success: the Charter (Article 23(2)) says that the organisations may request their governments to forward to the Council of Europe their comments on the Reports together with the Reports themselves, but up to now the response to this invitation to make the voices of the two sides of industry heard in the proceedings appears to have been meagre.

(d) The actual control mechanism of the I.L.O.[49] provides a paradigmatic example of the divergence between a constitutional text and a constitutional practice, or perhaps of Dicey's "Conventions of the Constitution" on an international plane. No one perusing the text of the I.L.O. Constitution could have the slightest inkling of what in fact happens at Geneva, no

more than anyone reading the Constitution of the United States forwards and backwards would have the shadow of an idea of what is happening in Washington. One of the interesting aspects of the Charter is that its authors – within the limitations imposed by the divergencies between the I.L.O. and the Council of Europe to which I have referred – attempted to codify in a constitutional text important elements of what had been evolved at Geneva through administrative practice.[50]

One of these elements is the dual scrutiny of the governmental Reports by a Committee of Experts and by a Committee of the General Conference. All the text of the Constitution (Article 23) has to say is that the Director-General of the International Labour Office must lay before the Conference a summary of the Reports, and the Committee of Experts as well as the Committee of Conference have been created *via facti*. In his authoritative analysis of these matters Dr. Nicolas Valticos[51] (to whose work I am very heavily indebted) makes it quite clear that in practice the role of the Committee of Experts is far more important than that of the Conference Committee which, normally, has no time to discuss more than about 10 per cent of the Experts' Comments.

The Charter expands this dual scrutiny to a quadruple scrutiny. Not only are the Government Reports (in theory together with the comments of the organisations on both sides) examined by a Committee of Experts (Article 24) and by the Consultative Assembly (Article 28), i.e. in fact by a committee it has elected. The Reports made by the Governments and the *Conclusions* of the Committee of Experts are subject to the further scrutiny of a Committee consisting of representatives of the States Parties to the Charter and appointed by them for this purpose – normally representatives of the Ministries of Labour. This Committee exercises the functions allocated by Article 27 of the Charter to what there appears as a Subcommittee of the Governmental Social Committee of the Council of Europe (in which all Members of the Council are represented, whether they are Parties to the Charter or not). The substitution of the independent Governmental Committee directly representing the Contracting Parties for a Sub-Committee of the Governmental Social Committee representing all Members of the Council shows how "Conventions of the Constitution" develop even in a body of comparatively recent origin such as the Council of Europe. To the meetings of this Committee "no more than two international organisations of employers and no more than two international trade Union organisations" are invited "to be represented as observers in a consultative capacity" – this is the marginal, one might say the vestigial, role the tripartite idea is allowed to play in the control mechanism of the Council of Europe. In view of the content of the Charter it can well be understood that international social welfare organisations may also be consulted by this Committee.

The Experts formulate their opinions – the English text of the Charter uses the gallicism "conclusions" – the Governmental Committee adds its own *"Conclusions"*, the Consultative Assembly (or its relevant committee) expresses its "views". All this goes – and this is the fourth stage – to the Committee of Ministers (Article 29), i.e. the Foreign Office Representatives, and this decides, by a two-thirds majority of those entitled to sit on it, whether to make any necessary "recommendations" to a Contracting Party to the Charter. No formal "recommendation" has up to now been made.[52]

(e) The emphasis of the procedure in practice is (as in the analogous case of the I.L.O.) very much on the work of the Committee of Experts of whom there must be no more than seven (Article 25). They are nominated by the Contracting Parties and appointed for six years by the Committee of Ministers. They must be "independent", "of the highest integrity", and "of recognised competence in international social questions". They are in fact judges and academics, citizens of States Members of the Council of Europe, but not necessarily of States Parties to the Charter: the President, M. Pierre Laroque, Head of the Social Section of the French Conseil d'Etat, has been a member and the President of the Committee from the beginning of its work in 1965, but it was only in 1973 that France ratified the Charter.

This Committee meets three or four times a year, and sometimes more frequently at Strasbourg for about a week. Its first task was to settle an elaborate questionnaire on each of the 72 provisions contained in the 19 Articles of Part II of the Charter. This questionnaire was approved by the Committee of Ministers: and the answers to it are the "form" in which, according to Article 21 of the Charter, the Governments must make their biennial Reports. In many cases the States concerned are also Parties to I.L.O. Conventions covering the same or a similar area as provisions of the Charter: if so, the questionnaire expressly allows them to furnish copies of their reports to the I.L.O. in lieu of a separate report to the Council of Europe. Since the Reports are biennial, the work of the Committee of Experts takes the form of "cycles" or "rounds" of scrutinies: at the moment it has reached the Fourth Cycle. The regularity of this rotation is however incomplete because three Members of the Council of Europe ratified the Charter at differing intervals after the Committee had started its work in 1966. These were Cyprus, Austria and France. Previously the Charter had been ratified by Denmark, Germany (Federal Republic), Ireland, Italy, Norway, Sweden, and the United Kingdom. The remaining Members of the Council of Europe: Belgium, Greece, Iceland, Luxembourg, Malta, the Netherlands, Switzerland and Turkey are not yet Parties to the Charter.

The work of the Committee is based on the careful, painstaking and thorough analysis of the governmental Reports by the Social Affairs Division of the Secretariat under its head, Dr. Hans Wiebringhaus. Representatives of the Social Affairs Division and of the Legal Division of the Secretariat always participate in the meetings of the Committee. So, as already mentioned, does a representative of the International Labour Office (see Article 26 of the Charter).

The governmental Reports are, as one has to expect, very unequal in value and comprehensiveness.[53] The Committee of Experts insists on factual as well as legal information, and especially on statistical data to show the actual working of the legal rules and institutions. To see how far a State has in fact given effect to the standards of social policy required by the Charter, it is by no means sufficient to know what legislation it has enacted. One knows too much about the tendency in some countries – not necessarily in Europe – to use high-sounding social legislation for political propaganda purposes to be satisfied with a communication of texts of statutes. In fact the Committee frequently receives summaries of judicial decisions and of administrative action, as well as statistics on collective agreements, on the effect of social security and welfare measures, etc.

It is in the light of the comprehensive information contained in the answers to the questionnaire that the Committee seeks to arrive at a conclusion as to whether the State has or has not satisfied its obligations under such provisions as it has ratified or whether the information supplied does not suffice to decide whether it has or has not done so, and what further information is needed. The conclusions are for each provision prepared by a *Rapporteur*: each Member of the Committee acts as *Rapporteur* for a number of Articles and for a number of countries and there is also a *Rapporteur Général*.

What emerges from all this is a fairly bulky document containing the Committee's *Conclusions,* arranged both by subject matter (the Articles) and by countries. The *Conclusions* are transmitted by the Secretary-General of the Council of Europe to the Consultative Assembly (Article 28), but in practice this is not done until the Governmental Committee has also formulated its *Conclusions,* and then the two sets of *Conclusions* go to the Consultative Assembly together. This practice – another example of an extra-textual constitutional development – was adopted by a decision of the Committee of Ministers at the request of the Consultative Assembly.[54] At the moment when they are thus transmitted to the Assembly, the *Conclusions* of the Committee of Experts are made accessible to the public in English and French, the two languages of the Council. As I have said, no formal "Recommendations" have as yet been made by the Committee of Ministers to any Government in the light of these *Conclusions,* although in its Resolution passed in May 1974 on the basis of the second set of *Conclusions* of the two relevant committees the Committee of Ministers does refer to the need for Parties to the Charter to take "action" "to make their national legislation ... comply with obligations deriving from the Charter". The reasons why, despite an express reference to the relevant Article 29 in the Resolution of May 1974, the Committee of Ministers has up to now not been able to go to the length of making formal Recommendations may perhaps have to be found in the fact that the attitudes of the Experts and those of the Representatives of the Ministeries of Labour are not on all occasions necessarily strictly identical. In the circumstances it is hardly surprising that a subtle shift in the functions of the *Conclusions* of the Experts seems to be taking place. From being an incidental stage in the supervision procedure, mere suggestions to the Committee of Ministers, the appear to be gaining a significance and a considerable authority of their own. They are communicated to all the States Parties to the Charter, and in some of these States the comments of the Committee of Experts have already clearly had an effect on legislative and administrative practice.[55] There has developed a *jurisprudence* (in the French sense) on the interpretation of the Charter. From the point of view of "jurisprudence" (in the English sense) it is quite fascinating to see how a – if the word must be used – "quasi-judicial" body tacitly and instinctively develops a rule of *stare decisis* without anyone in the world compelling it to do so. This comment on the Charter by a group of trained and skilled experts in social policy, in labour law, in social legislation, based as it is on careful scrutiny and deliberation and often (though not always) on the long experience of the corresponding body within the I.L.O., cannot fail to have the effect of an influential gloss, of an interpretation which, whilst not being "authentic" in the legal sense, is likely to enjoy a very high degree of persuasive authority. Whether and how far it is conducive to further action by other organs of the Council of Europe within the procedure provided by the Charter, is immaterial from this point of view.

Thus, whatever may be the future of the formal procedures provided for in the Charter, and even in the absence of formulated Recommendations by the Committee of Ministers, it is not unreasonable to expect that the Charter, supplemented by the Conclusions of the Committee of Experts may, in the fullness of time, bring about a measure of uniformity in the social and labour policies applied in a large part of Western Europe and of the Community Area in particular.

Since many aspects of labour law and social legislation are clearly outside the competence of the European Community organs, the Charter may thus eventually prove to be a valuable supplement to the law of the European Communities.

Notes

¹   There is a considerable literature on the European Social Charter. For a bibliography see Valticos, *Droit international du travail* (*Traité de droit du travail*, ed. Camerlynck, Vol. 8), 1970, No. 177, p. 159, Note 1. See in particular Valticos, *loc. cit.*, No. 177, and *passim*, also *Mise à Jour* 1973, p. 13; Lyon-Caen, *Droit social européen*, 2nd ed., 1972 (Précis Dalloz), esp. Nos. 113-130, pp. 83ff.; Wiebringhaus, *Annuaire français de droit international*, 1963, 709ff.; 1968, 784ff.; 1973, 928ff.; Rivista di Diritto Europeo, 1972, 169ff.; *The European Social Charter, Its Application and Implementation:* Duplicated Lecture at Edinburgh University, 1974; Kahn-Freund, *Labour Relations and International Standards. Some Reflections on the European Social Charter,* Miscellanea W.J. Ganshof van der Meersch, Vol. I, pp. 132ff., Brussels 1972; Tennfjord, *The European Social Charter, an Instrument of Social Collaboration,* European Yearbook Vol. IX, p. 71; Harris, *The European Social Charter,* 1 C.L.Q. 13(1964), p. 1076; Robertson, *Human Rights in Europe,* 1963, Chap. VIII, pp. 140ff.

²   In the case of the I.L.O. Constitution such General Principles are implied, but not formulated. See Valticos, *Un systeme de contrôle international: La mise en oeuvre des conventions internationales du travail,* Recueil des Cours 1968, I. 311, at 328.

³   Lyon-Caen, *loc. cit.*, No. 114, p. 84.

⁴   On the contrast between rules of law and general principles, there is a considerable literature in France. See especially Boulanger, *Principes genéraux du droit* et droit positif, Etudes G. Ripert, 1950, Vol. 1, pp. 51ff.; Jeanneau, *La nature des principes généraux du droit en droit français,* Contributions françaises au 6ème Conges de Droit comparé, 1962, Edition Cujas; Letourneur, *Les principes généraux du droit dans la jurisprudence du Conseil d'Etat,* Etudes et Documents 1951, pp. 19ff.

⁵   Esser, *Grundsatz und Norm in der richterlichen Fortbildung des Privatrechts,* 3rd ed., Tuebingen 1974.

⁶   *The Model of Rules,* 35 Univ. of Chicago L. Rev. 14 (1967) (also printed in *Essays in Legal Philosophy* (ed. Summers (1969)). See also Tapper, *A Note on Principles,* 34 Mod. L.R. (1971) 628.

⁷   Not the question of entry into the country which is, within the *corpus* of Council of Europe Conventions, governed by the European Convention on Establishment – see Appendix to the European Social Charter.

⁸   This preponderance of the labour law aspect may be due to the decisive influence of the Tri-Partite Conference of 1958 on the Draft of the Charter. See Harris, *loc. cit.* at p. 1078, Note 17. Some provisions of the Charter apply to self-employed as well as employed persons. This is the view of the Committee of Experts, and expressed e.g. in Article 19(10).

⁹   See on this problem my contribution to the Volume in Honour of Prof. Ganshof van der Meersch, *supra* Note 1, at pp. 145ff.

¹⁰   See for details Wiebringhaus, *Annuaire français de droit international,* 1973, at pp. 933ff.

¹¹   The Charter is woefully inadequate at this point. It fails to enact a precise maximum of hours of work, such as the 40-hour week required by the I.L.O. Conventions: see Lyon-Caen, *loc. cit.,* No. 117, p. 86; Harris, *loc. cit.,* p. 1079.

¹²   See e.g. Marty et Raynaud, *Droit civil,* Tome II, Vol. 1 (Sirey 1961), Nos. 468ff., pp. 503ff.; Kahn-Freund, Lévy and Rudden, *A Source-Book on French Law,* (Clarendon Press, 1973), pp. 391ff.

¹³   See above Note 1.

¹⁴   There Article 2, imposes an obligation, "by means appropriate to the methods in operation for determining rates of remuneration" to "promote, and, in so far as is consistent with such methods, ensure the application to all workers of the principle of equal remuneration for men and women for work of equal value", and Article 3 says that job evaluation shall be promoted "where such action will assist in giving effect to the provisions of this Convention".

¹⁵   See e.g. *Seventh General Report on the Activities of the European Communities,* 1973, No. 248, pp. 222ff.

¹⁶   The two requirements (ten Articles and 45 numbered Paragraphs) are, it seems, generally assumed to be alternative and not cumulative (see Valticos, *loc. cit.,* p. 159; Harris, *loc. cit.,* p. 1081, Note 34). The English and French texts (both of which are "equally authoritative") are not strictly identical. Article 20(1)(a) says in English: "provided that the total number of Articles *or* numbered paragraphs by which it is bound is not less than 10 Articles *or* 45 numbered paragraphs"; but in French: "pourvu que le nombre total des articles *et* des paragraphes numérotés qui la lient ne soit pas inférieur à 10 articles *ou* à 45 paragraphes numérotés". Fortunately this question has up to now been, and one hopes it will remain, academic.

¹⁷   The principle of the qualitative minimum (like the entire system of selective ratification) was foreshadowed by Part I of the I.L.O. Convention concerning Minimum Standards of Social Security of 1952 (for which see Valticos, *Droit international du travail, loc. cit.,* No. 421, pp. 393ff.) and, following it, by the European Social Security Code of 1964 (for which see Lyon-Caen, *loc. cit.,* Nos. 136ff., pp. 95ff.)

¹⁸   But, of course, if one of the seven Articles from which the five constituting the qualitative minimum are taken is only partly ratified, it does not count against the minimum: in the case of Austria, Article 6(4) having been excluded, Article 6 did not count against the qualitative minimum, but of course Article 6(1)-(3) counted against the quantitative minimum.

¹⁹   See on this Valticos, *loc. cit.* No. 615, pp. 544ff.; also *Revue critique de droit international privé,* 1955, 27ff.; Jenks, *The Application of International Labour Conventions by Means of Collective Agreements,* Festgabe fuer Makarov, 1958, 197ff.; Preface to *Inter-*

national Labour Code, II.L.O. 1952, Vol. I, LXXVIff.; Kahn-Freund, *Labour and the Law,* 1972, pp. 45ff.

20 It is of special significance that the English equivalent of *ordre public* is not "public policy", but "public interest". This gives rise to the question (not here to be discussed) whether *ordre public* in a document such as the Social Charter is or is not synonymous with *ordre public* in Private International Law (a question, as recent developments suggest, not without significance in European Community law).

21 The leading cases are of course *Van Gend en Loos* v. *Nederlandse Administratie der Belastingen* [1973] ECR 1; *Costa* v. *ENEL* [1964] ECR 585; *Walt Wilhelm* v. *Bundeskartellamt* [1969] C.M.L.R. 100. See for a survey Bebr, *Law of the European Communities and Municipal Law,* 34 Mod.L.R. (1971) 481.

22 On the problem of the internal effect of I.L.O. Conventions see Valticos, Recueil des Cours, *supra,* 1968 I, at pp. 343ff.; *Droit International du Travail,* Nos. 627ff.; Revue critique de droit international privé 1955, pp. 251ff.

23 As e.g. in the Netherlands (Article 66 of the Constitution), in Belgium (*Etat Belge* c. *S.A. Fromagerie Franco-Suisse Le Ski* 27.5.1971, Journal des Tribunaux 3.7.1971), and within certain limits, in France (Article 55 of the Constitution).

24 See e.g. *Grad* v. *Finanzamt Transtein* [1971] C.M.L.R. 1; *Van Duyn* v. *Home Office* [1974] ECR 1337.

25 For references see Soellner, *Arbeitsrecht,* 3rd ed. (1972), pp. 36, 78.

26 *Supra* Note 24.

27 Such as the problem of mass redundancies dealt with in the Council Directive of 17 February 1975 (O.J. 22.2.75) on the basis of the Council Resolution concerning the Social Action Programme of 21 January 1974, O.J. 12.2.74.

28 But here too there are numerous exceptions, e.g. Article 68 of the Coal and Steel Treaty, (see below), the entire problem of "equal pay for equal work", the problem of holidays (see Article 120 of the Treaty of Rome), the effect of mergers etc. on contracts of employment (see Draft Directive in O.J. of 9 September 1974), and, quite generally, problems of safety and health.

29 Fifth Draft Directive, presented by the Commission to the Council on 16 June 1970 (J.O. 1972, C7/11).

30 Statute of European Company: Proposal presented by the Commission to the Council on 30 June 1970. See Lyon-Caen, *loc. cit.,* No. 476.

31 For a succinct analysis of the legal limitations imposed by the Treaties on measures of social policy, and for the gradual evolution – within these legal limits– of a European Social Policy (leading up to the Social Action Programme of 1974) see Valticos, *Droit international du travail,* No. 191, p. 171, and *Mise à jour* 1973, Nos. 191 *bis, ter, quater.* The Social Action Programme (above Note (27)) envisages, *inter alia,* a regulation of working hours and of holidays, but it remains to be seen whether this can be achieved by a directive.

32 Part III, Title III, Chapter I. As the Editors of the *Encyclopedia of European*

Community Law, p. B 10102, note: "Of the articles in this Chapter only Article 119" (equal pay for equal work) "imposes any very specific obligation on anyone" – one might add Article 120 (holidays) also imposes an obligation, but it is anything but "specific".

[33] [1974] ECR 491.

[34] Despite the fact that three Community Members (the Benelux States) have not yet ratified it.

[35] *loc. cit.,* No. 177, p. 160.

[36] Thus Article 6(4) of the Charter (guarantee of right to strike and to lockout) has no equivalent in the I.L.O. corpus. The standards of the Charter are in some respects higher, and in others lower than those of the I.L.O. See Valticos, *loc. cit.,* No. 177, p. 160, Notes (2) to (4); Lyon-Caen, *loc. cit.,* No. 130, p. 92.

[37] One outstanding example (among many) is the parallel between I.L.O. Conventions 87 (1948) and 98 (1949) and Article 5 and 6 of the Charter.

[38] On the revision of I.L.O. Conventions see Valticos, *loc. cit.,* Nos. 125ff. (pp. 103ff.), with further literature p. 103, Note (3), and Nos. 242ff., pp. 246ff.

[39] Neither of which seems to have happened so far.

[40] See for the purposes of the Council of Europe its Statute Article 1, and for their analysis Robertson, *Human Rights in Europe,* 1963 and *European Institutions,* 1972 (also *The Council of Europe,* 2nd ed., 1961). The Statute is printed in Appendix I to the works of 1961 and 1972.

[41] It is elected by the Parliaments of the Member States. Statute, Article 25. See Robertson, *European Institutions,* p. 42.

[42] *Ibid.* Article 14. Robertson, *loc. cit.,* p. 40.

[43] *Ibid.* Article 15.

[44] For a detailed and very clear analysis of the origins of the Charter see Wiebringhaus, *La charte sociale européenne, Annuaire français de droit international,* 1963, pp. 710-713, also pp. 3ff. of the duplicated lecture at Edinburgh University mentioned *supra,* Note 1.

[45] I.L.O. Constitution Article 22.

[46] Valticos, *loc. cit.,* No. 664, p. 553; also Recueil, *loc. cit.,* p. 332.

[47] Article 19, para. 5(c) and (e) and para. 6(c) and (d).

[48] Article 23, para. 2.

[49] Wiebringhaus, *Annuaire français de droit international,* 1963, pp. 717ff.; 1968, pp. 783ff.; Rivista di Diritto Europeo 1972, pp. 171ff.; Valticos, Recueil, *loc. cit.,* pp. 335ff.

[50] But, alas, only as regards supervision *ex officio* on the basis of governmental reports, and not as regards a complaint mechanism. The I.L.O. has complaint procedures, so, of course, has the Council of Europe under the European Convention on Human Rights and Fundamental Freedoms. That the Charter has nothing even remotely similar is, as has often been pointed out, one of its major blemishes.

[51] *Droit International du Travail,* para. 642, p. 569; also Recueil, *loc. cit.,* pp.

341ff., esp. p. 343.

[52] Although, as pointed out below, there appears to be a certain development towards firmer action on the part of the Committee of Ministers, as seems to emerge from a comparison of its reaction to the first set of *Conclusions* with its reaction to the second set.

[53] For this and the following information see the published *Conclusions* of the Committee of Experts, especially their general introudctory remarks.

[54] I am much indebted to Dr. H. Wiebringhaus for drawing my attention to these facts.

[55] For examples see Wiebringhaus, Rivista di Diritto Europeo, 1972, p. 200. Thus the relevant authorities in the German Federal Republic have, in view of their obligations under Articles 18 and 19 of the Charter, exempted nationals of other Contracting Parties from the prohibition to engage for eign labour (which had been a response to the recent energy crisis), and reduced the waiting period for the reunion of the families of workers who are nationals of Contracting Parties from three years to one year (see Article 19(6)).